THE
National ⚾ Pastime
A REVIEW OF BASEBALL HISTORY

D1366935

THE NATIONAL PASTIME (ISSN 0734-6905, ISBN 0-910137-81-1), Number 19. Published by The Society for American Baseball Research, Inc., 812 Huron Rd., Suite 719, Cleveland, OH 44115. Postage paid at Birmingham, AL.

Editor
Mark Alvarez

Copy Editor
A.D. Suehsdorf

Designated Reader
Dick Thompson

The Society for American Baseball Research

History

The Society for American Baseball Research (SABR) was founded on August 10, 1971, by L. Robert "Bob" Davids and fifteen other baseball researchers at Cooperstown, New York, and now boasts more than 6,600 members worldwide. The Society's objectives are to foster the study of baseball as a significant American institution, to establish an accurate historical account of baseball through the years, to facilitate the dissemination of baseball research information, to stimulate the best interest of baseball as our national pastime, and to cooperate in safeguarding proprietary interests of individual research efforts of members of the Society.

The National Pastime

The Society published its first issue of **The National Pastime** in 1982. The present volume is the twentieth. Many of the previous volumes are still available for purchase (see inside back cover). The editorial policy is to publish a cross section of research articles by our members which reflect their interest in history, biography, statistics and other aspects of baseball not previously published.

Interested in Joining the Society?

SABR membership is open to all those interested in baseball research, statistics or history. SABR membership runs on a calendar year basis; if you join after October 1, you will be rolled over into the next calendar year. Membership dues are $50 US, $60 Canada & Mexico and $65 overseas (US funds only). Students and seniors can join for $30 ($40 in Canada & Mexico and $45 overseas). Members receive the **Baseball Research Journal**, **The National Pastime**, *The SABR Bulletin*, a Membership Directory and other special publications. To join SABR, send the appropriate amount and your name and address to the address below . Feel free to contact SABR for more information at the address below as well.

SABR
Dept. TNP
812 Huron Rd E #719
Cleveland, OH 44115
216-575-0500
www.sabr.org
info @ sabr. org

The Lost Art of Fair-Foul Hitting

Robert H. Schaefer

Baseball matured and came of age during the last third of the nineteenth century. The game improved as a result of suggestions made by a cadre of thoughtful sportswriters and managers who subjected it to critical analysis at the end of each season.

Captain Harry Wright, of the Boston Red Stockings, along with sportswriter Henry Chadwick, were the two most important personalities in this developmental effort. Chadwick's column was published in the influential New York *Clipper*, as well as other daily newspapers. His writings help us understand the reasons behind successful and unsuccessful proposed rule changes

One of the burning issues of the early 1870s concerned the rule for determining fair and foul hits. It stated that if a batted ball first bounced in fair territory, the ball was in play no matter where it rolled thereafter. This permitted a method of batting that became known as fair-foul hitting, a controversial art at the time, and one that today is vastly misunderstood.

Using the rule, a select group of clever hitters perfected a technique for deliberately striking the ball in a manner so that a spin—"English"—was imparted to it. After first touching the ground in fair territory the "English" caused the ball to twist sharply off into foul

After thirty-five years in the aerospace industry, where he was responsible for the human engineering aspects of the Apollo program and several versions of the Space Station, **Bob Schaefer** *has devoted his time to a project he calls |In Quest of .400." The focus of his research is to understand the circumstances surrounding each .400 season in terms of the extant rules, equipment, and ballparks. This article is an outgrowth of his research on the twenty-four individual major league .400 hitters and the thirty-five seasons in which that fabled batting average was attained.*

ground, far from the normal defensive positions of the infielders stationed within the foul lines. The ball was in play and the fielders were obliged to give chase as it skipped to the recesses of the foul grounds. The striker almost always earned first base, and frequently two bases, on this type of hit. Strikers who were skilled in the art of fair-foul hitting had a huge advantage, because it was impossible to post the infielders to defend against it and at the same time adequately cover the fair ground between the bases.

In the 1870s, the second baseman was usually stationed in the immediate vicinity of his base, a considerable distance from the first baseman. Scientific hitters attempted to exploit this large opening by poking ground balls between first and second.

The typical response to the threat of a fair-foul hit was to position the first and third basemen directly on their bases, with one foot in foul ground. This defensive posture only exacerbated the middle of the diamond even more. Thus, the mere existence of the fair-foul hit inflated the batting averages of all hitters, who could tap bouncers through what today we would consider enormous holes.

How it was done—Just how did a scientific hitter accomplish the art of fair-foul hitting ? First of all, the hitter had a colossal advantage in that, according to the rules of the 1860s and '70s, pitches he fouled off were not charged as strikes. He could make as many unsuccessful attempts at a fair-foul hit as he cared to without accumulating strikes. In addition, the striker had the privilege of calling for a high or low pitch—there was no single fixed strike zone.

When a hitter planned to make a fair-foul hit, he always called for a low pitch. Chadwick tells us that a fair-foul hit could never be made except from a low ball, and then the striker needed to step up so as to hit the ball down to the ground within the foul lines. The hitter's key for success was to hit down on, or chop at, the ball and deliver a glancing blow so that a spin was imparted to it. Spin was vital for the ball to veer sharply off into foul territory, beyond the reach of the fielders. The idea that a fair-foul hit was easy to make was, in Chadwick's succinct phrase, "absurd." Chadwick related that the slightest miscalculation on the part of the striker transformed the ventured fair-foul hit into an easily caught foul bound, or a chance to field the striker out at first base. The foul-bound rule provided that a striker was out should a player field the ball after its first bounce.

Making an accurate call of fair or foul on the first bounce was a daunting task for the umpire, who in the 1870s stood several feet off to the side of home plate, in foul ground. This offset location denied him an optimum view of the area in front of home plate, the spot where the fair-foul hit was likely to take its first bounce. In addition, his view of the ball was often blocked by the batter running toward first base, or by the catcher as he attempted to field it.

According to nineteenth century newspaper accounts, the creator of the fair-foul hit was Dickey Pearce, the innovative short fielder of the old Brooklyn Atlantics. Indeed, Pearce himself claimed this honor. Henry Chadwick provides strong evidence supporting Pearce's claim in his New York *Clipper* review entitled, "The Short Fielders of 1872":

> Dick is the originator of that strategic style of batting known as 'fair-foul hits', the most difficult balls to field, as well as to hit properly, that there are. Any muffin batsman can hit a fair ball to the out-field, but it takes considerable judgment, a quick eye, plenty of nerve and skillful batting to make first-base by a well hit fair-foul ball. When it is well done, it is a certain hit for first base, and any hit that ensures one base against sharp fielding shows skillful batting.

Chadwick shed additional light on the heritage of fair-foul hitting in an 1894 article by declaring that he himself had originated the concept. He said that the bunt grew out of fair-foul hitting and that he had suggested the idea of fair-foul hitting in 1864:

> I pointed out to Pearce the advantage of hitting the ball so that it should become a fair-foul hit, especially when a runner was on base; as, in such a case, even if the fielder got the ball to

first in time—which was usually impossible—the runner on first would easily get to second safely.

Pearce acted on Chadwick's suggestion and practiced the art of the fair-foul hit until he had it down flawlessly. He used the fair-foul with such regularity that the infielders would anticipate it and creep in close. Chadwick reported that Pearce would trick them by pretending to prepare for a fair-foul and then just tap the ball over their heads for a safe hit.

Other famous players, such as George Wright and Davey Force, duplicated Pearce's skill. The art of fair-foul hitting spread and by the early 1870s many strikers employed this style. Of course, some used it more often and effectively than others. Cap Anson described his 1874 Philadelphia A's teammate, James "Lefty" McMullen as a "rattling good batsman who excelled in fair-foul hitting." Levi Meyerle, twice the batting champion of the National Association, frequently used the fair-foul hit. Davey Eggler, also of Philadelphia, was another famous fair-foul hitter.

The excitement of a fair-foul hit is captured in this account of a game played on July 18, 1870, when the Harvard nine faced the vaunted Cincinnati Red Stockings in Cincinnati. Surprisingly, in the bottom of the ninth, the Harvards were leading the professional nine by six runs. Then with two hands out, and

> every base full, George Wright stepped to the bat amid 'a stillness as of death,' when the 'boldest held his breath for a time.' Every man, woman, and child on the ground knew that he was the right man in the right place. Not a nerve trembled as balls passed him, and he waited, though 'one strike', 'two strikes' came from the umpire. At length he was suited, and striking a 'fair foul' past third base took second for himself, and gave home to three men. There rose such a shout such as never before been heard on these grounds before.

The most renowned practitioner of fair-foul hitting was Ross "the Great and Only" Barnes, who won three batting titles in six years, and hit over .400 in four of them. Although history remembers him primarily for his masterful exploitation the fair-foul rule, in truth he was a complete hitter who did not rely exclusively on that technique for his success. However, the high regard for him as a fair-foul hitter is made clear in the following excerpts. On July 3, 1872, the Boston *Evening Journal* reported the match between the Red Stockings and the Forest City nine of Cleveland. We pick up the action in the ninth inning:

> There were now two hands out and no runs

made and the Bostons one run behind and it certainly looked as if it were all day with the invincible Reds but their friends were not to be disappointed in their favorites in winning a game when defeat seemed certain. Barnes was the next striker, and upon him depended the result of the game, as a base hit would at least bring in the tieing run. After waiting for a ball that suited him, he hit one of his favorite fair fouls, for which he is getting an enviable reputation, and as the ball traveled out toward the left field, Rogers and Harry Wright came dashing home and winning the game. Applause long and loud was awarded Barnes as he rested on second base, where his hit carried him.

On October 6, 1873, the Boston *Evening Journal* reported a match between the Bostons and the Philadelphia A's. We join them in the seventh inning, with two hands out, a man on second, and Boston losing to the A's, 2-1:

The excitement was now intense, the crowd being almost breathless with interest to see what Barnes would do. That sterling player showed his worth by hitting a fair foul to the left field earning two bases, bringing George [Wright] home and making the spectators wild with delight.

On July 22, 1872, Barnes made a clean home run on the Boston grounds on a fair-foul hit that rolled under the seats along the left side just behind third base. The ball remained in play while the fielders crawled under the seats to retrieve it, and Barnes scampered all the way around the bases. His homer bounced only a few feet in front of home, and including the roll, probably did not travel more than 100 feet. While many fair-foul hits earned two bases for the striker, Barnes' fair-foul home run was apparently unique.

Rule changes—Over time, the fair-foul hit caused several significant rule changes, and altered the diamond itself. For example, at the start of fair-foul era, there was no batter's box, nor any restrictions on where the striker was to stand to hit. To reduce the striker's ability to intentionally foul off a pitch, in 1867 a line was drawn through the center of the square home plate, from left to right, extending three feet to either side of the plate. This was called the line of home plate, and the hitter had to stand with one or both feet planted on this line when striking the ball.

In 1868, the rule was amended so the batter was required to stand astride the line of home plate. The penalty for hitting the ball illegally was a "foul" strike,

three of which would retire the striker.

The batter's line mutated into the batter's box in 1874. The box allowed the batter complete freedom of movement within a rectangle six feet long and three feet wide, centered on the line of home plate. The nearest line of the batter's box was one foot from the plate.

Until 1874, the cast-iron home plate was located in fair ground between the foul lines. A favorite trick of the fair-foul hitter was to bounce a ball straight down off the plate.

To prevent this, in 1875 the home plate was relocated in foul ground, with its forward point just touching the meeting of the foul lines. This denied it as a target for fair-foul hitters. To further handicap the fair-foul hitter, the batter's box was repositioned so it was no longer centered on the line of home plate, but was shifted a foot to the rear. A batter who was intent on making a fair-foul hit was thus located deeper in foul ground, making it more difficult for him to achieve a first bounce in fair territory. In addition, the hitter was limited to two "foul" strikes.

A final attempt to restrict fair-foul hitting was made in 1876, when the number of "foul" strikes required to retire a hitter was reduced to one. These constraints did not materially impact Barnes. He hit the horsehide for a .404 average (.429 by today's standards) and won the first National League batting crown. These changes to the diamond proved unsuccessful in preventing arguments resulting from fair-foul hitting as they were aimed at handicapping the hitter rather than assisting the umpire in distinguishing between fair and foul balls.

The main objection to fair-foul hitting lay in the umpire's limited ability to make the correct call of fair or foul. None of the opponents of fair-foul hitting thought it provided a hitter with a second-rate means of attaining first base, or that it was a cheap hit. Quite the opposite was true. It was universally regarded as requiring exceptional finesse. Only the most highly skilled strikers were able to execute it with consistency. The principal objection to it was that the umpire's decision usually precipitated disputes that degraded the quality of the game. Fair-foul hitting simply caused nasty arguments.

Observers of the game soon realized that a rule change governing fouls would ease the umpire's burden. But defining the most appropriate foul rule proved to be elusive. The first effort had been made at the 1873 National Association convention. A rule was proposed that would make all balls foul which struck the ground between home plate and a line reaching from the pitcher's position to first and third bases. Chadwick mocked the proposal and said it would only increase the number of chances to retire the striker by a foul bound catch. He estimated this proposed rule would cause the number of chances for foul bound catches to

Illness, Not Rules Changes, Ended Barnes' Career

Knowing full well that a new and livelier ball was to be used in 1877, the Cincinnati *Enquirer* boldly predicted that Ross Barnes would destroy League pitching. It assumed that Barnes would remain the League's supreme batsman, despite his loss of the fair-foul hit. On May 9, 1877, it wrote, "The mighty Barnes will be one of the glimmering lights in this year's ball field. Oh fair-foul, where is thy victory?"

The citizens of Porkopolis clearly weren't concerned that the loss of fair-foul hitting would be the end of the mighty Barnes, but his decline to .272 in 1877 has led many contemporary writers to conclude that the revocation of the fair-foul rule derailed his career. This notion overlooks the fact that Barnes played in only twenty-two games in 1877 due to "the ague," a malaria-like affliction characterized by alternating high fever and chills, along with a marked loss of strength, stamina, and vitality. Barnes tried to take his place with the team, but could not. A special dispatch to the *Enquirer*, dated Chicago, May 18, headlined:

BARNES TAKES A REST

The Chicago Club management today became fully convinced that Barnes was utterly disabled by long sickness, and was too weak to play the game. They therefore furloughed him, and he left at once for Rockford [his hometown] to recuperate. Smith will play second base in the St. Louis game tomorrow, and probably throughout the tour which begins Tuesday next."

The next day, the Chicago *Tribune* reported:

Barnes has been physically incapable of exertion; he is as weak, debilitated and worn as would be any strong man after a six months sickness. He has been willing, anxious and earnest to win, but his ability has been unable to keep pace with his desire. A remark of his, as follows, explains how he feels:

"I tell you, this is terrible, to be anxious to do a thing which you know you can do, and yet find that you are bodily unable to do it. I know what I can do, and what I have done, and yet I haven't the strength to do the same again."

The Boston *Daily Globe* picked up the story:

Barnes is not gaining. It is a matter now, not as to his playing ball this season, but whether he will be well enough to ever again attempt it. His last telegraph to the Chicago management says, "I seldom leave the house now. I don't feel badly, but I grow weaker every day."

Barnes never fully recovered from his bout with the ague. He was not re-engaged by Chicago, and unsuccessfully sued for unpaid wages. It was one of the first legal cases of this type brought by a ball player against his team. The suit was unsuccessful.

For 1878, he accepted the position of captain of the Tecumseh Club of London, Ontario, in the International League. His contract required him to play second base as well. Some historians consider this league to have been the equal of the National League during the late 1870s. Barnes batted only .235.

In 1879, Cincinnati captain Cal McVey took his old friend on as shortstop. Barnes responded by hitting .266. He led all shortstops in total chances per game with 5.8, and his fielding average was .864, a respectable number for those bare-handed days. Barnes wasn't in the National League in 1880. He popped up with Boston in 1881, once more playing for Harry Wright. He finished the year at .271, and committed more errors than any other shortstop in the league. Chadwick reported, "Barnes showed up well in the position, making some wonderful plays at times, but his errors…badly hurt his fine play."

It was his farewell appearance. At the age of 31, Ross Barnes was finished as a player. His final appearance on a ball field was as an umpire in the Players' League in 1890. He applied a rule incorrectly and was hooted off the field.

Because of the enduring and pervasive effects of his illness, we cannot accurately judge the effect that eliminating the art of the fair-foul hit had on Barnes' career. To place him in the proper perspective, Ross Barnes was distinctly more proficient at a very difficult style of hitting than any of his contemporaries.

—R.H.S.

triple. The rule was not adopted.

The tenth man—The next year Chadwick chastised the convention delegates because they wasted a full day trying to modify the code of rules in an attempt to end the undesirable effects of fair-foul hitting. He thought their effort was a waste of time because a mechanism was immediately available to provide a balanced defense against the fair-foul hit without amending the playing rules. To Chadwick, the solution was clear—add a tenth player.

Chadwick's scheme stationed the tenth player between first and second bases, a right shortstop, if you will. With a "right short" added to the infield the second basemen could cover his position up the middle, as well as part of the shortstop's. The shortstop could play nearer third, allowing the third basemen to cover the foul ground that was the target of fair-foul hitting. Here, Chadwick said, is a legitimate remedy for the objections of the opponents of fair-foul batting.

Using his column in The New York *Clipper* as a bully pulpit, he extolled the virtues of the art of fair foul hitting, and lobbied vigorously the ten-man, ten-inning game as a method to negate the associated problems. Chadwick persuaded his longtime friend, Harry Wright, to employ the ten-man, ten-inning concept in several exhibition matches during the spring of 1874. The record isn't clear precisely why Chadwick's ten-man, ten-inning game failed, but in retrospect, it is difficult to see how a tenth player would clarify the umpire's judgment of fair or foul.

In December of 1874, Chadwick had proposed a rule that required the batted ball to land in front of the batter's box in order to be fair. The purpose of this rule was to make it even more difficult to achieve a fair-foul. In this instance, Chadwick specifically stated that his proposal overcame the problem associated with the umpires' judgment, and would thus reduce arguments and delays of the game. His rule was not adopted.

Despite the fact that Barnes, the acclaimed virtuoso of the art, was his own star player, Harry Wright led the crusade against the fair-foul hit. During the winter of 1875, he had proposed a rule change to restrict it. It failed. Finally, in late October, 1876, the Bostons played an exhibition match using a new foul rule designed by Harry Wright. It made all batted balls that pass outside the foul lines before reaching first base or third base foul, and all batted balls that strike the ground and remain within the foul lines until they reach either first or third base fair. His proposed foul rule is instantly recognizable as the one in force today.

The *Clipper* reported that the result of play under the new rule was satisfactory to the spectators. Spectator satisfaction and acceptance were the ultimate criteria by which proposed changes were judged. The *Clipper* concluded, "of all the plans presented to obviate the difficulties that followed in the wake of fair-fouls, Harry Wright's proposed rule appeared to be the best." It is, the *Clipper* went on, "desirable that the vexatious doubts of the accuracy of the umpire in judging fair-fouls be removed in some way or other, and we know of no more feasible rule than this new one."

At the same time, Wright also proposed doing away with the foul-bound catch. A casual examination of games played during 1871-1876 indicates that about as many fair-foul hits were recorded as were foul-bound outs. It appears that these two events more or less cancelled each other out. Therefore, eliminating one but not the other would tip the scales in favor of either the offense or defense. Nonetheless, the foul-bound rule was retained by the National League until 1883.

Wright's foul rule, however, was adopted for the 1877 season. It had broad consequences. It instantly ended the era of fair-foul hitting, and it also allowed home plate to be moved back into fair territory, also in 1877.

On January 13, 1877, The *Clipper* observed that:

> Under the new rule the first and third basemen will not be required to stand as near to the foul ball lines as hitherto. Now the infielders will be able to consolidate their forces so as to secure more ground balls than they did before.

Keep your eye on the ball—This implied that batting averages would decline in 1877, as fewer ground balls would be able to penetrate the now concentrated infielders. Despite the impression left by Ross Barnes' decreased effectiveness (left), the reverse proved to be the case. With the fair-foul rule in full force in 1876, the National League posted a .265 batting average, and a slugging average of .321. Despite not having the advantage of the fair-foul hit in 1877, the League's batting average climbed to .271 and the slugging average increased to .338. These increases in batting were due to a change completely unrelated to the fair-foul rule: the selection of a newly designed ball. The ball used in 1876 did not have a rubber center. However, in 1876 use of this official dead ball was optional at the sole discretion of the home team. The 1877 National League convention selected a livelier official ball containing a one-ounce rubber center, and made its use compulsory in all league games. Then, as now, the goal was to make all games uniformly lively and attract more paying customers.

Bunts and Fair-Foul Hits

Who Was First?
Dickey Pearce
or Tommy Barlow?

To a great extent, the fog of history shrouds the precise identity of the player who made the first fair-foul hit, along with the precise date of the event. This information was, if not completely lost by the 1890s, was confused. At that time most base ball writers believed that origin of the fair-foul hit and bunt were related, i.e., one led to the other, but could not agree on which type of hit was invented first. Several sportswriters made a determined attempt to systematically answer this question during the winter of 1894. The lead investigator was William M. Rankin, of the New York *Clipper*. Based on his research Rankin concluded that the credit for originating both the bunt and fair-foul hit should be accorded to Dickey Pearce, the clever and innovative short fielder of the old Brooklyn Atlantics.

Rankin unearthed an account in the *Clipper* of a game played between the Atlantics and the Mutual nines that reported, "Pearce rolled a little one toward first base, which Galvin got and put out Pearce, although McDonald reached second safely on the hit."

This game was played on August 17, 1868, and in 1894 Rankin thought it was the first recorded instance of a sacrifice bunt. Rankin subsequently discovered a later game, played on September 10, 1868 between the Atlantics and the Unions of Morrisania, in which, "Pearce sent Ferguson home on a little hit which rolled towards third base, on which Dickey reached first base safely."

To conclusively substantiate Pearce's claim as the inventor of both the bunt and fair-foul hit, Rankin interviewed players who were participants in and eyewitnesses to the early history of baseball during the years just before and just after the Civil War. Here are their responses, as reported by Rankin.

Brooklyn born Bob "Death to Flying Things" Ferguson was well acquainted with Pearce. He told Rankin that he was under the impression that Tommy Barlow had invented the bunt. Barlow, Pearce, and Ferguson were all teammates on the Atlantics, 1872-73. Ferguson was certain that the bunt was based on the fair-foul hit. However, when informed of Pearce's claim to be the inventor of the bunt, Ferguson said that he would not dispute the point.

Herbert Worth played the outfield on the Star Club of Brooklyn in the late 1860s, and was briefly with the Atlantics in 1872 when he was twenty-five. Worth replied to Rankin:

Tommy Barlow was the inventor of the bunt hit, and was famous throughout the country for his skill. He had a short bat, not over two feet long, which when he hit the ball (if it could be called a hit) he imparted a wrist motion which gave the ball, when it came in contact with the bat, a sort of reversed twist and the ball after striking the ground would almost seem to remain where it struck and then dart off at an angle out of reach of the third baseman or the pitcher should they endeavor to field him out at first.

Worth went on to say that Pearce might have been the first to use the fair-foul hit. He thought that was probably the basis for Pearce's claim for inventing the bunt, as well as John Chapman's endorsement of Dickey's claim. But Worth was adamant that Pearce did not originate the bunt.

Both Henry Dollard, shortstop of the Star nine for several seasons, and Billy Barnie, another New York area player of the 1870s, agreed with Worth that Barlow was the inventor of the bunt. Dollard remembered that the bunt was once known as "Barlow's Dodo."

Now consider the testimony of John Chapman. Except for two seasons, 1867 and 1871, Chapman was the star outfielder of Brooklyn Atlantics from 1862 until 1873, overlapping Pearce's service with the club. Chapman stated unequivocally that Dickey Pearce invented both the bunt hit and the fair-foul style of hitting:

It was early in the sixties that he introduced the fair-foul and a few years later he adopted the bunt. I remember the late Tommy Barlow and how clever he used to make a bunt hit. Barlow always carried a little bat, about two feet long, and made a great reputation for himself in bunting the ball, but that was in 1871, when he was a member of the Star nine. Pearce, however, had made the bunt hit several years prior to that season. It was from Pearce that Barlow got the idea, although the latter had it down to such a science that he could not be beaten in making a bunt hit.

Who was Tommy Barlow ? His name and fame have dimmed over time. Certainly, he does not today enjoy the glory accorded to Dickey Pearce. Barlow's first season of professional base ball in the National Association was with the Atlantics in 1872, when he hit .310. Chadwick provides us with a description Barlow's batting style in 1873:

One of the best of the new style of strategic batsmen, and he last season earned many a first base through outwitting the pitcher by his peculiar style of making a base-hit. Whenever he made one of his patent hits—he simply allowed the ball to hit the bat—the

(hometown) crowd would laugh and applaud him; while, if any other club player of the out-of-town nines attempted such a thing, they would hiss him.

Not all the sportswriters were as enthusiastic about Barlow's strategic batting as was Father Chadwick. When the Atlantics played at the Boston grounds on September 8, 1873, The Boston *Globe* thoroughly denigrated Barlow's batting skill and ridiculed his attempts at bunting:

On the part of the Atlantics, Barlow acknowledged his weakness at the bat by attempting the black game, but Spalding got him out twice, and the attempt, which is rather a weak one for a professional club, was a failure.

Tommy Barlow's professional career came to a sudden end. After two successful seasons as the Atlantics catcher, in 1874 Barlow "revolved" to Hartford and shifted from behind the plate to shortstop. The transition was successful, and Barlow appeared in thirty-two games at his new position before being severely injured in a game against Chicago. He was given morphine for the pain, and became addicted. His career was ruined. After only one game at shortstop with New Haven in 1875, Barlow disappeared from the world of professional baseball. When Rankin conducted his interviews in 1894, several former teammates knew that Tommy had come to a tragic end, but the date location of his death are unknown.

The testimony of players who were his teammates supports Pearce's claim of inventing the bunt, as well as the fair-foul. Chadwick fully credits Pearce, who was born in 1836, and had been associated with base ball clubs since the mid-1850s, as being the first hitter to demonstrate the technique. Tommy Barlow, who didn't begin top-level play until 1872, certainly employed the bunt, but probably not until several years after Pearce dropped down the first "little one."

—R..H.S.

Ila Borders, Pitcher

Jean Hastings Ardell

On the night in June, 1999, that I arrived in Duluth, Ila Borders was sent in to pitch the ninth inning of a game that was far out of reach for the Duluth-Superior Dukes of the Northern League. Suddenly, the lights behind first base went dark for twenty minutes, a foreshadowing of her disastrous outing: six hits, six runs (three earned), a walk, and a wild pitch.

The Dukes put Borders on revocable waivers the next morning. Two days later, the Madison Black Wolf told her to catch the next Greyhound bus. She was to pitch for them the following night. Instead, I offered to drive her the 300-plus miles from Duluth to Madison. Bob Gustafson, the Dukes' general manager and a kind-hearted man, grabbed a fifty-dollar bill from his cash box, and sent us on our way. A mild-mannered Thelma and Louise, we drove through the Wisconsin countryside, munching popcorn and swigging mineral water as we talked of the vagaries of baseball. I left Borders at her motel with good wishes and the remainder of Gustafson's fifty dollars. Later, as I reflected on what it has been like for her to pioneer baseball's gender line, I came across these lines by poet Linda Mizejewski:

> In spring, my father
> Took me out at dusk
> To lots the boys had left,
> Seeing each year if I could spin
> The winning curve ball back to him
> And learn the catch, the grip and swing
> Of a missing son...

Jean Hastings Ardell *received the 1999* Baseball Weekly *Award for Research. Her book about women and baseball is forthcoming from Southern Illinois University Press.*

Mizejewski's poetry reminds me that baseball has always attracted women who find ways to cross the gender line to play. It has always been so, from pioneers such as Lizzie Arlington, who in 1898 became "the first woman signed to a contract in the minor leagues," appeared in one game, and was let go when she failed to draw the anticipated number of paying spectators; to the women of Philip Wrigley's All-American Girls Professional Baseball League, who played one another during the 1940s and early 1950s on modified diamonds wearing, God bless them, short-skirted uniforms; to the Colorado Silver Bullets, a team of women who grew up playing primarily softball before slipping away from their careers to play baseball against minor league, semipro, and college men's teams.

These experiences, while exotic, pale against those of Ila Borders who has played hardball day after day, year after year, with the boys and later the men of summer. She began at age ten in Little League baseball; at the age of twenty-four, she completed her third season in the minor leagues in September, 1999. You will find information on her pitching record in the table near the end of this article, but my purpose is to consider the social implications of her career. How does it affect the culture of baseball? Her teammates? Her coaches? Her fans? Herself?

Little League—When coaches saw Ila's strong arm and powerful hitting, they decided that a girl was welcome to play, especially if she was on their team. The parents in the stands were another story. "The Little League mothers were the toughest on me," Ila says.

"There was only one other girl playing…and they didn't think it was right for a girl to play a boy's sport."

Some of the milder comments included,"Go back to [your] Barbie dolls. Stick with your tea party. Who the…do you think you are?" Ila's father, Phil, still remembers this encounter:

"One gentleman said to me, 'What do we do? Put our sons in dresses and send them off to school?' But I always wanted Ila to be a girl, not like a boy. When she began pitching, her long hair bothered her and she wanted to cut it. I said, 'No. Keep it long.'"

The climate in the stands became so hostile that Phil Borders took to watching the game alone, down the right or left field foul line, a habit he continues today. But the hatred in the stands—that is what Ila calls it— brought father and daughter closer. A passionate student of the game, Phil Borders would become coach, mentor, friend, and agent to his daughter as she excelled on the diamond.

Ila Borders

Madison Black Wolf

Junior High—Borders attended Whittier Christian Junior High School, where her seventh- and eighth-grade teams went undefeated. She earned MVP honors both years. Her coach, Roland Eslinger, says she still holds a number of records in the school's Top Ten Record Book, including first place in innings pitched (40) and strikeouts (70); and fourth in ERA (0.44). With stats like that and acceptance from her teammates, this was her golden time.

"In junior high, things went OK," Ila recalls, "because it was still cool to be an athletic female." She calls Eslinger the first person outside her family who believed in her dream of making it to the major leagues. At the crucial time of puberty, when girls are prone to abandon their tomboy dreams, his encouragement had a salutary effect upon her confidence.

Ila was fourteen when she graduated from junior high school and her father felt that it was time for Ila truly to understand what the baseball life was like. He knew that potentially devastating challenges would face his daughter in the dugout and the locker room. Could she adapt to the life? Would she want to? That summer, he altered her birth certificate and signed her up on a semipro team. Today, she shrugs off the experience, saying that playing ball at age fourteen in the company of adult men helped toughen her resolve to continue with the game. Yet it also sensitized her to the adult cares with which her teammates contended. One man was married with a child. Ila saw his anguish as his wife endured a difficult pregnancy. When she entered high school that autumn, her classmates' adolescent worries over grades, dates, and appearance would seem shallow to her by comparison.

High School—When Ila arrived at Whittier Christian High School, the baseball coach already knew of her. Steve Randall had umpired a championship game in which she pitched. "She was a good pitcher but my concern was how she'd be accepted by the boys," he recalls. Borders came of age at a time when the Religious Right was debating women's proper role in American society. She had been raised in a Christian home and attended Christian schools. So I wondered whether any parents, students, teachers, or administrators had questioned on biblical grounds her entering so masculine an arena as baseball. Randall says that as far as he knows, that was not an issue. Borders says that she has been told the diamond is not the place for a woman, but not on religious grounds.

Randall believes that Ila's freshman year was made smoother because her teammates had grown up playing with or against her in Little League or junior high. Seeing her on the mound was no shock. The boys respected her mental toughness (Randall calls her a "warrior") and her self-discipline (on her own, she routinely arose at five a.m. to run and lift weights). In her senior year, Borders again won MVP honors. Randall says, "I often think that if more of the guys in the minors had her determination and commitment, they'd make it."

But away from the diamond, Borders encountered hard times. "In ninth grade, a lot changed," she says. "Everybody was worried about looking good." Caught between the girls' preoccupation with popularity and the boys' camaraderie on the field, she struggled to find her place. "I'm more of an introvert and didn't mind being on my own. Still, it bothered me, not fitting in socially," she says.

Randall thinks it was the girls' mixed reactions to her that gave her the most trouble. "Some really encouraged her, while some thought, 'What're you doing in a man's game? Or is it the publicity?' They questioned her motives, just as a lot of other coaches questioned my integrity: was I playing her for the publicity?"

And the Los Angeles *Times* reported:

> Girlfriends and mothers of opposing players are the worst.... They're the ones who've threatened her life, told her she'd better watch her back. Forced her to seek a kind and willing soul after the game to help her get to her car safely.

Despite—or, perhaps, because of—these difficulties, Borders immersed herself in baseball during these years, also playing senior division Little League and later Pony League ball. By graduation day, in June 1993, she had learned a few fundamentals about life on and off the diamond. She still loved the game enough to pursue what she knew would be a difficult quest. She was learning to recognize the value of mentors like Eslinger and Randall, both of whom she still keeps in touch with. She was also learning to expect a chilly reception from other girls. Today there are few women she trusts.

College—Phil Borders says he has always tried to be careful about whom Ila played for. Was she welcome? Would the coach want to play her? Well aware of the pressure on her, he has consistently sought quiet venues. During Ila's senior year in high school, she received several letters of interest from colleges. Ulti-mately, she accepted a partial baseball scholarship at Southern California College (SCC), a small Christian school about thirty miles from home.

Parents send their children to such a campus in some measure because they seek a shelter from the secular world. Certainly the Borders hoped that SCC would prove a haven in which their daughter could continue to develop as a Christian woman and as a ballplayer. The Golden State conference of the NAIA espouses high standards of sportsmanship, and Charlie Phillips, the coach and a former lefthanded pitcher, was a fan of hers, having told his wife, "I'm going to sign that kid someday. She's something special."

The signing brought another flurry of attention. To questioners, Phillips said, "I don't sign anybody who cannot pitch. I'm not in the game for publicity. If she can get outs, who cares if she's male or female?" Said Borders, "I just let [the criticism] go in one ear and out the other because I've worked pretty hard for this. If I can't handle the critics, I won't be set for college, or the majors, which is my goal."

On the day of her college pitching debut, more than 500 spectators and media overflowed the bleachers. Fox, ABC, NBC, CBS, *The Sporting News*, *Sports Illustrated*, and representatives from the Japanese media were there. The tiny campus had never seen anything like it. When the first batter flied out, he angrily spiked his bat, which hit his teammate in the on-deck area. Ila's presence on the mound would trigger this sort of response throughout her time with the SCC Vanguards. As a local sportswriter reported:

> Before games, opposing coaches would corner Phillips and whisper, "You're not throwing Ila today, are you?" Privately, not a single coach or player could stomach losing to a woman pitcher.

Familiarity did not increase her acceptance by opposing teams that season. After she threw 109 pitches in a 4-3 loss in March, SCC athletic director Pat Guillen complained of the opposing team, "Their players were very abusive. They were calling Ila names and using profanities throughout the game."

Creative epithets, of course, are a part of the poetry of baseball. Yet where do we draw the line? In the same way that we now wince at the racist remarks directed at Jackie Robinson and Hank Aaron during their ground-breaking years, some are troubled by the verbiage hurled Ila's way: When is it sexual harassment? (And would she sue)? It's ungentlemanly or plain coarse or un-Christian to speak so to a woman. What if my daughter was out there?

Whatever haven SCC offered did not include the diamond. Borders claims that during workouts she was frequently plugged in the back by hard-thrown balls from teammates who resented the media attention she received. But on the day of her debut, the Vanguards came alive after three mundane innings with inspired hitting and fielding behind her five-hit complete game, and posted a 12-1 win.

More than ever, Borders wanted to be seen simply as a pitcher, not as a female pitcher. Not a chance. The campus became a circus, with reporters calling at all times of the day and night. Her grades slipped and she began ducking interviews. I think it was then that she turned reticent toward the media.

Sophomore year was rocky in other ways. "My friends, who seemed to have been there for the wrong reasons, left me," she told a reporter. "I would call them to go out, but they always had other things to do. I felt completely alone."

Scouts wondered if she could take care of herself on the road. To prove that she could (and to continue working on her pitching skills), she played that summer in the Saskatchewan Major Baseball League. Traveling the open stretches of prairie and living in a basement room of her host family's home in the town of Swift Current (population 14,815), Borders says she came to terms with how lonely the baseball life can be.

Reading saw her through that solitary summer as it does now, for she is an avid book lover. She particularly identifies with Jackie Robinson's story. Sometimes other ball players ask why she reads so much. I think she is playing catch-up; during her childhood, baseball and her baseball-oriented parents permitted her little time for books.

When she returned from Canada, Charlie Phillips had been fired. With the new coach unreceptive to the idea of a woman on the team, she transferred to Whittier College, eventually earning a B.S. in kinesiology. She hoped to sign with an affiliate of a major league club. There were lookers but no bites. Then, in May 1997, Mike Veeck offered her a tryout with his St. Paul Saints of the independent Northern League. Borders left for Minnesota, anxious in every sense of the word to play professional baseball.

The Northern League—Summer warmth comes late to the upper Midwest and it does not linger. For the clubs of the Northern League, spring training begins in mid-May and the regular season ends in early September. In this unaffiliated league, the players know that their talents must flourish quickly and notably if they are to gain or regain the attention of a major league club and continue their careers.

Veeck already boasted a sold-out season and Phil Borders hoped that this would kill talk that Ila's signing was a gimmick. Still, Veeck found it necessary to defend his decision. "The fact it's going to be fun and a first is just an added bonus." Though true to his paternal heritage, he added, "It's not lost on me that fifty-four percent of the population is going to be pulling hard for Ila." One of Borders' greatest frustrations has been the enduring assumption that her career is some sort of gimmick. Her motivation has been questioned repeatedly. As one St. Paul commentator observed:

> Borders' only interest is playing baseball, just like the 26 men who will emerge from the home clubhouse next Thursday morning. But they will be presumed competent until their skills prove otherwise. Borders will be a side-show in the Saints' circus until her skills prove otherwise.

Just before she left for Minnesota, Ila says she received a letter from the president of a prominent women's organization who chided her. The message was that if Borders succeeded she'd be selling out women's sports, and if she failed she'd set back the cause of women's sports ten years. Borders shakes her head at such damned-if-you-do, damned-if-you-don't reasoning. As with the Little League mothers of her youth, women in the media tend to be her severest critics, she says. "My personal opinion about it is that we're taught to be victims. You can see it in women's magazines. When women see another woman out there being successful, they're threatened. Whereas I think many men, like my boyfriend, like to see a strong woman."

The doubts followed Borders when she was traded to the Duluth-Superior Dukes in June, 1997. The following season, Fargo-Moorhead Red Hawks manager Doug Cimunic expressed concern that Borders might "taint the quality of the league because Duluth retained her…after she finished 1997 with an ERA above 7.00." Borders responded by pitching six scoreless innings against the Red Hawks.

Playing ball in the Northern League has meant two notable changes from her earlier experiences. First, after the local media made much of her arrival, they settled into straightforward reports of her pitching performance. Today there are far fewer headlines about the hiring of a woman or the crossing of borders. Second, the fans have embraced her. When Mike Veeck traded Borders to Duluth, he faced considerable wrath from his young daughter. The fans tend to cheer her every appearance, good, bad, or indifferent, with chants of "Ila, Ila, Ila." Young girls from all over the country e-mail and write. One persuaded her father to drive from Tennessee to see her pitch. Adult fans fall for her, too. As Howie Hanson, a Duluth photographer and journalist, effuses:

> Ila is the Columbus of baseball who is proving the game square, square with old expectations

judged merely by statistics and performance on the field. I submit that the game is more than wins and losses, more than individual and team statistics, but about investing in the fans and communities who support the game. Ila invested her talent and heart in our community, and the fans appreciated it.

With the memory of Little League catcalls ingrained, Borders still registers surprise—even shock—at such benevolent outpourings.

On the fields of the Northern League, however, little has changed. The pressure to survive here is severe, and for many players, Ila's presence only makes it worse. Having her pitch in relief is like having your sister bail you out of a fight. Steve Shirley, who became the Dukes' pitching coach in 1999, says this:

Much of my work with this team has been psychological. Many of these players have recently been cut from affiliated clubs or are fighting back from an injury. They're not sure of themselves, and in baseball that hurts.

For opposing batters, the thought of striking out against a woman is dreadful. Mike Wallace happened to be in town to research a *Sixty Minutes* television interview (aired October 4, 1998) with Borders when she held the Red Hawks scoreless. Afterward, Chris Coste, the Red Hawks' all-star catcher, said to Wallace:

The only thing that was going through my mind was how I'm gonna see myself on SIXTY MINUTES striking out. I can't even tell you how many pointers guys were giving everybody. I mean, stay back, be patient, take it to right field, stride late, take a pitch…. And you know, you're on your way up to the plate, and you're actually thinking of this stuff…. It's almost unexplainable, the feeling you get when you look up at her and she's coming for her wind-up, her hair's flying around.

Facing Ila

Ila's pitching philosophy, as you would expect of a 5-foot-10, 165-pound pitcher, is to pitch with her head. "I change speeds and keep the ball low. I'm a close observer of every batter. During batting practice, I'll watch to see how he pumps the bat. Does he pump it high or low?—that's a natural preference. What are his strengths and weaknesses? Is he double-play material, tending to hit ground balls? When I throw the curve, does he flinch? I watch for the little things."

She says her best pitch is the screwball, which she uses against righthanded batters, along with the curve ball and the fastball (both cut and sinking). Lefthanded hitters can expect to see her slider, changeup, and the fastball (both cut and straight.)

Judging from the comments of players who have faced her in the Northern League, what they desperately want to do is to not strike out against a woman.

—JHA

Steve Shirley's daughter played baseball before switching to softball. She attended college on a softball scholarship. Shirley asks pragmatically, "How many young women are going to win a scholarship to play baseball?" It was my impression that out of compassion for what Ila goes through he wished that she had taken up softball, too.

Larry See was the Dukes' 1999 manager. In 1998, as player-coach with the Thunder Bay Whiskey Jacks, See faced Borders: "Coming up against her is a no-win situation. I mean, if you get a base hit, you're expected to off a woman. And if you don't…well, you look like a fool."

Asked how he fared against her, See immediately answered that he hit two home runs. As to other appearances against her, he mentioned a few grounders to the infield. Any other at-bats? There was a strikeout, "a called third strike on a pitch that was a foot outside," See said. "I thought the umpires in the league gave her a wide strike zone and others agreed with me."

Borders replies, "Actually, I struck him out twice. But when he came [to Duluth] to manage, he liked to remind me and others on the team of those two home runs. And you can't exactly say back to your manager, 'Hey, how about those strikeouts?'" Nor was her cause with her new manager helped during a recent poor outing when a chivalrous Dukes fan started riding See for leaving her in the game.

See says he often invited her into the locker room when the guys were watching TV to try to make her feel welcome. Borders preferred to sit outside. "It's hard to bring a team together, to bond, when you have that," See explains.

Fitting in is problematic. She does not shower or change in the locker room. She does that at home or in her motel room. When she comes to the locker room for a team meeting, she knocks on the door and calls out, "Housekeeping," to forewarn her teammates. Uncertain of their true feelings toward her and by nature a loner, she tends to keep to herself.

As a relief pitcher, she spends hours in the bullpen, where the conversation often turns to sexual encounters. "Don't you guys ever worry about getting a disease?" she has wondered. Rick Wagner, one of the Dukes' starters and a born-again Christian, says that he has chided other players for their language in her presence. "It just gets out of control sometimes—about women in general, and about her," he says. Meanwhile, Ila has seen enough of locker-room antics (though some she finds funny) and casual moral values to vow that she would never date a ballplayer. (She has since rescinded that vow but prefers to keep the details private). It is her blessing and her curse that she is treated, as she wishes to be, just like any ballplayer. "Sometimes I wish she'd look more like a girl," says Rick Wagner. "Wear a dress sometimes."

Borders smiles at the idea. "Wear a dress on a bus with twenty-five ballplayers? I don't think so. During the season, I want to blend in as much as I can. I live in my uniform, my warm-ups."

Off-season, it is different. Last year, Ila splurged on a pants suit from Ann Taylor. "I wore it and felt great in it," she says. "I wish to could do that more often, but playing ball keeps me broke…But someday…."

The consideration of what to wear faces any woman who competes in a male bastion. To fit in, many tend to dress, as much as is possible, as the men do. The businesswomen's "uniform" of the 1970s and early 80s was a straight-cut navy pinstripe suit jacket and skirt of modest length that camouflaged the figure. Once sure of their place, however, women relaxed their dress code. Today, many businesswomen wear more traditionally feminine attire. Hanging on in the Northern League, Borders wants camouflage.

Ila has another good reason for wanting to blend in: safety. With roughings up from her California days in mind, she recently said of her time with the Dukes, "I like living in Minnesota because there's no crime there. It's a huge relief to know I'm completely safe."

Though not entirely. As Borders sat in a visitors' bullpen, a scissors-wielding woman reached through the chain-link fence and tried to cut her hair. On the road, she once walked into a hotel room to be greeted by two strangers—male groupies exist, too. At her Madison, Wisconsin motel, when a receptionist handed her a room key in the crowded lobby and sang out, "Room [555] is right across the parking lot," Ila's response was immediate and sharp: "Rule number one on the road: never let anyone know what room I'm in." Wary of strange encounters, Borders wants to blend in.

This, then, is what it means to cross baseball's gender line: You shrug off the taunts of opposing players and teammates, some of which cut through the hide you have developed. You ignore the thought that life would be simpler for the other players, your coach and manager if you were gone. You try to keep up your confidence amid the comments that you're just a draw at the gate. (If the fans don't show, will you be gone, like Lizzie Arlington?). You put up with the press you don't trust. You know rather too much about how men behave away from the mediating influence of women. You see close-up the dark side of your own gender and choose female friends with caution. You often find acceptance among other minorities, individuals who have proven their loyalty: David Glick, a Jewish pitcher now with the Houston Astros; Bob Owens, an African-American football coach; a closeted gay man. To survive, you dress like the guys and try to blend in, keep aloof, and always watch your back. And when the chants of "Ila, Ila, Ila" stop and it is over, you hope that you will be remembered not as the game's "missing son" but as its fully-acknowledged daughter.

Firsts and Stats on Ila Borders' Career

September 1993:The first woman to be awarded a college baseball scholarship.

February 15, 1994: First woman to pitch a complete game victory in a college game. Southern California College v. Claremont-Mudd.

July 24, 1998: First woman to win a men's regular season professional baseball game, Duluth-Superior Dukes v. Sioux Falls Canaries.

1997-99: First woman to play three full seasons of professional men's baseball (the Northern League.

For the Record
Ila Jane Borders, Pitcher, Bats L; Throws L; Height: 5'10"; Weight: 150. Birthdate: 18 Feb. 1975; Birthplace; Downey, CA; Resides: La Mirada, CA. College: Whittier (CA).

1997 St. Paul Saints (Northern):
W:0; L:0; ERA:7.50; Games:7; Innings Pitched:6.0; Hits:11; Runs:8; Earned Runs:5; Walks:4; Strikeouts:5.
1997 Duluth-Superior Dukes (Northern):
W:0; L:0; ERA:7.56; Games:8; Innings Pitched:8.1; Hits:13; Runs:9; Earned Runs:7; Walks:5; Strikeouts:6.
1998 Duluth-Superior Dukes (Northern):
W:1; L:4; ERA:8.66; Games:14; Innings Pitched:43.2; Hits:65; Runs:45; Earned Runs:42; Walks:14; Strikeouts:14.
1999 Duluth Superior Dukes (Northern):
W:0; L:0; ERA:30.56; Games:3; Innings Pitched:2.1; Hits:10; Runs:11; Earned Runs:8; Walks:4; Strikeouts:1.
1999 Madison Black Wolf (Northern):*
W:1; L:0; ERA 1.67; Games:15; Innings Pitched:32.1; Hits:33; Runs:7; Earned Runs:6; Walks:10.

Strike Out

Bill Swank

They had the votes. They were ready to walk, but the strike struck out. The year was 1946. All indications pointed to a particularly contentious season between the ballplayers and team owners.

Early in the year, the Brothers Pasquel aggressively solicited American ballplayers with the promise of large paychecks if they would jump to the independent Mexican League. One of the stars who defected was pitcher Max Lanier of the St. Louis Cardinals. Lanier was 6-0 when he left the Redbirds, who would eventually claim their third World Series championship in five years in 1946.

Organized baseball threatened to expel the offending players from professional play in the United States for five years. When things did not work out in Mexico, the disillusioned players came home and found themselves at the mercy of baseball commissioner A.B. "Happy" Chandler. Most were allowed to return to rosters in 1949, after Danny Gardella threatened legal action, but the truce was uneasy and there were other issues yet to be resolved.

Player Al Niemiec sued the Seattle Rainers of the Pacific Coast League for releasing him two weeks into the season. A federal judge ruled that postwar reemployment rights of players who served in the military entitled them to a full year of pay at their former salaries. Niemiec got his money, but $667 was deducted from his check since he had earned this amount as a beer salesman for brewer Emil Sick, the Rainers

owner, following his release.

All the while, Robert Murphy, a Harvard-educated labor lawyer, was attempting to convince players to join his American Baseball Guild. The Pittsburgh Pirates showed the most interest with ninety-five percent membership, but team owner William E. Benswanger refused to bargain with Murphy over player grievances. Talks broke down and players were prepared to strike before their June 7 game with the New York Giants.

Pittsburgh manager Frank Frisch had already penciled in Honus Wagner, his seventy-two-year-old coach, to play shortstop. Although all of the players supported Murphy's goals, the team's three highest-paid players, Rip Sewell, Jimmy Brown, and Bob Elliott, led opposition to the strike. The final vote count was 20-16 in favor, which fell short of the required two-thirds majority necessary for a walkoff.

The most significant development from the labor unrest of 1946 was a pension plan proposed by St. Louis shortstop Marty Marion and the Cardinals' team trainer Doc Weaver. Players and teams would match contributions to a retirement fund that would pay a yearly annuity of $1,200 to ten-year veterans at age forty-five. Additional revenue would come from the All Star Game, World Series broadcasting rights and special exhibition games. Although some players were dubious, a pension plan was instituted that granted credit for previous years' service. To be eligible, a player had to be on a major league roster on the last day of the 1946 season or the first day of the 1947 season. This last requirement would prove to be a subtle distinction for those who jumped to Mexico.

Bill Swank *is the author of* Echoes From Lane Field, A History of the San Diego Padres, 1936-1957. *A crusader for old ballplayers, he has campaigned for years to get San Diego's first major leaguer, Dead Ball home run king Gavvy Cravath, elected to the Hall of Fame.*

Former Brooklyn Dodgers all-star second baseman Pete Coscarart was one of the more active Pittsburgh players to support the Guild in 1946. A nine-year major league veteran, Coscarart was immediately sold following the strike vote to San Diego in the Pacific Coast League. He would never play in the major leagues again.

More than fifty years later, Coscarart and his old Brooklyn teammate, Dolph Camilli, sued baseball for lost benefits and royalty rights they believed were denied them by Major League Baseball's multimillion dollar merchandising business. Apparently in response to similar pending litigation, MBL's executive council decided in 1997 to create a pension for Negro Leaguers who were unable to play in the majors long enough to qualify for the pension.

Later that year, this same offer was made to the pre-1947 players with four years in the major leagues. All of the players would receive $10,000 a year. Beginning in October 1997, sixty-seven former Negro Leaguers and fifty-one ex-major leaguers began receiving quarterly payments of $2,500. Several players were dissatisfied with this offer and rejected it on the basis that it did not provide for surviving spouses or medical expenses. They wanted benefits similar to those granted by baseball's existing pension program.

In February, 1998, a California jury awarded $85,000 to Coscarart and 383 other players for royalties they had been denied. After this judgment was announced, both sides claimed victory and both sides filed appeals. The plaintiffs would each receive $221.35 under this decision, but in the summer of 1999, the appellate court reduced the jury award. On October 18, 1999, the trial judge granted summary judgment to MLB, Major League Baseball Properties, and Phoenix Communications Group against the old-timers.

Bad guys?—The pension issues raised by the pre-1947 players are complex, emotional, and long standing. Major League Baseball and the current leadership of the Players Association, believe they have been unfairly portrayed as the villains in this scenario.

Don Fehr, head of the Players Association makes a critical point. "If pre-'47 players get a pension, it raises the question, what do you do with everybody else? Up til 1980, it took four years to be vested. Do members from '47 to '79 (with less than four years in the major leagues) have priority? They played during a period covered by the pension and the pre-'47 players did not. They were members of the Players Association and the pre-'47 players were not. The Baseball Guild did not become the Players Association. Under the law, unions cannot bargain for former employees. The legal significance is important. It would be nice for the old-timers to get a pension, but we cannot represent them."

The Major League Baseball Players Association was formed in 1953 primarily because the players were unable to receive an accounting of the pension fund. One of those post-1947 players who is not eligible for a pension is Bill Glynn, who played three years with the Cleveland Indians from 1952 through 1954. "I remember it so clear, because Al [Rosen] said they should drop the pension to three years instead of five for the guys who only stayed up for three years. I played over six years in Triple A and it was hard to get to the big leagues back then, because they only had sixteen teams. I remember Chuck Connors, the Rifleman, tried to get the pension for the guys who played in the minors. Al said the players who were up for eight or twelve years were getting bigger salaries and should be able to save some money for the future. He felt the three-year guys would need a pension more than the guys who played for a long time.

"I heard somebody say that if they took every old-timer who played just two years and gave them a small pension, they wouldn't even miss it. They must have a lot of money in that pension fund. I'd be glad to get $100 a month."

"You can't just amend a pension plan arbitrarily," argues former Players Association leader Marvin Miller. "There are federal statutes preventing discrimination. The pension plan began on April 1, 1947. You cannot arbitrarily adjust a pension plan, even if the employer agrees to bring into pension coverage the pre-'47 people, unless you bring in the post-'47 people."

Miller questions the lack of responsibility demonstrated by the post-1947 players who complain that their pensions have not been increased to their satisfaction. "They were the ones who knocked out the pre-'47 people. Consider what that means…you could have had a twenty-year man who was released just before the '46 season ended and he received nothing. They were responsible for excluding the pre-'47 players, yet both groups later blamed the present players.

"We moved the vesting from five years years to four years in 1969 and made it retroactive to 1947. We got it down to one day in the majors in the 1980 negotiations, but only prospectively."

The public is unaware of the in-fighting that occurs within the Players Association between today's ballplayers, the post-1980 players, and the retired pre-1980 players. Don Fehr humorously describes Hall of Fame pitcher and pre-1980s activist Early Wynn as "a man who could not take yes for an answer."

Marvin Miller adds, "The employer is the supplier of pensions. The notion that somehow the responsibility should shift to the players is absurd. Sportswriters bought this, too. I recall talking to reporters and asking if they felt responsible for the former writers of their publications, writers of thirty, forty years ago, whom they never met. The unanimous response was that they felt no obligation to pay for pensions for their predecessors since they were not the employer."

MLB spokesman Richard Levin states, "Baseball is very proud of its support of Major League Baseball players and other members of the baseball family. In 1997, the major league baseball clubs established two separate supplemental benefit plans to assist former players. To date, over $2,000,000 has been paid to former players under these two benefit plans. One-hundred and ninety-seven former players are currently receiving benefits under these plans and another twenty-seven have received benefits in the past."

Dreams and lawsuits—A tireless champion for the old-timers is Bob Locker, who pitched for ten major league seasons during the '60s and '70s. A dreamer, Locker suggests, "Baseball should have retirement homes for the old-timers in Arizona and Florida. They could be in the warm sun. They could talk baseball with their old friends. The old-timers would love to be around baseball and could talk with the fans. Think how much it would mean for the fans to talk with their heroes during spring training. It would be wonderful public relations for baseball."

Locker has crusaded on behalf of the pre-1947 players since his days as a player representative. "The Players Association was gathering some steam and we had a vote on the pension. We could max it out for ourselves or go all the way back. It turned out that I was the only one who voted for the old-timers. I had gone to an old-timers reunion in Florida and they made me aware they didn't have the pension. That just wasn't right. When I think about the pension that I get and what today's players will get and the old-timers get nothing...it makes me feel terrible. It just isn't right."

Max Lanier sued baseball and reportedly settled for $30,000 in 1998.

Marty Glick, a San Francisco attorney and baseball fan who represents Major League Baseball, does not consider Lanier to be a good example of the typical pre-1947 player. Lanier returned to the majors and played more than four years after 1949, which would have qualified him for a pension. "One of the salient facts is that when Lanier came back after the pension went into effect, he refused to contribute to the fund and it was a very minimal amount...two dollars per day during the playing season. If you didn't pay, you weren't in it. "

After his return to the Brooklyn Dodgers in 1949, outfielder Luis Olmo reportedly sent his contributions to the pension fund only to have the owners return his money. Max Lanier contends, "If we weren't on the roster the last day of '46 or the first (day) of '47, we couldn't get the pension. Luis Olmo and I played on the same team in Mexico. When I saw they wouldn't take his money for the pension, I thought what's the use of me sending it in?"

Glick confirms that Olmo initially contributed to the pension fund for approximately two years and his money was accepted. "Olmo himself decided to withdraw his contributions on August 8, 1951, and the money he asked for was sent back to him. Sal Maglie, Mickey Owen, and Fred Martin, for example, three players who also jumped to the Mexican League and reurned, contributed and all three received pensions. Mr. Lanier simply chose not to pay."

When Major League Baseball offered $10,000 a year to the old-timers, ninety-two-year-old Wally "Preacher" Hebert discussed the plan with his family and his former teammate, Pete Coscarart. "I knew at my age I wouldn't get much and didn't want to go to court. Pete was my roommate at Pittsburgh. I didn't want to hurt his case and he told me to take the money." Hebert died in December, 1999 and there are no survivor benefits for his wife from this program.

Eighty-seven-year-old Xavier "Mr. X" Rescigno, another Pirate teammate who played three years in the major leagues, recalls salary negotiations during the war years. "I sent my contract back to Benswanger. He was only going to give me $450 a month and I was making that in Albany! When the team came to New York, he wanted me to meet him at the Hotel New Yorker. I told him I could make that much working at my father's butcher shop. He said Albany was only paying me $250 a month, but I told him the owner was giving me another $200 under the table. He finally gave me $500. What could I do but sign? They were sure cheap. When your cap got dirty, they wouldn't give you a new one until you turned in your old one."

A reflective Coscarart notes, "The only ones left from the '41 Dodgers are Herman Franks, Mickey Owen, Newt Kimball, Ed Albosta, and myself and I'm the oldest of all of them [eighty-six]. Newt is eighty-three. Mickey is eighty-two. Herm is eighty-four, and Ed is only eighty. He's the young pup. I'm the old grandfather.

"I hadn't even thought of a pension when I was playing ball because there was none. Then Mr. Murphy came to the Pirates and started talking about organizing the guild for higher pay and the pension. We agreed it would take a two-thirds vote to strike. We didn't know how the vote would come out going into the meeting. I thought we'd have more votes. Rip Sewell and Al Lopez agreed with us, but they said we couldn't strike.

"The idea of going on a strike was scary, but we had to do something to shake them up. I always liked Mr. Benswanger. I thought he was a square shooter. Sewell, Lopez, [Bob] Elliott...all those guys felt that way. Benswanger was better than the other owners. All I could see was that we had to do something. The players weren't mad at each other. They all agreed, but they just wouldn't go on strike."

1941 National League Most Valuable Player Dolph

Camilli died in October, 1997. His widow, Molly, is very bitter. "Other ballplayers who were less famous than Dolph get a pension and he got nothing. They used Dolph's name and pictures and he wasn't compensated."

Mrs. Camilli is emphatic that "Dolph, Coscarart, and Gionfriddo were never offered the $2,500 every three months. A woman in Minnesota got one check. Her husband got sick and died. She had to give the second check back. [Then-acting baseball commissioner Bud] Selig is a liar."

Coscarart is more circumspect. "If we hadn't gone with Bob Murphy's plan, they might have never had a pension. It got the owners thinking when they thought we'd go on strike. We can look back now and realize that backing up Murphy's strike brought about the beginning of the pension that today's players have, but they have forgotten about the guys who made this all happen."

"Basketball, football, and hockey take care of their old-timers. Baseball, which is the number one game of the nation, has forgotten us," says the forlorn Coscarart. "They are just waiting for us to die."

It is doubly ironic that Pete Coscarart, one of the few remaining players who voted for the Baseball Guild in 1946, also filed the lawsuit against baseball that seemingly motivated Major League Baseball to provide a supplemental benefit program for the pre-1947 players. Once again, other ballplayers have benefited from Coscarart's courage and foresight.

In fairness, baseball has not forgotten the old-timers. Settlements have been reached with most of the pre-1947 players and perhaps in the near future Pete the Pirate will be awarded a share of baseball's treasure chest. Although Coscarart offered to drop his suit in September, 1999, the commissioner's office refused him the right to enroll in the $10,000 per year supplemental income program.

Sources:

Baseball Guide and Record Book (1947), J. G. Taylor Spink, Charles C. Spink & Son, 1947.

Baseball's Pivotal Era: 1945-1951, William J. Marshall, University Press of Kentucky, 1999.

The Imperfect Diamond, Lee Lowenfish and Tony Lupien, Stein and Day Publishers, 1980.

When The Boys Came Back: Baseball and 1946, Frederick Turner, Henry Holt and Company, 1996.

New York *Times*, Peter Gollenbock, July 27, 1997.

San Diego *Union-Tribune*, Phil Collier, September 28, 1997.

San Diego *Union-Tribune*, "In Brief," February 18, 1998.

Telephone interview with Wally Hebert, August 1, 1999.

Personal interview with Mollie Camilli, August 8, 1999.

Telephone interview with Bob Locker, August 15, 1999.

Personal interview with Pete Coscarart, August 16, 1999.

Telephone interview with Marty Glick, August 17, 1999 and letter dated October 26, 1999.

Telephone interview with Max Lanier, August 22, 1999.

Telephone interviews with Don Fehr, August 24, 1999 and January 31, 2000.

Letter from Richard Levin, August 25, 1999.

Telephone interview with Marvin Miller, August 29, 1999.

Telephone interview with Xavier Resigno, September 12, 1999.

Telephone interview with Bill Glynn, September 14, 1999.

Dick Higham

Larry R. Gerlach and Harold V. Higham

*R*ichard "Dick" Higham is simultaneously one of the best and least well-known figures in baseball history. He is widely known as the only umpire to be expelled from major league baseball because of alleged dishonesty. Yet his actual umpiring career is little known and the circumstances surrounding his expulsion have not received close scrutiny. Moreover, Higham's banishment has greatly obscured his accomplishments as one of the finest players of his day. Because he suffers from a unique historical opprobrium, it is especially important that his story be told thoroughly and accurately.

Conversations with Harold V. Higham beginning in 1997 convinced me that his great-grandfather has not been treated well by historians, myself included. As a result, we have collaborated to present as complete a study of l'affaire Higham as we could. Along with my historical account of Dick Higham's umpiring career ("The Historical Record") and a historiographical perspective ("Postscript"), Harry Higham has provided a lawyer's perspective on the case for his dismissal from baseball ("A Brief to the Bar of History"). Because Dick Higham had no legal representation during the hearing that led to his banishment, Harry Higham now asks questions likely to have been raised by defense counsel, questions that cause us to ponder the fairness of the proceedings and the validity of the case.

It is our hope that this unique conjoining of the perspectives and approaches of the historical and legal professions will sharpen sensibilities about what constitutes good historical research. Good history stems not only from gathering information from as many sources as possible, but also from asking challenging questions about the accuracy and meaning of the material. In the end, it is less important that historical questions be answered definitively than that they be asked critically. In times past, as in times present, things were not always as clear and simple as they might seem at first blush. The story of Richard Higham is a case in point.

—Larry Gerlach

THE HISTORICAL RECORD
Larry Gerlach

Like many other umpires, Dick Higham began his baseball career as a player. In 1870, at age nineteen, he joined the New York Mutuals, and during the life of the National Association played three years with the Mutes and single seasons with the Lord Baltimores (1872) and the Chicago White Stockings (1875). Following the demise of the Assocation, Higham played for the Hartford Dark Blues (1876) and Providence Grays (1878) of the National League, as well as the independent Syracuse Stars (1877) before concluding his playing career in 1879 with brief stints with two National Association teams, the Capital Citys of Albany and the Rochester Hop Bitters. (He also appeared in one game with the Troy Trojans in 1880.)

Dick Higham was one of the leading performers during professional baseball's formative decade. He was known as an outstanding batter, frequently leading his team in key offensive categories. An unusually versatile fielder, he mostly played catcher, second base, and right field, but eventually appeared at every position except pitcher. Several appointments as team manager

Larry R. Gerlach *is a professor of history at the University of Utah.* **Harold V. Higham** *is an attorney-at-law.*

and captain spoke to his leadership ability and knowledge of the game. He also was reputed to have associated with "undesirable characters" which, coupled with occasionally erratic fielding, led periodically to the suspicions of crooked play that clouded his reputation.

The Inaugural Season—When Dick Higham's playing career ended, he was not yet finished with professional baseball. On March 8, 1881, National League officials designated him as one of twenty-three men "of good repute and considered competent to act as Umpires" for the upcoming season.[1] At first his selection as an umpire seems inexplicable, given the persistent suspicions of "fixing" during his playing days in the National Association.[2] But in truth none of the rumors of "crooked play" was ever proved and no such allegations were voiced publicly while he was in the National League. Moreover, he was a recognized authority on playing the game, and had had some umpiring experience in the National Association[3]. Besides, competent umpires were in short supply. Only four of the twenty-four arbiters approved for 1880 were reappointed for 1881.[4]

Higham made his National League debut on May 2, 1881, as the umpire designee of the Providence Grays.[5] His initial outing passed without incident, but criticisms of the new arbiter arose during the rest of the five-game, home-and-home series with Boston. In one game he was charged with making "two or three decisions" that met with "determined and rowdyish opposition" from Providence fans, in another with "grossly one-sided umpiring," and in yet another with "two rank decisions" that incurred the "disapprobation" of Boston fans. However, the Boston *Globe* was impressed with the new arbiter: "Dick Higham is a perfectly fair umpire and knows every point, lets everybody hear his decisions promptly, and his occasional carelessness will be easily overcome."[6]

After calling the Grays and Wolverines series in Detroit on May 20-23, Higham, for reasons unknown, became the umpire designee of the new Detroit franchise. He umpired the Boston series in Detroit, May 25-27, substituted for Herm Doscher in Troy on June 8, and then did not umpire again until Boston returned to Detroit on July 9. On July 13, he experienced the danger of umpiring when Boston leadoff hitter Ross Barnes fouled off a pitch that hit Dick on the "left temple and cut it to the bone." After a surgeon arrived and stitched up "the gash," Higham and the game resumed.[7] On July 16, he switched to his hometown Troy Trojans, then rejoined Detroit on September 13 for the club's season-ending eastern trip. All told, he had umpired fifty-eight National League games, eight for Providence, eighteen for Detroit, and thirty-two for Troy.

Newspapers commented infrequently on umpiring, and then mostly to offer criticism. In Higham's case, there were no negative comments after the season-opening series between Boston and Providence. Following his initial series with the White Stockings in Detroit, the Detroit *Free Press* remarked on May 21 that "Higham is as good an umpire as he used to be [a] ball player." Two months later, the *Free Press* had not changed its assessment, declaring on July 15 that "Mr. Higham is one of the best umpires in the League." After his initial appearance with Troy, the Troy *Daily Times* on July 18 reported that Higham umpired the game "to everybody's satisfaction," and on August 8 commented that he had given "great satisfaction as an umpire." After the Grays defeated the Trojans, 2-1, in eleven innings on August 2, the *Providence Evening Bulletin* noted that "Higham umpired the game with excellent judgment."

Although known for "growling" as a player, Higham brooked no challenge to his umpiring authority. On July 26, he threatened Providence's Jack Farrell with a fine for arguing an "out" call, and on September 9 fined Harry Stovey, Worcester captain, $20 "for using ungentlemanly language and questioning the decision of the umpire."[8]

By all measures, he enjoyed great success in his first season as an umpire, capped off in early October when the "veteran ball player and gentlemanly umpire" received a "complimentary testimonial" in the form of an exhibition game between the home-town Trojans and a "picked nine."[9] Later that month, he solidified his association with Detroit by joining the Wolverines as a player for an exhibition tour to Richmond, Virginia.[10]

The Veteran Arbiter—National League officials again approved Higham for 1882, one of only six arbiters retained from the previous year.[11] (The American College Base Ball Association also approved him to work the June-July college season.)[12] His reputation was outstanding. Harry Wright, who switched managerial duties from Boston to Providence, thought Higham "first class," being "reliable and very even in his umpiring and always gentlemanly."[13] Delighted that Higham was rejoining the Wolverines, the Detroit *Free Press* on April 9 boasted: "Detroit's professional umpire is as good as anybody's."[14]

However, controversy arose after Detroit swept three games, May 1-3, from the Cleveland Blues to open the season. The Cleveland *Plain Dealer* contended that the Blues were "fairly" outplayed and at the conclusion of the series judged Higham "an excellent umpire," but the Cleveland *Herald* charged there was "nothing straight" about the "rather crooked" games.[15] While the target may have been players, as no allegations were levied against Higham, George "Foghorn" Bradley umpired the three-game series when Cleveland visited Detroit May 16-18. Newspapers gave no explanation for the substitution, the *Free Press* simply noting on May 16 that "Umpire Higham will witness the game today from the grand stand."

Higham made news. He was frequently complimented on his umpiring. For example, the Buffalo *Courier* on May 6 declared that "Higham umpired in a very satisfactory manner," and the Chicago *Herald* on May 21 noted that "although often accused of crooked playing when a league player," he "gave good satisfaction as an umpire." He was also criticized for misapplying a rule that affected the outcome of a game,[16] misjudging a home run,[17] and ignoring the official interpretation of a rule.[18] He also achieved recognition for being the first umpire to don a catcher's mask behind the plate. The first mention of him wearing a mask was during the May 20-23 series in Chicago, where the innovation drew negative comments from spectators who thought the "muzzle" might interfere with the arbiter's vision.[19] On June 10, the Worcester *Evening Gazette* commented: "Umpire Higham wears a mask when he and the catcher are under the bat—an exhibition of caution never seen here before." Higham's practice quickly caught on. By season's end "a majority of professional umpires" was wearing a catcher's mask.[20]

At approximately 3 o'clock on the afternoon of May 27, the Wolverines left on a road trip that ultimately would determine Dick Higham's place in baseball history. Interest in the eastern swing was high, as it began with a series between second-place Detroit and first-place Providence. William G. Thompson, mayor of Detroit and president of the ball club, accompanied the team as he had previously to Chicago May 20-23. En route to Rhode Island, the Detroits played an exhibition game, umpired by Higham, against the minor league Philadelphias, an Alliance club.[21]

On May 30, before 7,185 spectators, the largest crowd in Providence history, the Wolverines committed seven errors in losing, 4-0, to the Grays. The Providence *Daily Journal* attributed the miscues to "nervousness," while the Detroit *Free Press* cynically commented: "Next thing somebody will be saying the Detroits do not work in unison." Although Higham mistakenly denied the Grays a home run, the *Journal* thought his umpiring "intelligent and impartial."[22] The next day Detroit won, 6-4, and then dropped the series finale, 8-7, on June 2. The Wolverines then moved on to Boston, Worcester, and Troy.

On June 18, the Detroit *Free Press* announced that "the venerable Richard Higham, Esq." would umpire the Wolverines' next home game, but he did not return with the team after the June 17 game in Troy. Neither Troy nor Detroit newspapers gave any explanation for his sudden departure after umpiring twenty-six games for the Wolverines; the Detroit *Evening News* simply noted on June 20 that Dick Pearce would umpire the Providence series.[23] In fact, Mayor Thompson, had released Higham, suspecting him of dishonesty. Upon returning from the road trip, Thompson was given a letter purportedly written by Higham containing a code whereby he advised James Todd, a "well-known gambler," how to bet on the recent series in Providence and specifically how to wager on the first game.[24] The instructions matched the outcome of the contest and Thompson, who had just offered the Wolverines a $100 bonus for winning the championship, reacted with "the utmost indignation" and "immediately revoked" Higham's authorization to umpire for the team.[25]

As word of the Detroit club's investigation spread to league officials and some team owners, such as Chicago's Albert Spalding, Higham umpired for his home-town Trojans.[26] The switch to Troy was ironic given the circumstances, and the Troy *Daily Times'* assertion that Detroit's victory over the Trojans on June 17 was aided "by the umpire's favor on two close decisions." The paper also reprinted without comment a Buffalo *Express* article noting that Higham was "the last umpire to be chased into the swamps" and that the Troy newspapers claimed Higham's decisions in the last game with Detroit were "manifestly unfair, and that he cannot longer claim the distinction of being honest."[27] Be that as it may, he umpired three Trojans games in Buffalo, June 20-22, and was scheduled to umpire Troy games in Cleveland when he was summoned to Detroit and a rendezvous with history.[28]

The Hearing—Dick Higham return to Detroit to appear before a special session of the league's five-member Board of Directors, held at the Russell House on the afternoon of May 24, to answer charges of crooked umpiring brought by President Thompson. Neither Arthur H. Soden, president of the Boston club and interim league president following the death of William Hulbert in April, nor Secretary Nicholas Young of Washington, D. C., was present. Two of the four elected league directors, Thompson of Detroit and Freeman Brown of Worcester, were present. Josiah Jewett of Buffalo and A. L. Hotchkin of Troy did not attend, and were represented by club directors James Mugridge and Gardner Earl respectively.[29]

The circumstances of the hearing and the nature of the deliberations are shrouded in uncertainties, but the basic facts of the matter can be quickly summarized.[30] Higham "protested his innocence vigorously" and denied any collusion with gamblers to influence games. Thompson, an attorney by profession, then presented to the panel the incriminating letter and the opinion of three bank examiners expert in handwriting analysis that the handwriting was "identical" to that of another letter acknowledged to have been written by Higham. That was the only known evidence presented.[31] The meeting concluded with the Board of Directors voting unanimously that the charges against Higham were "fully sustained" and that he be "forever disqualified" from umpiring National League games.[32] Whether Higham was judged guilty of actually "selling," or merely "offering to sell," a game is unknown, but the league's rule prohibiting gambling covered either case.[33]

Newspaper reaction to the first expulsion of a major league umpire for dishonesty was curious. Despite the persistent concerns about gambling and umpiring voiced by the press, especially the New York *Clipper*, Higham's expulsion elicited surprisingly little comment. Some newspapers merely printed, verbatim or paraphrased, a brief Associated Press dispatch from Detroit.[34] Others offered cursory comments in support of the expulsion.[35] There was no outrage at the umpire's alleged dishonesty, no sense that the expulsion of an umpire protected the integrity of the game. However, as advocated by the New York *Clipper*, the National League, following the lead of the rival American Association, created in 1883 a staff of four salaried umpires as a means of enhancing the quality, independence, and financial status of the arbiters.[36]

For Dick Higham, a decade of fine ballplaying was obliterated in historical memory by a half-season of umpiring. A reading of newspaper accounts of virtually every game Higham umpired indicates that, occasional gaffs notwithstanding, he was a popular umpire and a good—even a very good—one. But sometimes good umpires, like good players, do bad things, even very bad things. Recurring suspicions of crooked play as player and persistent association with unsavory characters point to a pattern of probable behavior that correlates with the charges against him.

Dick Higham

The full story of Higham's expulsion remains untold and, pending the discovery of additional documentation, will never be known. There are discrepancies in, and omissions from, the record, and newspaper reportage at the time was not as complete or professional as it would become by the end of the century. Nor is it certain that Higham, if guilty, acted alone, since it is possible for an umpire or player to guarantee defeat, but impossible to guarantee victory.[37] Yet if the known case against Higham is not as complete as one would like, there is no indication that he was framed, was the victim of a personal vendetta, or was targeted as a scapegoat for the gambling ills then plaguing the game. Thus, from the perspective of traditional historical scholarship, Richard Higham stands guilty as charged and warrants the dishonorable distinction of being the only umpire expelled from major league baseball for dishonesty in the conduct of the game.[38]

However, given the opprobrium attached to being the only major league umpire dismissed for dishonesty, Higham deserves the day in court he did not have in 1882. Historians have both rushed to judgment and presented fundamentally flawed accounts of the explusion based primarily on the cursory research of Lee Allen.[39] The cautionary words of the Detroit *Post and Tribune* are as valid today as they were on June 25,

1882: "It is to be hoped that the action taken was not hasty. Higham has occupied an enviable position as an umpire, and has many admirers who refuse to believe him guilty. If the facts are incontrovertible the league directors are to be congratulated on their peremptory and speedy action. If not, it will injure the league." Thus, it is instructive to step beyond the bounds of traditional historical inquiry and to subject the record to legalistically discerning questions about the facts of the matter, as well as the procedures whereby Higham was found guilty.

A BRIEF TO THE BAR OF HISTORY
Harold V. Higham

It has been almost a century and a quarter since Richard "Dick" Higham was forever disqualified from acting as umpire in any game of ball participated in by a National League club. His "trial" took place at the Russell House in Detroit—and in the newspapers.

Since that time, many historians, reporters, writers, and editors have noted the event and its result. No one has ever raised a voice in Higham's defense.

What follows is a critical chronological exposition of contemporary newspaper accounts and of the National League's official "Minute of the Special Meeting" of June 24, 1882. I believe this is the first time this has been done.

This is not an attempt to prove Higham's innocence. It will, however, detail exactly what Richard Higham was accused of, and will raise the question of whether he was truly proven to have done it.

On June 24, 1882, the following item appeared on the front page of the Detroit *Evening News*:

A LEAGUE TRIAL

The board of directors of the national league of professional base ball clubs met at the Russell house this afternoon and went into secret session to try Richard Higham, of Troy, N.Y., one of the league umpires, on charges of crookedness in his decisions of games of ball between the Detroits and other clubs, preferred against him by president Thompson, of the Detroit club. Higham was present and the trial was entirely formal. It was concluded and the result sent to the league secretary, by whom the results will be promulgated, until which time the members all pledged themselves to profound secrecy. It has leaked out, however, that the charges were based upon letters written by Higham to gamblers in which the Detroit club played and he umpired; and that he was expelled from the league and list of umpires.

It was not until some eight to ten months later that the Official Minute of the meeting was made public, on page 103 of the *Spalding Guide* of 1883.

The *Spalding Guide*, particularly in the early days of the National League, was the official outlet for the dissemination of the league constitution, playing rules, minutes of board meetings, and other important League business, not the least of which was declaring the official pennant winner.

The Minute as published is exactly the same as the handwritten entry at page nine in the "Records of the National League of Professional Base Ball Clubs, 1881-1890," which can be found in the National Baseball Hall of Fame Museum and Library, at Cooperstown, New York. It states:

Special Meeting of the Board of Directors of the National League of Professional Base Ball Clubs held at the Russell House, Detroit, Mich.,
June 24, a. d. 1882.
PRESENT:
MESSRS. W. G. THOMPSON, FREEMAN BROWN, JAMES A. MUGRIDGE and GARDNER EARL, DIRECTORS. (The two latter representing the BUFFALO and TROY CITY CLUBS in the absence of MESSRS. JEWETT and HOPKINS.)
In the absence of President Soden and Secretary Young, MR. JAMES A. MUGRIDGE was elected chairman *pro tem.* and MR. FREEMAN BROWN, Sec'y *pro tem.*

PRESIDENT THOMPSON of the DETROIT CLUB preferred Charges against RICHARD HIGHAM, League umpire (letter marked "A") and in Support of same presented the following communication, (marked "B.") President Thompson by reason of representing the Club making the charges at issue, was excused from acting with the "Board."

Mr. Richard Higham, against whom the charges were preferred, was admitted to the meeting, and an opportunity given him to present his defence.

He denied the authorship of the letter marked "B" and made a general denial of all complicity with any person or persons to cause any game of ball to result otherwise than on its merits under the playing rules. The letter marked "B" having been submitted with a letter, the authorship of which Mr. Higham acknowledged to be his own, to three of the best handwriting experts in Detroit, and being pronounced identical with each other, it was *Resolved*, That the charges preferred by the Detroit Club against Richard Higham were fully sustained.

Resolved, That the said RICHARD HIGHAM be forever disqualified from acting as umpire in any game of ball participated in by a League Club.

On motion, adjourned
(Signed.)
FREEMAN BROWN,   JAMES A. MUGRIDGE,
Secretary *pro tem.*   Chairman *pro tem.*

From reading the Minute we learn that the League had trouble assembling its Board. Both the president and the secretary were absent, and substitutes had to be found for two members. Board member Thompson could not sit because he was the one preferring charges. Only one duly elected board member, Freeman Brown, acted. Article XI, Section 3 of the National League constitution required three directors to constitute a quorum. Any action taken by this assembly would have been on very shaky ground if challenged.

Based on the Minute, this is my analysis of what happened at the meeting:

1. President Thompson preferred the charges as embodied in a letter marked "A" and supported them with a "communication" marked "B."

2. Thompson was then excused from acting with the Board because he was representing the club making the charges.

3. Dick Higham was admitted to the meeting to present a defense. He (a) denied he was the author of the letter marked "B," and (b) denied any and all complicity with any person or persons to cause any game of ball to result otherwise than on its merits under the playing rules.

4. A comparison letter Higham admitted was in his own handwriting had been submitted along with letter "B" to "three of the best handwriting experts in Detroit." The handwriting on each was pronounced identical.

5. The charges preferred by the Detroit club were found to be fully sustained.

6. Richard Higham was forever disqualified from acting as umpire in any game of ball participated in by a league club.

7. The finding of the handwriting experts was apparently all contained in "A." The handwriting experts did not testify.

8. Only Higham testified in his behalf and had only his testimony to assist in his defense.

9. No one but Thompson and Higham testified.

10. Except for the comparison of letter "B" with a letter Higham admitted he wrote, no other evidence was offered to prove Thompson's charges.

11. Based on the process laid out in the Minute, Higham was disqualified for writing letter "B," not for complicity with others to cause a ball game to result otherwise than on its merits.

Letter "A," letter "B," and the comparison letter are not on file at the Hall of Fame with the Minute Book.

Newspaper talk—On Sunday, June 25, 1882, the day after the special meeting, the Chicago *Tribune* and the Detroit *Free Press* published what seemed to be coverage of the event. A close reading, though, shows they were actually written before the meeting took place. They were clear attempts to mold public opinion before the issuance of any official statements.

Chicago was the home of the White Stockings, as well as the headquarters of the National League, and Detroit was the site of the Special Meeting, but instead of being clear reports, they are both confusing and intriguing. The item in the Chicago *Tribune* states in pertinent part:

CROOKED UMPIRING
From a dispatch given below it will be seen that Dick Higham, by action of the League directors, has been expelled from the league list of umpires for collusion with gamblers in the umpiring of games.

It has been known for some time past that charges of the kind were Pending against Higham, but no publication has been made of it, lest an undeserved injury be inflicted. It seems, however, that the Directors found the charges fully sustained by the testimony, and by a unanimous vote expelled Higham. The charges were preferred by Mayor Thompson, President of the Detroit Club, as it was in Detroit that evidence was obtained through copies of telegrams showing that Higham was in communication with Eastern gamblers, that he indicated prior to each game how the money should be bet, and presumably governed his decisions accordingly, and that he is known to have received his share of the money thus won. Certainly grossly unfair decisions affecting the score and the results that were made by Higham at Detroit, coupled with the fact that his past record is not of the best, and his associates no better, led to a watch on his movements, with the results as stated above.

The Minute mentions no "testimony" except that of Thompson and Higham, no introduction of telegrams, no discussion of money. Interestingly, the same reporter states on one hand that he personally found Mr. Higham's umpiring to be competent and fair, and on the other that he thought Higham favored Detroit in an unidentified game by making "an unfair call."

The Chicago *Tribune* account also purports to quote the late NL founder William A. Hulbert, addressing the umpire's character, and saying: "I suppose I ought to have objected to the nomination then and there, for I had good reason to think that Higham was not a proper person for the league to endorse by electing him an umpire, but I forbore out of consideration for the gentleman who named Higham, and the nomination went through." Hulbert had died a little over two months before and was no longer available for comment.

As a counterweight, in a letter to the manager of the Union Base Ball Club, dated March 3, 1882, the profoundly respected Harry Wright, then with Boston, states in part: "...Of our League umpires I found Richard Higham to be first class. He is reliable and very even in his umpiring and always gentlemanly...."[40] Although Harry Wright was still alive and active throughout 1882, it does not appear that any newspaper sought any comment from him.

The item in the Detroit *Free Press* states::

There was quite a storm too, down town during the day, and it beat pitilessly upon the head of Richard Higham, the well-known league umpire, and it came from the board of league directors. He was summoned before them to explain a certain letter that was recently picked up in the Russell House and handed to President Thompson of the Detroit club. It bears no mail mark or stamp, and is supposed to have dropped from someone's pocket. It is addressed to James Todd, and proposes to arrange for a cipher dispatch by which Todd shall know when to bet on the Detroits and when on their opponents. It is signed "Dick." [All] the league clubs were represented at the hearing, which was held in the closest secrecy, and Mr. Higham was invited in to explain the true [business] of the letter. He denied that he wrote it. [The] members of the board, after a brief consultation, procured some letters, receipts, etc., from Higham and submitted them and the "Dick" letter to [four] bank experts, who all pronounced the writing to be identical, and a report of the case was sent to Secretary Young, of the league. The members of the board decline to give the full details of their deliberations, replying to all inquires [by citing] section 25, of the League Constitution, as follows: Any director who shall disclose, or publish any of the proceedings of the board, except officially [ ] in the report of the board, or when called upon by a vote of the league, shall forfeit his [place].
[brackets denote difficulty in reading the word from the copy of the microfilm.]

The leaks to the *Free Press* unlike those to the *Tribune*, do not mention suspicions, telegrams, testimony, eastern gamblers, or money received. We do learn that what is obviously letter "B," recently found at the very place where the special meeting was held, had fallen out of some unidentified person's pocket and was handed to Mayor Thompson. It was addressed to "Todd," contained a proposed cipher dispatch allegedly to be used for betting on Detroit's games, and was signed "Dick." On the record, at least, this was the sole basis on which Dick Higham was disqualified.

According to the *Free Press* reporter, it was *after* Higham testified that he did not write the letter that the Board gave comparision documents to four bank experts (not "three of the best handwriting experts in Detroit") to analyze.

Only insofar as the *Free Press* item speaks about a "Dick" letter, experts, and the "identical" appearance of letter "B" does it agree with the Minute. However, this insistence on the word "identical" casts the item and the proceedings in doubt. That the handwriting in letter "B" and the comparison letter were "identical" was more likely a layman's deliberate embellishment that could not be resisted by the Detroit *Free Press*, Mayor Thompson, the Board, or all three. In fact, no credible expert couches an opinion in absolute terms, and no true handwriting expert speaks in terms of "identical" letters or words.

Here is what a true expert writes about handwriting studies: "The identification of handwriting...is mainly based on the Principle that no person writes exactly alike and no two signatures of the same individual will be the perfect replica of each other."[41]

In any event, both the Chicago *Tribune* and Detroit *Free Press*, were quick to run innaccurate stories clearly based on advance information, not true reports of the meeting.

Perhaps they should have shown the same discretion as the Detroit *Post and Tribune* of the same day. It noted the accused had vigorously protested his innocence, and stated:

It is to be hoped that the action taken was not hasty. Higham has occupied an enviable position as an umpire, and has many admirers who refuse to believe him guilty. If the facts are incontrovertible the league directors are to be congratulated on their peremptory action. If not it will injure the league.

It also stated that manager Frank Bancroft of the Detroit Wolverines, testified, and that Freeman Brown —fill-in secretary of the meeting—had called to the attention of those in attendance that Higham had been seen in the society of a gambler when in Worcester.

The Minute, of course, makes no mention of Bancroft being present, let alone giving testimony. And if Brown, the only elected member of the board who was present, had said anything reflecting on the accused during the presentation of evidence, he should have withdrawn. This, of course, would have ended the meeting, because a quorum, even a broadly construed one that included substitutes for board members, would no longer have existed. If Brown said what is attributed to him and did not withdraw, then the special meeting was conducted in violation of the League Constitution. It would be fair to assume that the meeting, under those circumstances, was nothing more than a "kangaroo court" at which a finding for expulsion was agreed to in advance.

It would be interesting to know, along these lines of equity and fairness, what notice was given to Higham of the hearing and its purpose, and how much time and opportunity he was given to prepare a case and locate witnesses or experts to testify for him. There is no indication in the Minute or in any newspaper reports.

According to the New York *Herald* of June 23, 1882, Higham was in Buffalo, umpiring a game on the June 22 between Troy and Buffalo. Getting to Detroit would have taken him at least a day. If he was guilty and had been told in advance that he was going to be accused at a hearing in Detroit why would he have attended and put on such an empty defense, rather than simply resign and keep things quiet?

The letter—We do not have for review letter "A," letter "B," or the sample letter. We do have a most interesting item from the Detroit *Evening News* of Monday, June 26, 1882. That newspaper broke the original story on the day of the meeting and moved quickly at its conclusion, not before. It states:

WHY HIGHAM WAS BOUNCED.
On Tuesday, May 30, a well-known young man employed in a Woodward avenue retail house picked up the following letter, addressed to James Todd, Brunswick hotel:
Detroit, May 27, 1882.
Friend Todd:
I just got word we leave for the east on the 3 p.m. train, so I will not have a chance to see you. If you don't hear from me play the Providence Tuesday and if I want you to play the Detroits Wednesday I will telegraph in this way: "Buy all the lumber you can." If you do not hear from me don't play the Detroits, but buy Providence sure—that is the first game. I think this will do for the eastern series. I will write you from Boston. You can write me at any time in care of Detroit B. B. club. When you send me any money you can send check to me in care of the Detroit B. B. club, and it will be all right. You will see by that book I gave you the other day what city will [sic] be in.
Yours truly,
Dick.

Todd was known to be a man about town who lived largely by his wits, and the writer of the letter was suspected to be Dick Higham, who had been selected by the Detroit club to umpire their eastern games. The finder of the letter held it, only showing it to a friend, and awaited the result of the Detroit-Providence games, which sure enough turned out as predicted in the letter. On the return of the club from the eastern trip he showed the letter to president Thompson, who manifested the utmost indignation, immediately revoked the Detroit club's consent to have Higham for an umpire, and called a meeting of the league directors, who met at the Russell house and expelled Higham, as stated in Saturday's *News*. Higham denied the authorship of the letter, but other letters of his were produced and the signature "Dick" was declared by three bank experts to be the same. This prompt action on the part of the Detroit association clears their skirts of any insinuation of crookedness.

This newspaper item tells a different story about the finding of the letter as well as about the circumstance by which it came into the possession of President Thompson. It mentions a number of actions taken by President Thompson as a result of being apprised of the letter. It also mentions the pedigrees of the handwriting experts and gives a new finding by them. All this in addition to exhibiting what purports to be the body of letter "B."

If the well-known young man alluded to in the opening paragraph picked up or found the letter on Tuesday, May 30, 1882, chances are the Detroit-Providence game of that day was already underway, if not over. This fine young finder showed the letter to a friend, presumably the same day, although this is not stated, and they decided to await the outcome of both Detroit-Providence games before telling anyone they had found a letter addressed to a well-known man-about-town named Todd, who apparently was communicating with someone about baseball games.

Who was this fine young man and who was his friend? Why were either one or both not presented to the Board at the special meeting? Would it not be important to have either the fine young man or his friend verify how and where the letter was found? Its condition when found? Whether either or both attempted to return it to James Todd at the Brunswick? And why it was thought appropriate to hold the letter until the outcome of the games was reported? If Providence had lost Tuesday's game and Detroit had lost Wednesday's game, is it to be believed these fine young men would have discounted the contents of the letter entirely and either returned it to Todd or thrown it away?

As Mayor Thompson did not return from the Eastern trip until June 18, what did these fine young men do with the letter in the meantime? Where did they keep the letter? How did they make sure nothing happened to it? Why was it so important that they wait for the team to return? If a problem was discovered as early as May 30 with the games in which Detroit participated and Higham acted as umpire, why was not something done before he umpired another eleven League games?

What did James Todd have to say about the letter? Why was he not called before the board at the special meeting? Did any reporter seek his version? Did Mayor Thompson question him?

In 1882, only one umpire officiated in a National League game. He stood well back of the catcher, who crouched well back of the batter. With a runner on base, the umpire took a position in back of the pitcher, who stood in a rectangle fifty feet from home plate, so that he could watch the pitches and the base runner at the same time. The batter could request pitches high—between his belt and shoulder—or low—between his knees and belt. The pitcher was prohibited from releasing the ball above his waist. If the batter swung and missed, the pitch counted as a strike. If the pitch did not cross the plate in the area requested by the batter, it counted as a ball. In 1882, it took three strikes for an out and seven balls for a walk. All foul balls counted as strikes and a foul ball caught on the fly or on one bounce was an out. All the other basics such as stealing, tagging up, forcing the runner and the double play, were pretty much the same as today.

It is absurd to think that a lone umpire under those circumstances could "fix" a game. And Higham was never accused of acting in collusion with any manager or player.

How did the contents of the letter concerning the manner in which the writer wished to place two bets through Todd affect the outcome of either of the two games to which it refers? The author of the letter never says he has arranged the outcome of either game.

An athletic contest is not fixed by paying one side to win. It is fixed by paying one side to lose. The fixer must buy the loser. Where is the assurance to the gambler, Todd, that the losers have been bought?

Higham umpired the Tuesday and Wednesday games in Providence. The home team won on Tuesday, 4-0, and the Boston *Daily Globe* of the next day said, "The umpiring of Higham was excellent." The May 31 edition of the Providence *Daily Journal* carried an eyewitness account of this first game and stated: "The umpiring was intelligent and impartial, and contributed largely to the success of the game." Detroit won the Wednesday game, 6-4. Accounts in local papers and the Detroit *Evening News* make no comment about the umpiring.

In the letter, betting on both these games was provided for on a contingency basis. If the fix was in, the "lumber" message must have been sent to Todd. Where is the telegram?

Telegraph messages are written out or dictated and an operator transmits them over public wires. A copy of the message would have been on file at the office of the point of origin, where it was paid for by the sender, and at the receiving office in Detroit, and the copies would have included the names of the receiver and sender. Did either of the fine young men, or anyone from the board, or anyone from any newspaper, go to the telegraph office in either Providence or Detroit to inquire about a message instructing Todd to buy lumber?

The *Post and Tribune* article states that "other letters of his were produced," the Minute says that only a "comparison" letter in Higham's handwriting and letter "B," the incriminating letter, were placed before the Board. The article also states that in comparing the two letters, the experts declared only the signature "Dick" to be the same. The Minute indicates that letter "B" was the sole evidence on which the Board relied in making its finding.

How did the "experts" go about their examination, from June 18 to June 24? Did they compare all the handwriting in the "comparison" letter with all the handwriting in letter "B?" Why did they comment only on the signature? What was their opinion, if any, concerning who wrote the text of letter "B?"

Apart from whether Dick Higham would have wished to ask these questions in his own defense, wasn't the Board bound to ask them? And shouldn't the Board have heard from the fine young men, and "three of the best handwriting experts in Detroit" (or were they merely "three bank examiners") to insure that "the action taken was not hasty" and that "the facts are incontrovertible?"

At the very least, wouldn't the presence of these witnesses at the special meeting have afforded the board an opportunity to make the facts clearer? Shouldn't the media have sought out these witnesses in an attempt to obtain clarification?

Let's look closely at the letter. The author not only dates it, but also notes that it was written in the "City of Detroit." He further mentions leaving for the East on the 3 PM train.

Why does Todd need to know that the note is written in Detroit? Assuming improper activity, why does the writer use Todd's name, especially preceeded by the polite salutation of the day, "Friend?" Would it not have been more in keeping with a plot to merely jot "J" or "T"—or perhaps not provide any form of address at all?

May 27, 1882, the date on the letter, was a Saturday. The first game of Detroit's Eastern trip was on Tuesday, May 30, at Providence and the second game was on Wednesday, May 31, also at Providence. The author had already arranged a bet with Todd on Providence to win the Tuesday game. As of May 27, he is betting on Providence to win the Wednesday game as well, but if he changes his mind, he will send Todd a coded telegraph message switching his bet to Detroit. He will next write to Todd from Boston.

The author had given Todd a book that seems to include a schedule. Any time Todd needs to contact the author, he can write to him in care of the Detroit Base Ball Club. In fact, Todd can send him money—even checks (presumably his winnings)—via the ballclub and "it will be all right."

In 1882, the rules of the National League provided for the first time that umpires, as well as players and managers, were prohibited from gambling. It is highly unlikely that a member of any of these groups would want it known that he was in communication with a known gambler. Conversely, any person traveling with the Detroit team on this Eastern trip in May, 1882, who was not a player or manager or umpire, could receive such mail and/or checks without fear of being accused of violating league rules.

If this is indeed letter "B," is it not clear that its author is *not* fixing games? In a fix, cash is the medium of exchange. Would the fixer arrange to receive the related money in care of the team with which he is associated? Would he be willing to receive checks at all?

The letter makes it clear that its author is betting on baseball games, sometimes on Detroit and sometimes not. Because he is associated with the Detroit team and is traveling with it on this eastern trip, it may be unseemly for anyone to know he occasionally bets—or more important, that he sometimes bets on the opposition. Hence the need for a code on this occasion.

In sum, there is no evidence at all that Richard Higham was involved in fixing games, even assuming that he was the gambler who wrote letter "B." Leaving aside the important technical issue of the missing quorum, the process itself was still far from what we today would consider fair. We know that Higham was disqualified. What we really don't know—either from the record or the newspaper coverage—is whether he should have been.

POSTSCRIPT
Larry Gerlach

Upon his death in 1905, Richard Higham passed into the annals of history. In writing about Higham, historians have virtually ignored his ballplaying career and focused instead on his brief tenure as an umpire, and then almost exclusively on his expulsion for dishonesty. Moreover, they have read back from the banishment, assuming dishonorable conduct throughout his umpiring career and suggesting that it portended his eventual dismissal.

Higham's contemporaries would have been surprised by history's treatment of his career and expulsion. The question of guilt or innocence aside, the lack of extensive coverage of his banishment and subsequent commentary in newspapers suggests that contemporaries did not think the expulsion of an umpire for alleged crookedness had major implications for the integrity of the game. Neither did contemporary historians. Alfred H. Spink, publisher of *The Sporting News*, did not mention Higham in *The National Game* (1910), the first baseball history. Albert G. Spalding, who wrote extensively on the evils of players and gambling in *America's National Game* (1911), the first detailed, comprehensive history of baseball, knew the circumstances of Higham's dismissal but merely noted that in 1882 "Richard Higham was expelled on charges preferred by the Detroit Club, for collusion with pool-sellers" without mentioning that he was an umpire or commenting on the significance of the banishment. And in his *History and Records of Baseball* (1914), Francis C. Richter, publisher of *The Sporting Life,* cited as the two "memorable events" of 1882 the death of William Hulbert and "the expulsion of Umpire Higham, at a special meeting in June, charge of collusion with pool gamblers, preferred by the Detroit Club."[42]

Nor did the expulsion damage Higham's baseball reputation, for he was remembered upon his death in 1905 primarily as a fine ballplayer. The headline of the most extensive of the four known obituaries, in the Chicago *Tribune* on March 19, announced: OLD TIME BALL PLAYER DIES; WAS STAR IN EARLY '70S. The obituary mentioned that he was "one of the stars" on the famous Mutual club, "could fill almost any position on the ball field," and caught without a mask or chest protector. It also noted that gambling on games was "popular" during Higham's day and that a "quite a number of star performers were expelled for being in the employ of the gamblers," but did not mention his umpiring career or expulsion. The Detroit *Tribune*, the lone Detroit newspaper to note Higham's passing, commented on March 21 that he was "widely known" as a player for the Mutuals and White Sox, but did not mention his umpiring or expulsion. *The Sporting News* on March 25 also simply noted the death of "a star player of the '70s" who "became famous" as a member of the Mutuals. On the other hand, *The Sporting Life* on March 25 reprinted verbatim much of the *Tribune*'s obituary, but headlined the notice, DICK HIGHAM DEAD. ONLY UMPIRE EVER EXPELLED FOR CROOKEDNESS, and replaced the *Tribune*'s comments about players and gambling with the comment that Higham "became a National League umpire and was expelled upon charges of crookedness." The absence of references to the expulsion in the Chicago *Tribune*, Detroit *Tribune*, and *The Sporting News*, along with cursory mention in *The Sporting Life*, suggests that Higham's banishment was not considered a defining moment in baseball history.

The different emphases and perspectives accorded Higham's career and expulsion over time are understandable. Modern historians are acutely sensitive to gambling's threat to the integrity of the game because of the Black Sox Scandal of 1919, whereas during the nineteenth century wagering on baseball was popular, openly conducted, and generally tolerated. Moreover, with the abandonment of the single-umpire system and the receipt of greater authority, twentieth-century umpires assumed a primary role in the conduct of the game, whereas during the nineteenth century they had relatively little control or influence over it. Thus gambling by players, not by umpires, was the principal concern of the times.

It is said, in truth, that each generation writes its own history according to current interests and sensibilities. We hope this study of Dick Higham provides a balanced assessment of his umpiring career as well as the proper context for assessing the circumstances of his being the only major league umpire to be expelled for dishonesty.

Notes:

1. Higham was listed third on the 23-man roster behind Herman Doscher and Charles Furlong, indicating that he was an early choice. League umpires were chosen as follows: Each club sent nominations to the league secretary; league officials then compiled from the nominees a list of approved umpires numbering three times as many as there were clubs. *Spalding's Base Ball Guide and Official League Book for 1881* (Chicago: A. G. Spalding & Bros., 1881), pp. 76, 93, 96. He assuredly was Providence's nominee, having played for the Grays in 1878 and spent enough time in Providence for the American College Baseball Association to think he lived in the Rhode Island capital. Higham then lived in Troy, New York. Was Herm Doscher, who lived in the adjacent community of Lansingburg and had umpired National League games in 1880, many for Boston and Providence, instrumental in Higham becoming an umpire?

2. Commentary in the New York *Sun,* June 25, 1882, about Higham's expulsion corroborated feelings held by league president William Hulbert: "His expulsion, involving as it does the question of trusting to the promises of reformed players, brings out the soundess of the views of ex-President Hulbert of the league, who based his determined opposition to the reinstatement of players expelled for dishonest conduct on the point his experience had taught him, that 'there was no trusting such fellows.'" Although never expelled as a player, Higham left the White Stockings in 1875 under a cloud of suspicion while Hulbert was the principal owner of the club.

3. Higham had umpired six games in the National Association, where umpires, especially in the early years, were unpaid volunteers, usually players chosen from nonparticipating clubs but sometimes from one of the teams playing in the game. While on leave from the Baltimore club to visit his ill father, Higham made his umpiring debut with the Mutuals and Atlantics on July 8, 1872. **(When James Higham died on July 9 at age 45, the Baltimores were in Cleveland. New York *Times*, July 9 and 10 1872; New York *Times* and the New York *Tribune*, July 10, 1872.; New York *Clipper*, July 20, 1872,)** He later umpired for the Mutuals at Middletown on July 27, 1872; Boston at Atlantics on June 2, 1873, when Theodore Bomeisler withdrew after a second-inning argument; Philadelphia at Boston on June 17, 1873; Boston at Atlantics on October 7, 1874; and Hartford at Mutuals on August 24, 1875. See the New York *Times* and New York *Tribune*, June 3, 1873; Boston *Globe*, June 18,1873; New York *Times*, October 8, 1874 and August 25, 1875. Comments about his umpiring appeared in the newspapers only after his first two outings. Of his initial appearance as an arbiter in the Mutuals and Atlantics game on July 8, 1872, the New York *Times* noted that "the umpiring was remarkably strict." His second outing,

Mutuals at Middletown, CT, on July 27, prompted sharp criticism. The Middletown *Daily Constitution* on July 29 simply stated that "the decisions of the umpire forced the Mansfields to play against heavy odds" without identifying Higham as the arbiter. But the Middletown *Sentinel and Witness* on August 2 declared that Middletown's recent defeat was "due almost wholly" to Higham's decisions, which were "all made in favor of the Mutuals, and so grossly wrong" that the spectators "hooted and even insulted the umpire" and that "it required great efforts on the part of the police and managers to keep the crowd from mobbing him." The paper also stated that Higham "afterwards boasted of his decisions and that the Mutuals acknowledged his marked judgments in their favor." For further details on the incident, see David Arcidiacono, *Middletown's Season In The Sun* (privately published, 1999), pp. 95-96. Just how Higham's impartial umpiring affected a 29-9 defeat is unknown. Thanks to William Ryczek for a photocopy of the *Sentinel and Witness* article.

4. *Spalding's Base Ball Guide and Official League Book for 1880* (Chicago: A. G. Spalding & Bros., 1880), p. 96. The carry-overs were Al Barker, George Bradley, Thomas Gillean, and Daniel F. Sullivan.

5. Normally umpires were chosen by mutual agreement of the clubs at least seven days in advance of the game. Absent agreement, the home team selected the umpire from a list of seven submitted by the visiting club at least five days in advance. If neither of the above occurred, the home team chose the umpire. *Spalding's Base Ball Guide...for 1881, pp,* 75-77. In practice, clubs sought to engage the services of a particular umpire (one of those they had submitted to the league) thereby ensuring good umpiring for the team and frequent, predictable work for the arbiter. But as with players, umpires occasionally switched their designated teams during the course of the season, perhaps to reduce travel. There were so few good umpires that a de facto league umpiring staff quickly emerged as clubs readily agreed upon arbiters. For example, in 1881, a total of thiry men umpired NL games. Ten umpired one game, five called two games, and only six umpired more than nine: Edward Callahan, 22; W.W. Jeffers, 24; Philip Powers, 27; George "Foghorn" Bradley; Dick Hogham, 58, and John "Herm" Doscher, 79. Because Doscher, Bradley, and Higham were so highly respected, they worked both home and away games for their respective clubs.

6. Providence *Journal*, May 5, 1881; Boston *Daily Globe*, May 6 and 8, 1881. A Providence "crank," evidently not knowing that the Grays hired Higham, asserted: "Last year, Boston claimed the umpires lost them games, so this year they are starting under the kindly protection of umpire Richard Higham, who has already presented them with two pure gift games. Even Boston pa-

pers say his work is bad, and the Providence club the sufferer." Quoted in Preston D. Orem, "Baseball (1845-1881) From the Newspaper Accounts" (Altadena, CA., 1961), p. 346.

7. Detroit *Free Press,* July 14, 1881.

8. Troy *Daily Times*, July 27 and September 10, 1881. Stovey's heavy fine was later remitted.

9. *Ibid.*, September 30, 1881. The reason(s) for the "testimonial" game are unknown; it was scheduled for Wednesday, October 5, but no report of the contest appeared in the newspapers.

10. Higham and Providence's Bill McClellan replaced second baseman Joe Gerhardt and third-sacker Art Whitney on the trip. New York *Clipper*, October 15, 1881.

11. Since Higham appears as eighth umpire on the list, it can be assumed that he was elected at the December 8, 1881, meeting instead of being one of those added on March 7 to complete the 24-man roster. *Spalding's Base Ball Guide and Official League Book for 1882* (Chicago: A. G. Spalding & Bros., 1882), pp. 91, 94, 100. The other returnees were Herman Doscher, Williams Hawes, Thomas Carey, Joseph Dunnigan, and Charles Smith.

12. Higham, listed as living in Providence, was one of 20 umpires approved to umpire college games. Six other professional umpires—Billy McLean, Dick Pearce, John Kelly, Joseph Quinn, Timothy Donovan, and Williams Hawes—were also selected. *Ibid.*, p. 44.

13. Wright to Manager Brown, Union Base Ball Club, March 3, 1882. Wright Correspondence, Spalding Collection, New York Public Library.

14. In addition to working exhibition games, Higham found time in the preseason to take the field against the Detroits as a member of a "picked nine." He played first base, batted fifth, got one hit, and committed one error; he did not strike out. Detroit *Free Press*, April 27-29, 1882.

15. Cleveland *Plain Dealer*, May 2-4, 1882; Cleveland *Herald* as quoted in the Detroit *Free Press*, May 6, 1882.

16. During a May 20 game against Chicago, with Wolverines on second and third base, Detroit's George Wood hit the ball over the left field fence. Hooking to the left, the ball passed over the fence in fair territory, but landed outside the foul line. Instead of allowing the two runners to score and placing the batter at second, Higham ruled the ball "foul" thereby causing a "pretty severe" storm of protest. Chicago won the game 5-2, and Higham subsequently checked the rule and admitted his error that cost Detroit the game. Detroit *Free Press*, May 24, 1882.

17. On May 30, Providence's Paul Hines hit a ball over the left-field fence, but when an "officious outsider" threw the ball back, Higham, "thinking it came back on the bound from the top of the fence, declared it to be a two-base hit only." New York *Clipper*, June 10, 1882. The blown call notwithstanding, the Boston *Globe*, May 31, felt "the umpiring of Mr. Higham was excellent."

18. Confusion initially existed over the status of a batter who did not run to first base after a dripped third strike, but Higham announced he would ignore the official interpretation of the rules by declaring the batters "out" if they fail to run to first, thereby negating the possibility of a double- or triple-play. The Buffalo *Courier* on June 17 advised: "League clubs who engage Higham as umpire should make a note of this." For an explanation of the rule, see *The* New York *Clipper*, June 3, 1882. The *Clipper* article was reprinted in the Detroit *Free Press,* June 5, 1882. When catchers began deliberately dropping third strikes to set up a potential double- or triple-play depending on the bases occupied, batters attempted to nullify multiple-out attempts by avoiding the catcher's tag instead of running to first. Hence Rule 57 (6) adopted in 1882 stipulated that batters who did not run to first after a dropped third strike were "out" without having to be touched. Batters then stopped running to first, thereby precluding force plays. Some umpires, like Dick Pearce and Higham, ignored the amendment; their interpretation proved correct, as the league in 1883 amended the rule to eliminate the possibility "force plays" if the batter did not run to first after a dropped third strike. *Spalding's Base Ball Guide... for 1883* (Chicago: A. G. Spalding & Bros., 1883), pp. 29, 83.

19. Orem, "Baseball," p. 41.

20. New York *Clipper*, February 10, 1883.

21. Philadelphia *Inquirer*, May 29 and 30, 1882. Owners frequently accompanied their teams on road trips, as A. G. Spalding did with the White Stockings for a series in Detroit. Chicago *Herald*, May 28, 1882.

22. Providence *Daily Journal,* Providence *Evening Bulletin,* Detroit *Evening News*, and Detroit *Free Press*, May 31, 1882. The *Free Press* noted on June 1: "Such errors as were made by Farrell, McGeary, Troy and Hanlon would not occur again in a year." For the home run gaff, see footnote No. 16.

23. Charles Maddox umpired Monday's game against Chicago. Detroit *Free Press*, June 20, 1882.

24. No information about Todd has come to light. Detroit city directories for the period contain no listing for a James Todd.

25. Detroit *Evening News* June 26, 1882; New York *Herald*, June 20, 1882.

26. Chicago *Daily Tribune's* reported on June 25 that it "had been known for some time past that charges of the kind were pending against Higham, but no publication has been made of it, lest an undeserved injury be inflicted." On June 23 A. G. Spalding, owner of the Chicago White Stockings, queried in separate telegrams to Thompson and A. H. Soden, Interim President of the National League: "What official League action will be taken about Higham. Notice he umpired yesterday. He was to umpire here July fourth. Answer." Chicago Cubs Records: Correspondence, Chicago Historical Society.

27. Troy *Daily Times*, June 18 and 21, 1882. The assertion also appeared in the *Chicago Tribune*, June 25, 1882.

28. The Cleveland *Herald* on June 24 mentioned that Higham was to have umpired that day's game against Troy, but instead had left "for New Haven to umpire the great Yale-Dartmouth College contest. He will be here for games next week." Higham probably mentioned going to New Haven as a cover for the trip to Detroit, as the college season had ended on June 24 with a Princeton vs. Yale game in New York City. The Yale-Dartmouth contest in New Haven was played on June 3. In any event, the next day the *Herald* printed a notice of Higham's explusion along with the cryptic aside: "Higham will *not* umpire to-day's game."

29. The president was an ex officio member of the Board; the other four Directors were annually elected. "Constitution of the National League. . . ." in *Spalding's Base Ball Guide... for 1881* (Chicago: A G. Spalding & Bros., 1881), p. 42. Hotchkin may have excused himself because of an earlier confrontation with Higham. See ft. 34. Mugridge was a partner with his father in George Mugridge & Son "steam bakery." *The Buffalo City Directory for the Year 1881* (Buffalo, NY: Sampson, Davenport & Co., 1881). Earl was a partner in Earl & Wilson, collar manufacturers. *The Troy City Directory for the Year 1882* (Troy, NY: Sampson, Davenport & Co., 1882).

30. The most extensive newspaper accounts of the hearing appear in the Detroit *Evening Press*, June 24, 26, and 30; the Detroit *Free Press*, June 25 and 27; and the Detroit *Post and Tribune*, June 25.

31. The Detroit *Post and Tribune,* June 26, reported that Freeman Brown, Secretary of the Worcester Ruby Legs, mentioned that Higham had been seen with a gambler when the Detroits were in town, and that Wolverines manager Frank Bancroft "testified" during the hearing. Brown may have made such a comment during the discussion of the case, but there is no evi-

dence that Bancroft appeared before the Board. According to the June 27 Detroit *Free Press*, Bancroft subsequently learned on June 26 that Higham had in fact left a letter at the Brunswick Hotel to be delivered to Todd.

32. *Spalding's Base Ball Guide… for 1883* (Chicago: A G. Spalding & Bros., 1883), p. 103.

33. Adopted in 1879, the rule was explicit as to the grounds for permanent expulsion: "Any League Umpire who shall be convicted of selling, or offering to sell, a game of which he is Umpire, shall thereupon be removed from his official capacity and placed under the same disabilities inflicted on expelled players by the Constitution of the League." Rule 67, "Playing Rules of the National League… ," *Spalding's Base Ball Guide… for 1882*, p. 78.

34. For example, the Boston *Daily Globe*, Buffalo *Courier*, New York *Herald*, New York *Times*, June 25, 1882; *The Inter-Ocean* (Chicago) and Cleveland *Plain Dealer*, June 26; and the New York *Clipper*, July 1, 1882.

35. The Providence *Daily Journal* and the Providence *Evening Bulletin* on June 26 reported that "it was also proven that Higham's associations in the various cities he visited gave strong suspicions that he was catering to the gambling element." The Troy *Daily Times,* June 26, felt Higham's banishment was "well merited" and thought "it will be remembered that much fault was found with Higham's decisions in two of the Detroit games in this city, the Wolverines having his especial favor," particularly when calling balls and strikes as "his judgment was invariably erroneous." The paper also declared that A. L. Hotchkin, an official of the Troy club, "openly informed Higham that he was believed to be crooked." The June 26 Worcester *Evening Gazette,* noting that "Higham will be remembered as the umpire of the Detroit victories over Worcester, one of which resulted from his allowing a questionable triple-play by the Detroits," reported favorably "the expulsion of an umpire whose associations have led to strong suspicions that he was working in the interests of the gamblers, and who was finally almost certainly detected in ways that were dark." The Cleveland *Herald*, June 25-27, printed wire service reports as well as an extensive story appearing in the *Chicago Tribune* on June 25. The Chicago *Tribune*, June 25, said "certain grossly unfair decisions affecting the score and the result that were made by Higham at Detroit, coupled with the fact that his past record is not of the best, and his associates no better, led to a watch on his movements." *The Sun* (New York City), June 25, 1882, commented on the need to rid the game of gambling.

36. The umpires received $1,000 for the season. New York *Clipper*, November 25, 1882; *Spalding's Base Ball Guide…for 1883*, p. 87. The Higham affair also may have had at least a temporary affect on behavior. On June 30 the Detroit *Evening News* reprinted the following from the Saginaw *Courier*: "The young men of this city have ceased betting on the base ball league games. They have been "given a pointer on that" by Dick Higham, the expelled and popular umpire of the Detroits."

37. Could Higham have been the organizer of fixes or the contact person with gamblers? After all, umpires then traveled with the club, stayed in team hotel, and socialized with players—circumstances promoting familiarity rather than independence. It is impossible to discern from the box scores and cursory game reports patterns of play that would suggest the involvement of particular players. However, the Wolverines shortstop and captain Mike McGeary, was long rumored to be guilty of crooked play. Dasher Troy at second and Alonzo Knight in right were very erratic fielders.

38. Higham was not the first professional umpired accused of dishonesty on the field. In 1878 the Buffalo *Express* charged International League umpire George Campbell with selling the June 12 Rochester at Buffalo game to gamblers. Campbell subsequently sued the paper, but when the case came to trial on April 20, 1880, Campbell and his lawyers failed to appear, arguably an

admission of culpability. See Joseph M. Overfield, "A Dishonest Umpire?!!!," *Baseball Digest,* (May, 1963), pp. 47-49.

39. Former Hall of Fame historian Lee Allen wrote the long-accepted version of the incident in a chapter on crookedness in early baseball entitled "The Wansley Affair" in *The Hot Stove League* (New York: A. S. Barnes, 1955), pp. 184-85. Allen stated that Thompson was "sick and tired of watching his Wolverines lose games at which Higham officiated" and because of his suspicions" hired detectives who succeeded in intercepting two letters that Higham had written and posted." Others have followed Allen's lead, most notably Daniel E. Ginsburg, *The Fix Is In: A History of Baseball Gambling and Game Fixing Scandals* (Jefferson, NC: McFarland, 1995), p. 56, who writes that the meeting resulted after Thompson, concerned that "every close play seemed to go against Detroit," hired detectives to investigate Higham. There is no evidence to support these basic assertions. With Higham as umpire, the Wolverines were one game behind league-leading Providence, 16-9-1 overall and 6-3-1 after the questionable series with the Grays; any public criticisms of his umpiring were overwhelmingly that he favored Detroit. The Detroit *Evening News*, June 19, observed that the club was "well satisfied with their eastern trip in which they won 7 out of the 12 games played and retained their position next [to] the leader." Moreover, there is no evidence that Thompson hired detectives to investigate Higham, and Allen's assertions that the incriminating letter was "posted" and the handwriting verified by a single expert are incorrect. Additionally, Orem, "Baseball," p. 42, errs both in saying that Higham "confessed" when presented with the evidence against him and was expelled on June 30. Richard Bak, A Place for Summer: A Narrative History of Tiger Stadium (Detroit: Wayne State University Press,1998), p. 30, states inaccurately that Thompson "ordered" Higham's expulsion after it was revealed he was "in cahoots with a group of Detroit gamblers." Former sports writer William D. Perrin wrote a remarkable version of the incident in a series of newspaper articles about early baseball in Providence, Rhode Island. In the June 16, 1928 edition of the Providence *Evening Bulletin,* Perrin claims the incriminating "note," containing the names of local persons involved in the fix, was found by a maid at the Narragansett Hotel in Providence where Higham was staying and that she gave it to the hotel manager, who then handed it over to baseball authorities. He further says that Higham signaled the gamblers how to bet by placing a broom at various angles in the window of a jewelery shop. The article also appears in *Days of Greatness: Providence Baseball, 1875-1885* (Cooperstown, NY: Society for American Baseball Research, 1984), p. 21. Other than stating that the "note" was signed "Dick," Perrin's version is fundamentally at odds with what is known about Higham's expulsion. However, the specificity and accuracy of his accounts of other baseball events, combined with the facts that there were numerous jewelry shops near the Narragansett Hotel and that Higham spent an appreciable amount of time in Providence, raises the possibility that Perrin, writing 36 years after the fact, either confused the immediate events of 1882 with earlier gambling activities in the city or had been given inaccurate information by those familiar with local baseball history.

40. Spalding Collection, Harry Wright Correspondence 1878-1885, Volume 4, Item 35.

41. *Identification Of Handwriting & Cross Examination Of Experts*, M.K. Mehta, Examiner of Questioned Documents, 4th Edition, N. M. Tripathi Private Ltd., 1970, page 235.

42. Spink, *The National Game* (St. Louis, MO: The National Game Publishing Co., 1910); Spalding, *America's National Game…* . (New York: American Sports Publishing Company, 1911), p. 239; Richter, *Richter's History and Records of Base Ball….* (Philadelphia: privately published, 1914), p. 56.

My Start in the Newspaper Business

Eddie Gold

When my brother Mickey fired me as an usher at the Oriental Theatre, that ended my career in show business. I then entered the world of journalism in the exalted position of copy boy at the Chicago *Sun-Times*. The date was January 12, 1951.

I was in awe as I glanced around the city room. At one desk was chief photographer Tom Howard. He once strapped a camera to his ankle and flashed the execution of Ruth Judd, a shot that went around the world.

At another desk was crime reporter Ray Brennan, who chronicled the exploits of John Dillinger, Al Capone, and Roger Touhy and was ready to spring into action whenever another bullet-riddled body was discovered in a trunk.

Huddled near the phones were a pair of Jacks, rewrite man McPhaul and police reporter McGuire. They had freed Mazcek from Stateville in a murder case that later became the film *Call Northside 777*, starring James Stewart.

It seemed as if every copy editor sported green eye shades and had a cigarette across the ear, one in the mouth and another in the ash tray—all lit at the same time. If you looked closely, you could spot the whiskey eating through their cups of coffee. Many chewed tobacco and the joint was sprinkled with spittoons. It was nearing the end of the era of the street-smart reporter who didn't sport any college degrees, but you could fire a cannon through the city room without hitting a female reporter—sorry, Roz Russell.

One of my tasks was accompanying a photographer to ball games. I would lug "Big Bertha," which must've weighed about thirty-five pounds. It was used to zoom in for closeups of baseball action. One time at Wrigley Field, Cincinnati Reds manager Rogers Hornsby was hitting fungoes and a ball skipped past him. I put down Bertha, raced over, scooped up the ball, and tossed it to Hornsby. The Rajah's eyes were sparkling when he said, "Nice play, son."

I got my first byline at age seventeen. Herman Kogan, our book editor, tossed *The Chicago White Sox*, by Warren Brown, on my desk and told me to review it, and added, "Let's see if you can write."

I sat at my typewriter and just stared. I didn't start typing until I was sweating blood. I wrote about the Hitless Wonders, the Black Sox scandal, and went all the way to the Go-Go Sox era. The next day I was going to hand it in, but retreated when I saw Kogan at his desk. I waited until he departed before turning the piece in. He never said anything to me, but that Sunday, my review appeared in the book section. I still have the clipping.

A couple of days later my phone rang and it was the dour Warren Brown. He said, "Good writeup," and hung up. Imagine getting a call from the sports columnist of the Chicago *American*, who must've been an apprentice to Gutenberg.

The following winter, I got a $3 raise (up from $2.80) and was assigned to the sports department. I took scores and race results, answered the phones, and went for coffee. But I got a chance to rub elbows with such baseball writers as Edgar Munzel, Jack Clarke, Jerry Holtzman, and John C. Hoffman, who took a liking to me.

Eddie Gold *is a semi-retired sportswriter who still can't finish a beer.*

One wintry evening Hoffman brought a visitor to the sports department. He was a burr-headed, craggy-faced gent named Bill Veeck, owner of the downtrodden St. Louis Browns. Veeck was already known for pumping life and fun into the game and knocking the stuffiness out. He was a character, an innovator, a gagster, a man who lost a leg in World War II but kept on smiling. He used his peg leg for an ashtray.

Anyway, Hoffman nudged Veeck, and said, "Eddie's the world's greatest Cubs' fan."

"Oh, a horticulturist," said Veeck, who had planted the ivy at Wrigley Field.

After putting the paper to bed, we all retreated to the Pall Mall Lounge, which was next to the *Sun-Times* building. Although I was eighteen and looked fifteen, I always carried a card of some guy born in Rock Hill, Kansas, in 1927. I took a sip of beer, and at the same time, Veeck put down his empty bottle. It was then I realized I was out of my league.

The talk got around to Rollie Hemsley, a fun-loving catcher who made stops with the Cubs and six other teams during the 1930s and '40s. The Cubs were in New York for a series against the Giants and Dodgers. "He was arrested three times in one night for being drunk and disorderly," recalled Veeck.

"[Cubs traveling secretary] Bob Lewis and I bailed him out the first two times. When the desk sergeant called the third time, we said, 'We never heard of him' and let him sleep it off."

My next advancement was helping to dummy the pages. Hoffman once walked in and found me flustered by a lack of hot news items. "I'll call Frank Lane [the White Sox general manager] and see if we could make a trade with the Browns," said Hoffman. Lane then swapped infielder Willie Miranda to Veeck.

Several weeks later, I was short of juicy items. I asked Hoffman if we could get Miranda back. Lane and Veeck obliged me and Willie was back with the Sox. How often does a pencil-pusher wield such power?

Veeck soon sold his Browns and the franchise was shipped to Baltimore. I was shipped to Korea.

I remember sitting in my bunker, reading the *Stars and Stripes*. One line caught my eye. It read: Home run–Cubs: Banks.

I said, "Who the hell is Banks?"

The original Sidd Finch

Baseball has produced more false messiahs than any other sport, from Ebenezer Beatin, "The Allentown Wonder," to Mo Solomon, "The Rabbi of Swat," to Clint "Floppy" Hartung. But somehow we never quite abandon our faith that there is, somewhere out there in the wilderness, the phenom who will appear to lead our team to victory. It is at the core of baseball mythology. About the closest we'll ever come (and who needs to come any closer?) is a big, ugly kid from behind the walls of a training school in Baltimore, a "Babe" who redeemed the game in a dark time.

In baseball literature, this theme has been treated with reverence—Malamud's Roy Hobbs. But there is perhaps an even longer tradition of poking fun at our faith, as George Plimpton did with is April Fool's phenom, the unhittable would-be Met, Sidd Finch.

In 1887, the Chicago Mail *introduced a prototype for Sidd Finch in the form of Teang Wong Foo, a "Coolie" from the village of Uwăchu in the Chinese province of Kiangton rumored to be bound for the White Stockings.*

"It is extremely probable that when the Detroit baseball club again faces the Chicagoans, it will meet with such a terror in the pitcher's box as has never been known in baseball circles."

The unknown writer offers this eyewitness account: "Yesterday afternoon the big pitcher was brought out in Hip Lung's cockroach pit and prepared to show what he could do. Three posts had been erected in a line ten feet apart. In line with them was a nail half driven into an oak plank. Teang Foo took his position a few feet away from the first post, He then looked over his left shoulder three times and then throwing his head around until he looked squarely behind him, he at the same time delivered the ball. With a hum like a buzz-top the ball gracefully curved around the three posts, and then, taking a straight shoot, hit the nail squarely on the head. Four times Teang Foo sent the ball cavorting around the posts and on to the nail."

As yet, there is no listing for Teang Wong Foo in the Baseball Encyclopedia. Maybe he's having some kind of visa problem.

—David McDonald

The Polo Grounds

Stew Thornley

In any sport but baseball, identifying a specific stadium by the diagram of its playing area would be difficult, perhaps impossible. Standardization is a staple in stadiums and arenas for sports like football, hockey, and basketball. But baseball, from the beginning, has felt less confined in determining its outer reaches. In the days before enclosed stadiums, a river or copse of trees could intrude upon a playing area. When fences were erected, it was for the purpose of charging admission to the game, and no standards existed for their height, their distance from home plate, or for the shape they imposed upon the outfields.

Through most of baseball's history, the contours of playing areas have been distinctive. Often it has been a matter of necessity. Ballparks wedged into the confines of existing city blocks emerged with strange shapes. Quirks in street schemes produced otherwise inexplicable crannies. Where a building remained because team owners were unable to acquire and demolish it, the outfield simply took a detour around it. The result is that fans can tell where they are, whether it's Fenway Park in Boston or Wrigley Field in Chicago. Sometimes just a glance at a stadium diagram is sufficient.

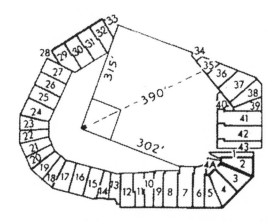

Fenway Park, Boston

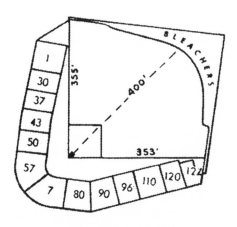

Wrigley Field, Chicago

Stew Thornley *is the author of* Land of the Giants: New York's Polo Grounds, *to be published by Temple University Press in fall, 2000. This article is excerpted from his slide presentation,* The Polo Grounds—A Tale of Four Stadiums, *which received the* USA Today Baseball Weekly *Award as the best research presentation at the 1998 SABR National Convention in San Francisco.*

But even in a sport known for its curiously configured stadiums, one in particular stands out.

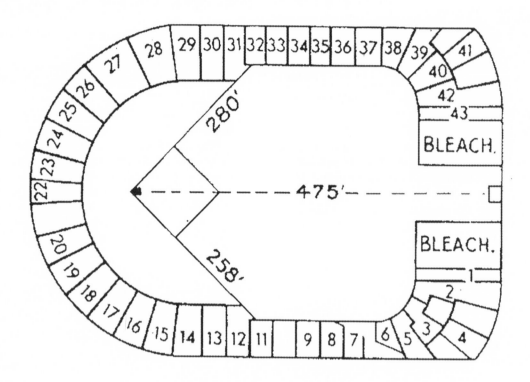

Polo Grounds, New York

The Polo Grounds, an odd name for an odd stadium, was home to several teams, most notably the New York Giants until the team moved to San Francisco following the 1957 season. Its horseshoe-shaped grandstand and elongated playing area provided for ridiculously short distances down the foul lines and equally ridiculous long distances to the power alleys and center field.

So short were its foul-line distances that inches were sometimes included in the measurements—279 feet, 8 inches to left; 257 feet, 8 inches to right. As for the distance in feet to center, the figure almost could have been rounded to the nearest hundred.

But there's much more to the Polo Grounds than its peculiar profile. Just as the New York AL team was identified with its home, Yankee Stadium, and the Dodgers were linked to Brooklyn's Ebbets Field, the Giants were identified with the Polo Grounds.

The Polo Grounds over a few decades became a massive edifice, tucked in between the Harlem River and an lofty outcropping of mica schist known as

Coogan's Bluff. The vicinity of the escarpment, in Upper Harlem, a portion of northern Manhattan, was part of a farm granted by the British Crown to John Gardiner in the early 1700s. It received its name after one of Gardiner's descendants, Harriet Gardiner Lynch, married James J. Coogan, a politician who would become Manhattan borough president in 1899.

When the New York Giants moved into Coogan's Hollow in 1889, the area was considered the outskirts of town. Only in the past thirty years had the city even begun laying out streets on the eastern portion of Manhattan north of 155th Street, the southern boundary of the region. Not only that, it had been barely fifteen years since the area occupied by the Polo Grounds was anything more than river-bottom wetlands that were more often than not covered with water. Landfilling has changed the size and shape of Manhattan ever since the Dutch settled the area, and some of the island, including this portion of it, sits on fill that was dumped into the river.

But while land and streets were relatively new, this part of town did have public transit, providing a way for fans to get to the games. Elevated railroads first served the area in the 1880s, followed by subways in the twentieth century.

Several parks bore the Polo Grounds name. The final three were located beneath Coogan's Bluff. But the first stadium to use the name, and the only one on which polo was actually played, was at the corner of 110th Street and Fifth Avenue, just north of Central Park. Outdoor polo in America was first played here in the 1870s, although the site was eventually taken over by baseball. In 1883, these Polo Grounds became home to two major-league teams—the Metropolitans of the American Association and the National League team then generally known simply as the New-Yorks.

The teams shared the venue over the course of three seasons, and the main diamond in the southeast corner of the property had a lavish and expansive grandstand. During much of the 1883 season, though, the Metropolitans played their games on a far-inferior diamond toward the southwest corner of the property.

When both the Metropolitans and the National League team played at home at the same time—there were a couple of stretches during the 1883 season when this happened—a flimsy canvas-covered portable fence was brought in to separate the diamonds. Under rules of the day, batted or thrown balls going under the fence remained in play, causing the odd scene of an outfielder emerging into the opposing field in pursuit of a ball. Outfielders proved agile and adept at getting under the fence and to the fugitive balls. Although batted balls frequently made it under the canvas divider, none ended up as a home run.

However, the canvas fence did restrict the field of play to the point of producing the first over-the-fence home runs at the Polo Grounds. It even caused some batters to adjust their batting style. Regarding one National League game when the barrier was up, the New York *Tribune* said, "'Sky-scrapers' were more numerous than 'daisy-cutters'…There was little scientific place batting."

The Giants played at 110th and Fifth until 1888. In early 1889, the city cut a street through the site and ended the life of the original Polo Grounds.

The Giants moved uptown to the southern parcel of Coogan's Hollow. Also known as Manhattan Field, from the beginning it was called the New Polo Grounds. The park was hastily constructed and was in barren condition when the Giants moved into it in July, 1889. Construction continued, and by 1890, the park became a fairly elaborate structure.

In 1890, the Giants had a new next-door neighbor. The New York Players' League club built its stadium immediately to the north of the Polo Grounds. When the league folded after a single season, the Giants abandoned their diamond and moved north into Brotherhood Park, which became the Polo Grounds as the abandoned park reverted to Manhattan Field. The older strucure remained throughout the 1890s before being torn down. Even as a vacant lot, the site was still referred to as Manhattan Field, and it hosted cricket matches and other events.

The Giants used this third Polo Grounds for more than twenty years. This was the ballpark of Christy Mathewson and the 1905 World Series and Merkle's Boner. But in 1911 the grandstand burned. It was replaced, on the same spot, by a steel and concrete structure, the fourth Polo Grounds—the one modern fans remember, the Polo Grounds of Carl Hubbell and Bobby Thomson, and the Amazin' Mets.

Its odd dimensions, with extremes of both shortness and length, raise the question of whether the Polo Grounds was a park that favored hitters or pitchers. The answer is both. In terms of overall offense, the Polo Grounds was about neutral, perhaps even favoring pitchers. But in terms of home runs, it was a haven for the long ball. It was the friendliest home run park of any post-1914 baseball stadium until Coors Field came along in Denver in 1995.

One of the factors contributing to home runs at the Polo Grounds was the upper deck in left field, which overhung the lower deck by twenty-one feet. That's an incredible overbite, which turned a lot of seemingly easy fly balls into home runs as they'd settle into the upper deck when they may not otherwise have reached the seats in the lower deck.

The Polo Grounds was also used for football. It was the home of pro teams such as the Giants and the AFL Titans/Jets and was a regular host for the Army-Navy game for many years and the site of many Notre Dame football games, including the one in which the Four Horsemen were christened. Through the years, this Polo Grounds was the site of boxing matches, auto races, winter carnivals with ski slopes erected, religious rallies, rodeos, soccer, tennis, and opera.

The Mets expected to use the Polo Grounds only in their inaugural season of 1962. But when Shea Stadium wasn't ready for 1963, the Polo Grounds got a reprieve. It was torn down in 1964.

A housing project, the Polo Grounds Towers, now occupies the site. Many of the residents are too young to remember the Polo Grounds, but a plaque erected to mark the approximate site of home plate at least provides them with a reminder of how hallowed this ground is.

Polo Ground Park Factors

Polo Grounds I as used by National League (Giants) 1883-1888 (Southeast diamond)
Run factor: 92   Home run factor: 71

Home (360 games)	Road (357 games)
Runs/game: 9.90	Runs/game: 10.74
Home runs/game .370	Home runs/game .529

Polo Grounds II, used by Giants 1889-1890
Run factor: 98   Home run factor: 54

Home (129 games)	Road (137 games)
Runs/game: 11.22	Runs/game: 11.60
Home runs/game .333	Home runs/game .628

Polo Grounds III used by Giants 1891-1910
Run factor: 97   Home run factor: 134

Home (1,478 games)	Road (1,449 games)
Runs/game: 9.47	Runs/game: 9.79
Home runs/game .445	Home runs/game .333

Polo Grounds IV, as used by Yankees 1913-1922
Run factor: 101   Home run factor: 197

Home (762 games)	Road (741 games)
Runs/game: 8.19	Runs/game: 8.08
Home runs/game .819	Home runs/game .420

Polo Grounds IV, as used by Giants 1911-1957
Run factor: 97   Home run factor: 170

Home (3,596 games)	Road (3,610 games)
Runs/game: 8.72	Runs/game: 9.00
Home runs/game 1.58	Home runs/game .932

Polo Grounds IV, as used by Mets 1962-1963
Run factor: 110   Home run factor: 162

Home (161 games)	Road (162 games)
Runs/game: 9.33	Runs/game: 8.26
Home runs/game 2.28	Home runs/game 1.37

Total Polo Grounds IV, all teams 1911-1957 and 1962-1963

Home (4,519 games)	Road (4,513 games)
Runs/game: 8.65	Runs/game: 8.82
Home runs/game 1.47	Home runs/game .864

Polo Grounds Players

Babe Ruth
1920-22 Polo Grounds

	Games	HR/G	BA	OBP	SA
Home	197	.38	.379	.505	.849
Road	207	.35	.349	.490	.751

1923-32 Yankee Stadium

	Games	HR/G	BA	OBP	SA
Home	714	.31	.355	.489	.708
Road	704	.33	.355	.485	.715

Mel Ott
1926-47 Polo Grounds

	Games	HR/G	BA	OBP	SA
Home	1,368	.24	.297	.421	.558
Road	1,362	.14	.311	.407	.510

Willie Mays
1951-52, 1954-57 Polo Grounds

	Games	HR/G	BA	OBP	SA
Home	381	.25	.319	.391	.592
Road	381	.24	.304	.386	.579

Harry and Stanley

Dave Anderson

Before the Niekros, Phil and Joe with 539 wins; before the Perrys, Gaylord and Jim with 529 wins; came the brothers Coveleski with 296 wins. Most baseball fans know of Stanley Coveleski's 215-win Hall of Fame career, but few know much about his older brother Harry, who was a baseball hero in his own right.

The clan Coveleski lived in Shamokin, Pennsylvania, where the patriarch was a Polish immigrant coal miner. Like many big league stars of the early twentieth century, Harry and Stanley used their considerable baseball talents to escape the grime and danger of the mines.

Harry Coveleski was one of the first Polish-Americans to make the big leagues. He was 1-0 in 1907 with the Philadelphia Phillies, but made his mark the next year. The 1908 season was one of the most exciting in baseball history. Both pennant races involved multiple teams and went down to the last game of the season. In the National League, the Chicago Cubs won the pennant—and went on to take their last World Championship. That could not have happened without the efforts of Harry "The Giant Killer" Coveleski.

Virtually a rookie, Harry's first start of

Dave Anderson *is is the author of* More Than Merkle, *a book about the 1908 baseball season. It was published by the University of Nebraska Press in early 2000.*

Harry Coveleski

Transcendental Graphics

1908 was against the Giants. He was bombed and sent back to the minors for seasoning. In September he came back up and in one of the most astonishing feats of late-season clutch pitching ever, won his nickname by beating New York three times in five days.

(Coveleski was not the only player to earn the nickname in 1908, Cub pitcher Jack Pfiester, the Cub starter in the infamous Merkle Game in September, was dubbed "Giant Killer" by the Chicago *Tribune* after he won key games during July and August.)

Harry's first win came September 29 in the second game of a doubleheader. He threw a six-hitter before a Polo Grounds crowd of 19,000, winning, 7-0

Two days later on October 1, he took the mound against the Giants in Philadelphia, again in a second game of a doubleheader. This time he threw a four hitter, winning 6-2. The frustration felt by the Giants and New York fans is evident in this comment from the New York *Herald*:

> The only way in which McGraw can beat that gentleman with the Russian suffix to his name, which is pronounced like an automobile with its muffler off, running on three cylinders, is to dress the team in kimonos and disguise them as Japs. Then, if the same disguised ballplayers make a noise like the Mikado's army, Coveleskie might dig for the tall timber.

The writer's reference to the Japanese was in the context of that nation's victory over Imperial Russia in the recent Russo-Japanese War.

Coveleski's next win came after a day of rest, against none other than the immortal Christy Mathewson. Matty won 37 games in 1908, with eleven shutouts and a microscopic 1.43 ERA. But it was his error in the fifth inning that let in the Phillies' winning run. The Giants did not go down easy. Leading 3-2 in the ninth, Coveleski was in a jam. New York had runners on second and third and none out.

The Giants batter was "Turkey Mike" Donlin, one of the best hitters in the league and fearsome in the clutch. Donlin and his .334 batting average were retired on a pop fly. The next hitter, Cy Seymour, grounded into a fielder's choice when the runner on third, "Moose" McCormick, was retired in a rundown. Art Devlin struck out to end the game and give Harry something to write home about.

Again the New York *Herald* expressed chagrin:

> If the Giants lose the pennant, Coveleski deserves the credit for defeating them. He seems to have the Indian sign on the stickers, big and little, from Coogan's Bluff. He hails from Shamokin, Pennsylvania, in the coal field, and is a Polak.

Harry's 4-1 mark in 1908 was his best effort in the National League. In 1909 and 1910, he was 6-10 and 1-1. He did not return to the majors until 1914. As a member of the American League Detroit Tigers, Coveleski won 22 games in 1914, 22 in 1915, and 21 in 1916. He retired in 1918 with an 81-55 career mark.

A measure of mystery surrounds Coveleski's departure from the National League and the rapid loss of his skill. It may have had something to do with psychological warfare conducted by Giant manager John McGraw who wrote the text for the "don't get mad, get even" school of thought. McGraw never forgave nor forgot what Harry Coveleski did to his ball club.

Giants players claim they ran Coveleski out of the league because of Harry's habit of chewing on sausage during games. He allegedly kept the kielbasa in his pocket. New York outfielder Fred Snodgrass says McGraw told them to ask Harry for a chew of sausage. The repeated requests so unnerved him that he lost his edge as a pitcher.

The Coveleski clan vehemently denied the tale. Stan was fond of saying, "In baseball it's tomorrow that counts. You worry all the time. It never ends. Lord, baseball is a worrying thing." One thing Stan did not worry about was the story about his brother. He bluntly said it was a bunch of bull.

As Harry's career was winding down, Stan was beginning to assert dominance in the American League. For eleven consecutive years, his wins were in double digits, and he notched 20-game seasons for Cleveland from 1918 through 1921. During the 1920 World Series Stan won three games with a 0.67 earned run average, and in one game against Brooklyn threw only 72 pitches. He was traded to Washington and was 20-5 for the American League Champion Senators in 1925. He was 0-2 in the World Series against Pittsburgh.

The Coveleski brothers were close. They faced each other only once, and that was in an exhibition game. While they were both in the American League, Harry and Stan refused to pitch against each other, arguing that no matter who won there would be fans who believed the loser was not giving an honest effort.

Stan's selection to the Baseball Hall of Fame in 1969 was richly deserved. His 215 wins, a reputation for pinpoint control, and his 1920 World Series performance gave Harry's younger brother baseball immortality.

Harry died in Shamokin in 1950 at the age of 64. Stanley passed away in South Bend, Indiana, in 1984. He was 94 years old. Coveleski Regional Stadium stands in South Bend today, home of the South Bend Silverhawks, a Class A affiliate of the Arizona Diamondbacks. The facility also hosts high school games and is an Indiana State High School Baseball sectional and regional site.

The careers of the Coveleski brothers were a landmark in early baseball history. They were among the

Stan Coveleski

Transcendental Graphics

first Polish-American baseball stars, preparing the way for successors such as Al Simmons (Aloys Szymanski), Stan "The Man" Musial, "Moose" Skowron, Ted Kluszewski, Greg "Bull" Luzinski, Carl Yastrzemski, and others. Among brother combinations they rank fifth all time in wins, and hold the distinction of having eight twenty-win seasons between them. Not bad for a couple of mining town kids.

The Hawaii Winter League 1993-1997

Frank Ardolino

The following short history of the Hawaii Winter League does not attempt to trace the pennant races or to detail the feats of individual players and teams. Instead, it describes the steady growth the league experienced from its inception in 1993 to its unfortunate demise after the 1997 season. The story of the league follows the exciting pattern of a fledgling organization with high hopes slowly creating an international flavor by attracting top major league prospects and players from Asian countries. The most interesting aspect of the Hawaii Winter League was the effort its officials and players made to develop a sense of community support for the league. The five years of its existence, during which attendance rose by forty percent, were characterized by innovative promotional and ticket policies, improved facilities, and the introduction of a new team playing at a historic ballpark. All indications were positive—until the sudden folding of the league.

So much in Hawaiian sports history concerns unfortunate endings. The centrally located Honolulu Stadium, which served as the major venue for sports events from 1926 to 1975 and is now a heavily used urban park, has been replaced by a rusting, cavernous, and disadvantageously located Aloha Stadium, which excites no close community identification. The departure of the minor league franchise Hawaii Islanders in 1987 after twenty-seven years in the Islands left a big gap in the Hawaiian professional baseball scene. The

heralded appearance in April, 1997 of the St.Louis Cardinals and San Diego Padres in a three-game series that counted in the standings drew 77,432 fans, but the promised return of teams for more big league games in subsequent seasons has not occurred. Only the Hawaii Winter League was providing regular professional games and when it folded paradise was indeed diminished.

1993—The Hawaii Winter Baseball League was established as a third alternative to the Latin-American leagues and the Arizona Winter League. It was a league to which the majors could send their A and Double-A prospects. It was also viewed as the means of returning professional baseball to Hawaii. After a false start in 1992, Duane Kurisu, a local boy from Hilo who made his money in real estate, launched the new league, which he hoped would not only be profitable but also socially useful. "I look at this as less of a business and more of a dream, a chance to make a positive difference in the world...Hawaii Winter Baseball will bring people together...I want it to be like in *Field of Dreams*. One of the players will say, 'Is this heaven?' And I'll say, 'No it's Hawaii.' It's a cliché that Hawaii is a melting pot—but now this is a melting pot for baseball."

Bob Berg, the president of the league, declared that "Everybody is going to want to send their prospects here. I see this as a step toward having a true World Series."

In the first season, seventeen major league teams and six Asian teams sent ninety-six players, who were organized into four teams on four islands: the Hilo Stars (Hawaii); the Honolulu Sharks (Oahu); the Maui

Frank Ardolino *teaches Shakespeare at the university of Hawaii. He is researching the appearance of Shakespearean quotations in sports films..*

Stingrays, and the Kauai Emeralds. The Hilo Stars, whose roster was composed of players from Japanese teams, were managed by Tim Ireland of the Milwaukee Brewers and played at Vulcan Stadium, capacity 1,415. The Sharks, managed by local hero Lennie Sakata of the Anaheim Angels, who appeared in the 1984 World Series for the Orioles, played at the University of Hawaii's Rainbow Stadium, capacity 4,312. The Stingrays, managed by Carlos Alfonso of the San Francisco Giants, played at War Memorial Stadium, capacity 3,112. The Emeralds, managed by Trent Jewett of the Pittsburgh Pirates and composed of a mixture of players from the United States, Korea, and Taiwan, played at Lihue's Vidihna Stadium, capacity 551, which had no lights. The season consisted of fifty-four games played over ten weeks from mid October to mid-December.

League officials hoped to draw about 100,000 spectators for the season. The first week's attendance of 9,859 was close to the goal of 10,000 a week, but the league never fulfilled its financial expectations, attracting only 53,383 and sustaining a six-figure loss. The big hope was Rainbow Stadium, where the Sharks had thirty-six home games. Instead of drawing the projected 1,500 per game, the Sharks averaged only 648. The Maui Stingrays were the most popular team, averaging 865 fans for twenty-three home games. Traffic jams, lack of publicity, and bad facilities at several of the fields contributed to the attendance problems.

Because of the financial problems, rained-out games were not rescheduled. As a result, the teams ended up playing an unequal number of games. The Hilo Stars, who won the championship by two games, played only forty-eight games compared to the second-place Sharks' full season of fifty-four, while Kaui and Maui got to play fifty-two and fifty games, respectively. Despite the problems, Brent Lutz, the Sharks' first baseman, summed up the players' perspective on the international quality of the league when he said, "Baseball is a common language. The guys on the teams said they really enjoyed playing with the foreign players. I met a lot of new guys, made some friends and learned a lot."

1994—The second season was notable for the increased number of teams sending players, the introduction of season ticket packages and an All Star game, and the signing of two women players. The league provided more innovative promotional ploys such as $75 season-ticket packages that included bingo games for winning trips to Las Vegas, Hawaii's favorite vacation spot. The Sharks doubled their season ticket holders from 500 to 1,000. In addition, there were ten-game packages ($50 reserved, $35 general admission) and a $17 youth pass for the twenty-seven home games and All-Star Game.

The number of major league teams sending players increased to twenty-one with the inclusion of the Dodgers, Marlins, Red Sox, and Yankees. In addition, six Korean and six Japanese teams provided a total of twenty-six players, who were spread among the four teams, instead of being concentrated on the Hilo squad.

The ninety-seven players represented a mixture of hopefuls, local heroes, and famous names. The Sharks had four members who had played scholastic ball in Hawaii: Matt Apana, Todd Takayoshi, Ben Agbayani, and Joey Meyer. Meyer, who played in the majors for two years (1988-89) with the Brewers, was a great favorite in the Islands, noted for his prodigious home runs. Players with famous names included third sackers Aaron Boone, son of Bob Boone, and Preston Wilson, stepson of Mookie Wilson; pitcher Todd Blyleven, son of Bert Blyleven; and Craig Griffey, brother of Ken Griffey Jr.

The biggest innovation for 1994 was the signing by the Maui Stingrays of Julie Croteau and Lee Anne Ketchum, who became the first women to play on a men's professional team. Both women had played for the Colorado Silver Bullets the previous summer, and both had extensive experience competing in embattled situations. Croteau, a twenty-three-year old, 5-foot-8, 130 pound first baseman, lost a court battle to play on her high school boys' team, but she became the first woman to play for and coach NCAA men's teams—Division III St. Mary's College in Maryland and Division III Western New England College in Massachusetts, respectively. The twenty-four-year-old Lee Anne Ketchum, a 5-foot-4, 150 pound righthanded pitcher, did get to play for her high school boys' team for two years and compiled a record of 12-5 with six saves. With the Silver Bullets, who were 6-38 for the season, she won five, and in one game she struck out 14, throwing her fastball in the 80s.

Although they received a lot of publicity when they signed to play in the Hawaii Winter League, the two women did not get much playing time. Croteau appeared in ten games and went 1-for-10 with no RBIs, no runs scored, one walk, and two Ks. Ketchum pitched in eight games, had an 0-0 record, with no saves and an ERA of 7.71. She yielded ten runs, six earned, 15 hits in seven innings, three homers and four walks, and struck out three.

In the inaugural All Star Game played before 2,263 fans at Rainbow Stadium on November 18, the USA team defeated the International squad, 6-4, in ten innings. In the final and deciding game of the season, the Kauai Emeralds won the championship by defeating the Sharks, 2-0, on second baseman Hiroki Kokubo's two-run homer. The Emeralds, who overcame a dismal 1-6 start, finished at 29-21 (.580) to win by three percentage points over the Maui Stingrays. Kokubo was the league MVP, winning the batting title with a .370 average, getting the most hits (74) and most doubles (21), and compiling the best on-base percentage (.429).

The 1994 season provided proof that there was a rising market for the Hawaii Winter League, as attendance increased by 16,150 to 69,533. Another indication of the league's success as a professional showcase was evinced by the naming of seventeen of its players to the forty-man rosters of their respective major league organizations.

1995—Total attendance increased forty-seven percent to 106,787, not only as a result of the league's growing popularity but also because of the replacement of the Kauai team by the West Oahu CaneFires. The Kaui Emeralds had averaged fewer than 100 fans per game at their tiny ballpark. The CaneFires, on the other hand, played their home games at historic Hans L'Orange Park in Waipahu, which had a capacity of 2,200, plus additional seats on the grass for $1. Hans L'Orange Park was named for the son of a Norwegian sea captain who came to Hawaii in 1912 and began working for the Oahu Sugar Company. He convinced the company to give him several acres of low-yield sugar fields to build a community center and field in 1924. The field was renamed in honor of L'Orange in 1955, two years before he retired after forty-five years with the company. In 1995, the field was renovated for the CaneFires and quickly became an ideal Hawaiian site to watch ballgames. To help the fans root for the CareFires, City Councilman Mufi Hanneman composed a local Hawaiian version of the baseball anthem, "Take Me Out to the Ballgame":

> Take me out to the ballgame,
> Take me out to Hans L'Orange.
> Buy me some li hing mui and spam musubi,
> You can bet that I'll always be back.
> So its root, root for the CaneFires, if we don't win, we make A.

The season ended with Maui defeating the Sharks, 4-3, in the newly instituted championship game between the two teams with the best records. Before 1,846 fans at Hans L'Orange Park, former University of Hawaii pitcher Joey Vierra held the Sharks to seven hits, striking out six and walking only one, and was voted the MVP of the game.

1996—Additional promotional ploys were created. A new ticket program, entitled "Baseball Bucks," featured charitable organizations selling booklets of four general admission tickets for $20, with half of that sum counting as a charitable donation. Also, players increased their school visits, and a half-hour weekly TV program, "The Road to the Show," featured highlights of the games and profiles of the players.

The major leagues demonstrated their continuing interest in the Winter League by signing a three-year extension of their agreement. Twenty-one big league and Asian teams sent 104 players, and the rosters of each team were increased to twenty-eight to accommodate more players and to expand the pitching staffs in order to save arms. The quality of league play was enhanced by the assigning of nine top draft picks and ten first-round choices. The league also began a new divisional format, with the Sharks and CaneFires in the Outrigger Division, and the Stingrays and Stars in the Volcano Division. The championship was won by Maui, which defeated Honolulu, 6-4. As a result of these measures, attendance increased by 7,000 to 113,000, even with eight rained-out games that were not replayed. League officials speculated that attendance would have been 120,000 over a full season.

1997—Corporate sponsors such as the Bank of Hawaii and the First Hawaiian Bank played bigger roles in special promotions. One of these involved a "Picnic at the Park," where for $25 a fan was treated to barbecue chicken, hamburger, and hot dogs, plus corn on the cob, baked beans, soda and/or beer. As another gastronomic incentive, hot dogs were sold for a quarter each at all Wednesday games with a limit of four per order. The four teams hired new managers, all with major league experience: Dave Anderson (Sharks), Tom Lawless (CaneFires), Joe Ferguson (Maui), and Jim Byrd (Hilo). In addition, the league signed five pitchers who had high school and college baseball careers in Hawaii: Matt Apana, Paul Ah Yat, Mike McCutcheon, Onan Masaoka, and Kyle Kawabata. There was TV coverage of the games in Japan. In the title game, the Honolulu Sharks finally won the championship by defeating Hilo, 9-8, before 12,000 fans at Hans L'Orange Park.

When the season ended all the signs pointed to growing popularity and success. The attendance had risen by twenty percent to 136,270, fifty-two players from the league had earned major league roster spots, and expansion to six teams was in the offing.

In light of all this, fans were stunned to learn that the Hawaii Winter Baseball League was folding. The cause was financial disagreement with the major leagues. The Winter League wanted the major leagues to pay more than ten percent of players' salaries. The league already had to pay ninety percent of the salaries for players, umps, and coaches, as well as all expenses for bats, balls, per diems, and transportation and housing costs. As a result, league expenses ran from $750,000 to $1,000,000 per annum, with losses from inception totaling between $5 and $8 million. League officials argued that the Hawaii Winter League was the only minor league in the United States that had to pay salaries and expenses, and if the big leagues paid $10,000 to $20,000 per team, the operation would be solvent. The majors refused, and Duane Kurisu pulled the plug.

The end came not with a bang, but with nary a whimper. The major leagues never explained their stance, and there was little public reaction from disappointed fans.

Hawaii Winter League officials did express their anger at the lack of recognition from the big leagues. Perhaps league president Frank Kudo said it best: "This is about equity. They are treating us like Venezu- ela or the Dominican League. We felt like we were sub- sidizing Major League Baseball. It should be the other way around."

The league kept an office open for two months after its closing in the forlorn hope that the major leagues would supply the needed money. They never did. Appropriately, the office was on the second floor of a building overlooking what used to be right field in old Honolulu Stadium.

Hawaii Winter League Leaders

Team Champions

1993	Hilo Stars
1994	Kauai Emeralds
1995	Maui Stingrays
1996	Maui Stingrays
1997	Honolulu Sharks

Batting Champions

Year	Player	Team	AVG
1993	Chad Fonville	Maui	.336
1994	Hiroki Kokubo	Kauai	.370
1995	D.J. Boston	Honolulu	.347
1996	Brad Fullmer	Honolulu	.333
1997	Nobuhiko Matsunaka	West Oahu	.372

Home Run Champions

Year	Player	Team	HR
1993	Ernie Young	Kauai	11
1994	David Kennedy	Kauai	13
1995	Derek Gibson	Maui	8
1996	Gabe Kapler	West oahu	7
1997	Calvin Pickering	Maui	10
	Jim Chamblee	West Oahu	10

RBI Champions

Year	Player	Team	RBI
1993	Ernie Young	Kauai	37
1994	David Kennedy	Kauai	36
1995	Preston Wilson	Maui	30
1996	Brad Fullmer	Honolulu	41
1997	Nobuhiko Matsunaka	West Oahu	37

Lowest Earned Run Average

Year	Player	Team	ERA
1993	Joe Ganote	Honolulu	2.04
1994	Hidekazu Watanabe	Kauai	0.98
1995	Noe Najera	Honolulu	1.87
1996	Masao Teramae	Honolulu	1.50
1997	Darrin Babineaux	Maui	1.35

Most Wins

Year	Player	Team	W-L
1993	Brian Harrison	Honolulu	5-3
	Dukyeoma Ka	Kauai	5-3
1994	Hidekazu Watanabe	Kauai	8-0
1995	Ryan Hancock	West Oahu	5-1
1996	Masahiro Sakumoto	Maui	5-0
	Keizaburoh Tanoue	Maui	5-0
1997	Paul O'Malley	Hilo	4-4
	Luther Hackman	Maui	4-3
	Keith Evans	West Oahu	4-3
	Shinji Kurano	West Oahu	4-5
	Philip Grundy	West Oahu	4-3

Most Strikeouts

Year	Player	Team	SO
1993	Dukyeoma Ka	Kauai	55
1994	Hidekazu Watanabe	Kauai	77
1995	Joey Viera	Maui	59
1996	Hideki Okajima	Honolulu	46
1997	Junichi Kawahara	Honolulu	68

Most Saves

Year	Player	Team	SV
1993	Jeff McCurry	Kauai	9
1994	Barry Goldman	Honolulu	10
1995	Bryan Wolff	Honolulu	8
1996	Justin Speier	West Oahu	10
1997	Ryan Kohlmeier	Maui	8

Finding Andy Nelson

Bob Tholkes

There are only a few remaining baseball "mystery men" —players who appeared in the big leagues since 1900 about whom we have no basic biographical information. Until recently, Andy Nelson was one of them. This is Andy's story, and the story of how we dug it—or most of it—out.

Swede Hollow was an immigrant settlement which squatted for a century in Phalen Creek ravine on the east side of St. Paul, Minnesota. The city pretended officially that it was not there. Newcomers found a polyglot of wooden dwellings, unhampered in their construction by building or sanitary regulations and undisturbed by the usual city services. When they were financially able, residents moved "up the street" and out of the ravine, a tangible manifestation of upward mobility.

We now know that Ole and Elna Nelson and their four children arrived in St. Paul from Sweden in the early 1880s and found their way to Swede Hollow. Two more children were born there, Andy on November 30, 1884, and Frank in 1891. When the older children could work and pay rent, the family moved "up the street" in 1893.

Baseball permeated the summers of St. Paul boys at the turn of the century. In May, age-group teams would form and advertise in the papers requesting that captains of other teams contact their captains to schedule games. Boys often had older brothers or fathers playing either on independent nines or industrial league teams.

Bob Tholkes *is active in Minnesota's Halsey Hall Chapter and on the Biographical Research Committee. He founded the Chapter's vintage baseball team, the Quicksteps.*

This was undoubtedly Andy's background when he surfaced in May, 1903, as a pitcher for the Parlor Clothing Company. At age eighteen he was competing with adults for the first time. A family picture taken at the time shows a strapping fellow of 6 foot 2 or 3. Parlor Clothing played other independents and town teams. Andy was competitive, winning a few and losing a few. The remainder of his amateur career is a blank. In 1906, if not before, he began playing semipro ball in the Dakotas. The connection with that area may have been older brother Nels, who sometime during the decade moved to Dickinson, North Dakota.

Andy pitched for Leeds of the North Dakota Central League in 1907. By the time the club's season ended on July 19, he was exhibiting more stuff than the average Central League team could handle, striking out 21 Lakota batters in a game on July 1. The earliest of the fifty postcards that Andy sent home during his travels depicts a match in progress between Leeds and its rival from Cando. Only players, a bench, and an umpire are in camera range. The field is apparently a converted patch of prairie, with not a tree or a building in sight.

This exposure was sufficient to earn Andy the attention of the Chicago White Sox. In March, 1908, owner Charles Comiskey dispatched veteran hurler Roy Patterson, who was nursing a sore arm, to look the youngster over. Comiskey seems to have considered the Upper Midwest his particular scouting ground. He had operated the St. Paul team in the Western League before transferring it to Chicago in 1900. Players from Minnesota and Wisconsin dotted his lineups. Patterson, himself from St. Croix Falls, Wisconsin, liked what he saw, and in early April, Nelson was off to Sioux City, Iowa, to join the White Sox seconds, hopefuls who had accompanied the regulars to spring training in California, and were now working their way back, stopping to play exhibitions. A few would be kept on after the start of the regular season in case the regulars faltered or injuries occurred.

What made such a raw recruit worth a tryout? He was big, strong, and lefthanded. Major league teams at the time commonly took young players with potential under their wings. Besides, the White Sox were making only a minimal investment. Nelson could be released without further compensation at any time. At twenty-three, he wasn't particularly young, but shaving a year or two off his actual age would certainly have been in keeping with baseball tradition.

After debuting in relief at Omaha, Nelson started at Burlington, Iowa, and pitched a complete-game, two-hit shutout, striking out eleven. The Burlington *Hawkeye* declared that he "plainly had ability enough to land in high company," and the Chicago *Daily Journal* wrote that the "big Swedish southpaw from St. Paul" had "astonished the natives of Burlington, Ia.," and described him as "the real goods and a genuine wonder" and as a "large Scandinavian…with the speed of Waddell and good control." Typically for the times, much was made of Nelson's ethnicity throughout his baseball career.

Andy pitched again in Decatur, Iowa, and reached the big city around April 15. Chicago made an obvious impression on him. The event worth recording on his postcard of April 18 was that 18,000 people had attended the opener. This postcard, like the others, was sent to sister Ingrid Johnson and her husband Nels at their apartment above Nels' saloon. References in the postcards indicate that Nelson was writing letters as well as sending the penny postcards, which mostly featured pictures of local sights. The failure of these letters to survive is unfortunate. The postcards indicate that Andy was an interesting, articulate writer.

Nelson had shown enough, and the White Sox were short of healthy pitchers. He was retained. In May, he was placed on the roster, and accompanied the team on its first eastern swing. Postcards came from each new city. He wrote that he "played Broadway off the boards," whatever that meant in 1908. In Washington, he visited the other St. Paul east-sider in the majors, Hank Gehring of the Nationals. His hometown newspaper meanwhile had noticed his success. The St. Paul *Dispatch* on May 14 notified the public that he was with the Sox but, instead of extolling his promise, humorously emphasized his ethnicity:

Nelson…was taken on the Eastern trip with the Sox…Nelson is said to have new Swedish movements of the curved variety, besides more speed than ever before shot out of

Stockholm. Mr. Nelson is a modest youth. Comiskey asked him how he fooled the batsmen. "Dat is easy," answered Mr. Nelson. "Aye peetch dat ball so fast dat de catcher skal have it before da batter is on de yob." "But what if they are hitting speed?" queried the Old Roman. "Den," said Mr. Nelson, "Aye tak two throws at dem, and de two throws togedder skal mak de speed twice so fast as one."

In Boston, he got into his first game, a lopsided 16-5 loss on Tuesday, May 26, in front of Ban Johnson and a crowd of 6,323. He pitched the seventh and eighth innings. Gavvy Cravath walked to lead off the seventh but was caught stealing. Fielder Jones then made a spectacular running, barehanded catch of Doc Gessler's liner to right-center. With two outs, if rather unconvincing ones, under his belt, Nelson then struck out Bob Unglaub. In the eighth, Heinie Wagner singled with one out, but Nelson retired the eighth and ninth hitters to finish his first assignment unscathed.

From Boston the White Sox headed back to Chicago. Nelson made his second and last appearance at home, starting on Saturday, June 6, against Washington as a last-minute replacement for veteran lefthander Nick Altrock, who was having arm troubles. This was a great opportunity. He would have the support of the home crowd, and the Nationals were a weak-hitting team whose starting lineup had several lefthanded hitters.

While the crowd was friendly ("Salvos of applause greeted Andy Nelson," the Chicago *Tribune* reported), there were about 15,000 in the park watching his every move. His career was on the line, and this wasn't Leeds or Burlington. Nelson was nervous. Charlie Dryden of the *Tribune* wrote, "Our southpaw performed like an inmate, pacing up and down his little cell, and the game dragged horribly." In the first, Clyde Milan walked. Ollie Pickering bunted safely. Jim Delahanty lined to left and Otis Clymer forced Pickering, but Gabby Street singled in Milan. Nervous or not, Nelson then steadied sufficiently to prevent further damage until the fourth inning. With one out, Dave Altizer walked, stole second, and an out later scored on Jerry Freeman's single to right. There were two further runs, unearned, in the seventh. Pickering led off with a single. Nelson then couldn't field Delahanty's bunt to the right side, which rolled past him to second baseman George Davis, who picked it up and threw it into right field for a three-base error, Pickering scoring. Nelson then caught Clymer's foul pop himself, but Street squeezed Delahanty home. Altizer then singled but was caught stealing to end the inning.

With the White Sox then trailing 4 to 1, that was it for Nelson. The crowd went home happy, since the Sox scored two in the eighth and two in the ninth for the win. Andy had surrendered two earned runs on three walks and ten hits—a "quality start" by today's standards, but plainly unsatisfactory, especially the walks, in 1908, a year when American League batters hit .239 and, coincidentally, pitchers had a collective ERA of 2.39.

The Washington *Post* was critical but correct about Andy's state of development: "Nelson, a young man who hails from somewhere in the woods…is a green lefthander who knows nothing about fielding bunts, and made a mess of several…he did not seem to have much speed, and only an ordinary curve ball."

The White Sox, meanwhile, were getting back some of their injured veteran pitchers, like Patterson and Altrock, and could dispense with Nelson's services. On a tailender, his results—two earned runs in nine total innings— may have earned him more innings, but the White Sox intended to be contenders. Comiskey had an informal relationship with the Des Moines Boosters, who were struggling to escape the Western League's cellar. Nelson had almost landed in Des Moines in April—the Des Moines *Daily News* announced his acquisition—and on June 12 he was sent out. By the end of the season he was certainly Des Moines property, but in his postcard home on June 17 Andy writes that he was "loaned to Des Moines for a couple of months…Comiskey wants me back before September".

Nelson was belted around in that first game in Des Moines, but was recognized to be out of condition. He had not pitched regularly all season. It was mid-July before he finally won a game, but when the Western League season ended on September 15 his record was seven wins and eight losses for a last place team, with two five-hitters and a shutout. He batted .284, but finished last in pitchers' fielding with a percentage of .879. With the White Sox in the midst of the American League's incredible four-team pennant race of 1908, there would be no recall to Chicago.

Nelson presumably returned to St. Paul for the off-season, and reported to Des Moines in April, 1909. The Boosters had acquired several new pitchers. Despite throwing a no-hitter at a college team, Andy didn't get in a game after the start of the regular season and was loaned to Fond du Lac of the Wisconsin–Illinois League on May 19. Before leaving Des Moines, he appeared in a team photo. This photo shows a distinctly huskier individual than the lean, firmly-muscled young fellow in the family photo. Nelson's off-season training may have been confined to Nels Johnson's saloon.

Fond du Lac was a large step backward. The few postcards home that summer were critical of his teammates. They finished sixth of eight. Andy was a workhorse, third in the league in games pitched with 32, winning 17 and losing 15. His effectiveness waned toward season's end, perhaps from pitching too frequently. The Fond du Lac *Commonwealth* criticized team management for overworking its few effective

starters. The paper assigned him the nickname "Battler" because he worked out of many tight situations; perhaps he was having control problems or was not bearing down on every hitter. The name was also a takeoff on the popular lightweight champion "Battling" Nelson. The paper noted at season's end that he remained on Des Moines' reserve list.

Nelson did not go straight home after leaving Fond du Lac. As the *Commonwealth* reported two weeks later, he went to Ishpeming, on Michigan's Upper Peninsula, to pitch for an independent team. The paper also published a report that he had been signed by the Philadelphia A's, evidently only a rumor. By October 1, the season was over and Nelson was on the road again, back to St. Paul according to more postcards, and then west to North Dakota and Montana in November and December for reasons unknown.

The spring of 1910 saw Nelson resume his baseball career. Still Des Moines property, he was loaned out for a spring training tryout with Fort Wayne, Indiana. He pitched little after arriving on April 20— a postcard mentions that he was "stiff as ____" from hard training, so he may have been behind in his conditioning. His first outing was for three innings in an exhibition against Duluth of the Minnesota-Wisconsin League, and he was touched for two runs. His problems with fielding continued. The Fort Wayne *Sentinel* described an error in detail:

> Nelson passed Buzinski in the third and then came in too fast on Kenny's bunt and it popped over his head. Then he lunged for it, slipped and fell and with his breadbasket in contact with the sloppy field he attempted to make one of those do-or-die heaves and he pegged to center field in an attempt to catch a runner at second when said runner had passed the station without even slowing down and was legging for third.

After surviving the first few cutdowns, Nelson was released just before the start of the regular season. According to the *Sentinel*, Des Moines would not agree to compensate Fort Wayne if he was recalled during the season, so rather than take a chance on being left suddenly short a player, he was cut. It probably didn't help that he was still not taking a regular turn in exhibition matches, evidently not in shape to open the season at full effectiveness.

Meanwhile, Wausau, Wisconsin, had released his brother Frank, also a pitcher. How Frank had ended up trying out with Wausau is unknown, but it was probably through the same connection that Andy was then signed on to replace him. Here Andy was given a chance to pitch himself into shape, but after losing his first four starts, he was released. The Wausau *Herald* mentioned that he had shown sufficient stuff but had trouble with his control. There were no further postcards that summer, so perhaps he went home. Unless he caught on with some semipro team that year, this seems to have been the end of Nelson's baseball career.

Andy's whereabouts from this point can be traced only for as long as the postcards continued. September, 1910, found him in Salt Lake City, working his way west with three friends, looking for work. These postcards suggest that alcohol had become a significant part of his life. He reports that two of his buddies had "recuperated after a couple of days jag and went to Bingham Canyon to work," and he wrote in October from San Francisco, commending the strong beer to be found there. He headed back toward St. Paul in November, stopping in Dickinson to see brother Nels, but by November 29 was back in California. He particularly liked Los Angeles, and spent the winter there. His last postcard, dated April 18, 1911, from Los Angeles, mentioned that he was heading for Salt Lake City.

St. Paul had little attraction for Nelson thereafter. He dropped out of sight until 1925, when he is listed in the St. Paul city directory as boarding with brother Henry and working as a laborer. Father Ole Nelson had died in December, 1924. It is most likely that he returned for the funeral and hung around for a while. Andy's whereabouts after 1925 and his final fate are unknown. He is not listed among surviving family in brother Frank's obituary in December, 1941, and the family was unable to locate him in 1948 at the time of his mother's death.

The search—Collection of biographical information on former major leaguers began not long after Andy Nelson ended his career. Ernie Lanigan, the most prominent pioneer, knew him only as Nelson. Hy Turkin and S.C. Thompson in their landmark 1951 baseball encyclopedia added his first name but confused him with an older contemporary who had pitched for the Minneapolis Millers, veteran minor leaguer Peaches Nelson.

That is where matters stood at SABR's founding in 1971, when a systematic effort began to trace the many former major leaguers whose biographical information was unknown. In one respect, at least, Andy Nelson now began to prove exceptional: he combined all the factors that make information about an old-time player hard to find. His name is common. He had only a brief career in baseball. And, as we now know, he did not settle down anywhere. Thus, he survived as a mystery while more or less complete information was obtained on virtually all his contemporaries. In the early 1980s researchers Bill Haber and Rich Topp between them succeeded in distinguishing him from Peaches Nelson, and after combing contemporary Chicago newspapers

and discovering his connection to St. Paul, enlisted me for the next step: finding references to him in his home city.

Unfortunately, his Chicago press coverage had noted only that he had spent the 1907 season at Leeds and that he had been sent to Des Moines in June, 1908. No biographical information. Since the 1908 St. Paul city directory listed sixteen Andrew Nelsons, and since the Chicago newspaper reference to St. Paul was unsubstantiated anyway, a search for more newspaper coverage was the best option. I eventually used microfilmed collections of local newspapers, and the "trade" papers, *Sporting Life* and *The Sporting News*, available from SABR's lending library, to follow Andy through the seasons of 1907, 1908, and 1909. However, the sketchy personal information I found was usually misleading. The Leeds, North Dakota, paper listed Andy A. Nelson, which was helpful, but also gave his hometown as Minneapolis rather than St. Paul, which resulted in much wasted effort. Networking with other SABR members—always a valuable piece of the research process—resulted in a major break when fellow Halsey Hall Chapter member Fred Buckland came across a history of St. Paul amateur baseball which listed an Andy Nelson. More newspaper scanning identified him as a pitcher. Since Andy now had to be identified from among the general population, refocusing the search on the most likely locality, St. Paul, became the next best direction.

The sources of information familiar to genealogists are familiar also to SABR's biographical researchers: state and national census data; city directories, which list adult residents alphabetically, with addresses and occupations; local and state birth and death records; the Social Security Death Index (SSDI), and the immense Mormon Genealogical Library, to list only the best known. Lack of birth information for Andy Nelson, or even a definite age, complicated matters.

I compiled a list of "candidates," cross-checking the St. Paul directories in the years around 1908 with the 1900 Minnesota census to identify Andy Nelsons in the right age range who lived in the right place, optimally the east side of St. Paul, at the right time. Nothing was more important to this effort than the existence of a Soundex census index for the 1900 census. Available for the U.S. censuses of 1880, 1900, and 1920, a Soundex is an alphabetical arrangement on microfilm of the census cards collected for each household in each state for those years. Since names are subject to spelling variations, sound-alike names are grouped together. Names, addresses, birth month, year, place, and relationships are listed, and the card is filed under the name of the head of household.

More than one candidate emerged from the Soundex, but when the city directory identified one of these as Andrew A. Nelson, and when this individual disappeared from the listings at the time that Andy began traveling around playing ball, I had a clear favorite.

Since he did disappear, however, instead of conveniently remaining under the occupation "ballplayer," and did not reappear in the SSDI, there remained only the hope that his family could be traced and would know about their ballplaying ancestor. After ninety years, this was a long shot, but so were all the possibilities. In its favor was the fact that ballplayers tend to be family celebrities. The Biographical Research Committee has even had a few cases where mystery players were found when the player's descendants have contacted SABR looking for information.

Family tracing is a matter of completing three steps for each individual traced: following him or her through the years in the city directory until the name stops being listed, often when the person died; obtaining a death certificate from the locality or state; and using the death date to find the obituary with, we hope, surviving relatives listed. The cycle is then repeated with the survivors. In Andy Nelson's case, this worked, since his descendants, though few, did not inherit his fondness for roaming the continent. As it turned out, though only one of his siblings had any children, and though she married a Johnson (another nightmare name for a Minnesota researcher), she was, through Andy's mother's obituary, traceable to *her* obituary. Her son, Andy's nephew, lived and died in St. Paul, and also had children, so through *his* obituary a living relative, Andy's grandniece, was located, having wandered only as far as Iowa.

I needed more luck at this point. Player descendants receiving calls or letters out of the blue by a baseball historian may be excused for being nonplussed, at the least. In this case, however, the "family celebrity" theory operated, in spades. Not only was Andy Nelson's baseball career known, but the family had saved the collection of postcards described above, and there was a family picture which matched Andy with a newspaper drawing that appeared in Chicago in 1908. The family's cooperation was unstinting, and let me put together the story of his baseball career, and to nail down the date of his birth. Unfortunately, as also noted above, even the family doesn't know what happened to Andy, or where and when he died.

In the case of Andy Nelson, the biographical research process produced one of its typical success stories: a pot of gold, not at the end of a rainbow, but at the end of a long process of digging. It turned up a story as classically American as those of other immigrants' sons, like Babe Ruth and Joe DiMaggio, who found greatness and lifelong public adoration. If Andy's baseball career ended far more typically—a brief escape from obscurity—it may be said that none began more humbly. Maybe someday the story of the Swede Hollow boy who reached baseball's major leagues will be concluded.

Van's dandy
Rookie pitcher Van Lingle Mungo broke in with the dodgers in a special way in September, 1931. He hurled a three-hit shutout, 2-0, over the Braves, striking out 12. Van also unloaded a triple and a single at bat. It was the type of performance that caused "Mungo Fever" in Brooklyn every spring. But Van never won 20 games in the majors.

Super cycler
Joe DiMaggio hit for the cycle, including two home runs, as the Yankees ripped the Senators, 16-2, in a 1937 game. Eleven years later, in 1948, Joe did the same thing—hit a single, double, triple, and two homers—as the Yankees blasted the White Sox, 13-2.

Long time coming
In 1934, the Tigers won their first pennant since 1909 and the first American League flag for a "western" team in fourteen years. The Indians finished first in 1920.

—Don Nelson

Pepper

Joel H. Hawkins
Terry Bertolino

Playing pepper has always been a part of baseball, but no one made it an integral part of the game quite like the House of David. With their wild flips, sleight of hand movements, and fake tosses, the House of David put top-notch showmanship into the game. Their version of pepper was almost an art form.

Benjamin Purnell, a former wandering evangelical preacher, started the House of David as a religious colony in Benton Harbor, Michigan, in 1902. Baseball was introduced around 1914 as a form of day-care as well as a physical

Joel H. Hawkins *and* **Terry Bertolino** *are very active with remaining House of David members, and were initial contributors to the City of David (H.I.D.) Museum located on Colony grounds, as well as participants in the reopening of the City of David to the public for individual and group tours. They anticipate a late fall release of their book,* The Original House of David Baseball Club: An Illustrated Journey, *from Arcadia Publishing. Visit their webpage at www.peppergame.com, which is solely devoted to research on the House of David baseball team (s).*

> **Pepper: A fast paced pregame bunting and fielding drill among small clusters of players playing at close range. One player chops at the ball with a brisk, bunt-like stroke. The batted ball is pitched back to the batter by the man who fields it.**
> **—The Dickson Baseball Dictionary**

> **House of David pepper: Several players with gloves got together in front of the stands and started to toss a ball among themselves. They tossed the ball behind their backs, between their legs, over their shoulders, or faked a throw with one hand while flipping the bll with the other. Faster and faster the ball—and gloves— were tossed among the players. Suddenly, the ball would disappear from the swirling action. The players, acting puzzled, looked for it everywhere. Then the batter, joining the search, would grab one player by his beard, lift it up, and out would drop the ball.**
> **—Tom Dewhirst**

activity for the younger members of the colony around 1914. Later, the colony started charging admission to local crowds that gathered when the long-haired members played.

The House of David pepper game was created on October 16, 1922, as a way to kill time while waiting for a visiting team to appear. The hilarious exhibition put on by outfielder-pitcher Jesse Lee "Doc" Tally and infielder Walter "Dutch" Faust had the audience rolling in the aisles. Knowing a good thing when he saw it, team manager Francis Thorpe used pepper as a way to increase attendance. Billing it as a special attraction, he moved House of David pepper from the beginning of the contest to the middle of the fifth inning.

Eventually, boisterous first baseman Long John Tucker was added to the game. When Faust left the colony in 1927 to pursue a career in professional baseball, third baseman George "Andy" Anderson took his place. This House of David pepper trio stayed together for fifteen years and it's the one most people remember.

Australian-born George Anderson came with his family to the House of David colony in November, 1920, at the age of ten. It didn't take him long to adapt to his new national pastime, and he soon made it his game of choice. He realized early on that making the House of David traveling team would allow him to see the country, and at age seventeen he got his opportunity.

Anderson broke in as a catcher, but quickly added second base, shortstop, and third base as positions he could play well. It was at third base that he excelled and where he stayed for many years. Known as a slap hitter, Anderson hit over .300 during his House of David career.

John Tucker had a similar start. Born in Tyler, Texas, in 1902, he arrived at the House of David in 1915. His family was immediately assigned to work at the lumber operation on High Island in Lake Michigan. There, John and many of the other children kept themselves busy playing baseball.

In 1919, Tucker, who had been "scouted" at his childhood games, was summoned to play for the House of David home team, which played at the colony's amusement park while the traveling team took to the road. In 1923, he got his shot with the traveling team, and by 1925 he was the team's full-time first baseman.

Known as a prankster and the team comedian, Tucker caught balls behind his back and between his legs during games, and his chatter from first base kept hitters on their toes. His unbridled enthusiasm for baseball made him a natural for the pepper game.

Doc Tally was the catalyst and patriarch of the trio. He was eighteen years old when he arrived in Benton Harbor in 1914 to live at the colony. He and his brothers turned House of David baseball into a money-making endeavor. A great outfielder and righthanded knuckleball pitcher, Doc pitched the team to a county championship in 1915 during its first full season. Batting lefthanded, he had great power, hit for a high average, and could bunt when the team needed a sacrifice or a squeeze.

The breakup—On November 19, 1927, House of David founder Benjamin Purnell died after a long illness. His widow, Mary, and colony secretary, Judge Harry T. Dewhirst, waged a war over control of the colony, and the result was a split. In 1929, each faction fielded a baseball team and claimed to be the "true" House of David team. Manager Thorpe sided with Mary Purnell, along with the famed pepper game trio of Tally, Tucker, and Anderson.

During the spring of 1930, the colony formally divided into two separate groups. The Dewhirst colony retained the name "House of David," while Mary Purnell's colony adopted the name "The Israelite House of David as Reorganized by Mary Purnell," but was usually known as "The City of David." Both colonies use "House of David" for promotional items and newspaper articles.

The pepper game also went through a change. Over the years, many House of David players had learned the craft, often performing it at home games while the traveling team with Tally, Tucker, and Anderson were on long barnstorming tours. After the colony division, the number of players performing the exhibition increased. The House of David entered into an arrangement with promoter Ray Doan to send three teams on the road during the 1930s. Each team featured its own version of the pepper game. Since the teams had new players each year, the quality of pepper declined.

> You know the House of David were the first ones to play "pepper"—they invented it. They used to have a big routine like the Globetrotters before the game and they'd pack the park. They'd toss the ball around to each other, behind their backs, all kinds of tricks. It was something to see.
>
> —Ted "Double Duty" Radcliffe,
> 36 Years of Pitching & Catching
> in Baseball's Negro Leagues (McNary).

Photos courtesy of the authors.

Above, left to right: George Anderson, John Tucker, and Jesse Lee "Dock" Tally around 1935. Facing page: the same three in the same order, showing off House of David pepper.

The most consistent players on the Dewhirst House of David team and in its Pepper Game were Tom Dewhirst, Dave Harrison, Lloyd Dalager, and Dutch Faust, who returned to the colony after two injury-filled seasons in the minor leagues. Not a House of David member but a long-term employee of the colony, Eddie Deal was considered one of the best pepper players.

While the House of David tinkered with its teams, the City of David continued its baseball-playing excellence. The team lost its home park in the split, and was constantly on the road. In 1932, it was third in the famous Denver Post Tournament.

In 1934, long-time manager Thorpe returned to the colony to assume a greater res-ponsibility in day-to-day operations. The enthusiastic Tucker took over as team manager. The team started traveling to new places and playing longer seasons. This strong squad played 192 games in 1934, compiling a 142-50 record. It also barnstormed through Mexico and Hawaii, playing pepper—and drawing crowds —all the way.

As the '30s wound down, the House of David stopped sending teams out on the road, focusing instead on local leagues and day trips around Michigan and Indiana. During the war years, the House of David stopped playing altogether. These were hard times for the City of David, too, and the club folded in 1942, when Anderson was drafted and Tucker left the colony to play for the local auto manufacturer, Auto Specialties.

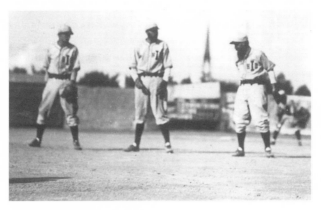

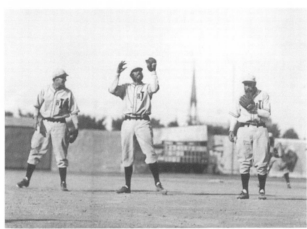

After the war, Anderson and Tally revived the team with Anderson as manager. On January 25, 1950, Tally died suddenly at the age of fifty-three. He had been gearing up for his thirty-sixth season. Anderson finally called it quits in 1955 at age forty-five, after his twenty-eighth year of baseball. He left the colony in 1962 to pursue a position with the city of St. Joseph's school district.

Tucker managed the Auto Specialties team that won the 1947 National Semi-Pro Championship, and played until the manufacturer stopped fielding a team in 1957. He managed a local American Legion team until his retirement in 1967. Altogether, Tucker spent forty-four years in baseball. After retiring, he moved to Holiday, Florida, where he passed away at the age of eighty-nine in March, 1991.

Anderson now spends his time between Michigan and Florida where he and his wife, Exa, enjoy their roses—over 300 prize varieties in two states. Into his late eighties he often played two rounds of golf in a day.

The kind of cheerfully anarchic pepper the House of David made popular became an attraction for many teams. Especially during the '20s and '30s, touring Negro Leagues teams featured similar exhibitions, and even the world champion St. Louis Cardinals of 1934— the famous Gas House Gang, put on a wonderful pregame pepper show.

George, John, and Doc were all instrumental in the development of the House of David Basketball Team... but that is another story.

In Name Only

Dick Thompson

Chick Stahl

Jake Stahl

Both photos: Transcendental Graphics

This is a story I became interested in more than a decade ago, and I suppose it would make a great work of fiction, as it contains many of the essential elements of a good novel or television soap opera. The facts, however—the sex, suicide, high finance, attempted murder, and mistaken identities—are all true. It is the tale of Chick and Jake Stahl, two prominent figures from baseball's Dead Ball Era whose early deaths later confused several generations of baseball historians.

During their playing days, and for several decades that followed, the Stahls were two distinct baseball entities. Yes, they shared the same last name and were briefly teammates, and yes, they both managed the Boston American League franchise. Beyond that, they had little in common.

When Hy Turkin and S. C. Thompson published *The Official Encyclopedia of Baseball*, the Stahls became something they never were: brothers.[1] And brothers they would remain, at least in the circle of baseball history, for close to thirty-five years. (The Stahls were not the only victims of fallible research. Bill and Patsy

Dick Thompson *lives in Bridgewater, Massachusetts, hometown of Mickey Cochrane. He would like to thank Ray Nemec, Bob Richardson, A.D. Suehsdorf, and Glenn Stout for assistance with this article.*

Donovan for a time were also incorrectly listed as brothers.)[2]

While doing some early Red Sox research in the mid-1980s, I noticed that I never found in contemporary sources the usual references to the Stahls being siblings. This seemed odd considering the prominence of the pair. The only plausible explanation I could come up with was that they were not related, but that ran counter to most baseball reference works.

In the spring of 1986, I ran into Glenn Stout, today a noted sports historian and writer who was then working at the Boston Public Library. Glenn was in the process of researching his article on Chick Stahl's suicide, "The Manager's Endgame," which appeared in the May, 1986, issue of *Boston Magazine*. Glenn had also noticed the lack of reference to a Stahl familial relationship.

I next wrote to Bill Deane, then senior research associate at the Hall of Fame, asking his opinion. Bill wrote back, "Your theory on the Stahls is interesting, and appears to be correct. I checked through every bit of material in each of their files, and could find no mention at all of their being brothers."

Chick—Charles Sylvester "Chick" Stahl was a star. He played on four major league pennant winners and twice hit over .350 during his ten years in the big show. His beginnings, though humble, seemed fairly standard for a ballplayer of his era.

His birth date and place, as given in early baseball encyclopedias, was January 10, 1873, in Fort Wayne, Indiana. Chick claimed that there were twenty-four children in his family, "We had enough in our family to make a couple of nines—eighteen boys and half a dozen girls."[3] At least one of his brothers, Fred, appears to have played minor league ball.[4]

The family, then living in Avilla, Indiana, appeared in the 1880 U.S. census, where forty-two-year-old Pennsylvania native Ruben Stahl, the family patriarch, listed his occupation as "huckster." He and his wife Barbara (Stadtmiller), thirty-seven, had been married since 1865, and at the time had nine children, four boys and five girls ranging in age from three to sixteen. By 1885, the family had relocated to Fort Wayne, where Ruben was listed in the city directory as a carpenter. Several newspaper accounts appear to confirm Chick's birthplace as Avilla, but a true birth record has never been located.[5]

Fast forward to 1906. The Boston Americans, flag winners in '03 and '04 and winners of the first modern World Series, had hit bottom. Jimmy Collins, Chick's best friend and roommate, was let go as field manager late in the season. In a decision that would prove fatal, Chick took over command of the team.

Stout felt that Stahl, like generations of players before and after him, took full advantage of the fast fame, fast money, and fast women that came with being a major league star, so it came as somewhat of a surprise to his friends when he married Miss Julia Harmon in Boston on November 14, 1906. The newlyweds left on a honeymoon trip that took them to Virginia, Hot Springs, Arkansas, and Buffalo, New York, to visit with Collins before finally heading to Fort Wayne where the couple planned to reside.[6]

Stahl, for the most part, appears to have led a sedate lifestyle during the off-season in Indiana. Known to be a liberal spender, he had also invested wisely in real estate, owning at least three houses in addition to business property. He also set up at least one of his brothers in business, and provided carefully for his mother and new wife, having $9,000 in life insurance.[7]

Spring training started uneventfully for the Bostons that year in Little Rock, but Stahl abruptly resigned as manager in Louisville, Kentucky, on March 25. Talked into running the team until a successor could be found, Stahl took the team to West Baden Springs, Indiana, for an exhibition game.

The morning of March 28 seemed like a good day for baseball. Stahl was out of bed early, ate breakfast, and then headed for the local field to check on playing con-ditions. He walked back to the hotel, went to the room he was sharing with Collins, and drank a bottle of carbolic acid. Collins entered the room to hear his long-time friend's last words, "I couldn't help it, Jim. I did it. It was killing me and I couldn't stand it." Help was called for but nothing could be done. Stahl's death certificate listed the cause of death as "carbolic acid poisoning (15 minutes)."[8]

Stahl's body, accompanied by his brother Perry, arrived in Fort Wayne on the morning of March 30, and the remains were laid to rest in the city's Lindenwood Cemetery the next day. The funeral was one of the largest ever seen in Fort Wayne. The widow, a bride for less than five months, was overcome with grief. No clergy were in attendance as Stahl, a Catholic, had committed suicide. The services were organized by the local Elks and Eagles Lodges and the eulogy was given by Congressman James Robinson.[9]

The Boston players took it hard. Cy Young tearfully addressed the team in his role as new interim manager, "It is mighty tough, boys. I never dreamed of such a thing. In fact, none of us could imagine Stahl doing away with himself. Players may come and go, but there are few Chick Stahls."[10]

Young's words were the expected response from protective teammates. Certainly the Boston players wouldn't speak unkindly of a newly deceased teammate, but they probably felt some type of guilt for either ignoring or misreading the visible signs. Stahl's wife, expecting to rejoin Chick for the opening of the regular season, had returned to Boston at the start of spring training. Collins, sensing his friend's depression, urged Chick to send for Julia. In Little Rock, Stahl said to a photographer who snapped his and Collins' picture, "Well, I guess that will be the last picture ever taken of me."[11] Rumor had it that a few days prior to his death teammates had taken another bottle of carbolic acid away from Stahl in Louisville.[12]

Initial statements by the Boston press indicated that Stahl's suicide was caused by the pressure of the managing the team. One writer, Frederic P. O'Connell of the Boston *Post*, hinted otherwise. He indicated in his stories that baseball was only a supplementary cause in Stahl's death. O'Connell was the only member of the Boston press who seemed willing to investigate the affair on a deeper level. Just as he seemed poised to print the whole truth, and he indicated that many in baseball knew it, he was suddenly stricken with pneumonia and died, as had Stahl, in West Baden.[13]

Causes—At this point Stout and I differ in our conclusions. Stout's theory was that another woman appeared from Stahl's past, blackmailing him with the claim she was pregnant with his child. Noted baseball scholars Harold Seymour[14] and David Voight[15] also gave credence to this theory. The theory is that, forced to deal with the potential scandal from this woman, Stahl opted to take his life. Stout felt this was the story that O'Connell was ready to tell.

This is possible. At seven o'clock on the evening of January 26, 1902, Chick was walking past Granneman's drug store in Fort Wayne.[16] He was accompanied by an unidentified friend, probably female. Lying in wait with a loaded revolver was his recently deposed flame, a twenty-year-old stenographer named Lulu Ortman. As Stahl passed the drug store, Lulu confronted him on the street, demanding an explanation. Chick, not wishing to discuss his affairs in public, suggested the trio remove themselves from the busy street. After doing so, Miss Ortman then reached into the folds of her dress and pulled out her gun. Chick quickly grabbed the pistol before any shots could be fired. As fate would have it, a police officer was passing by and observed the ensuing scuffle. All three individuals were taken in, and after the circumstances were investigated, Stahl was released while Lulu's father, evidently to teach her a lesson, or maybe to allow Chick time to make his getaway, let her sit all night at the Fort Wayne City Hall. Chick declined to press charges.[17]

Stout based his conclusions on extensive research in the many Boston papers of 1907, but I feel the real answer is to be found in Fort Wayne, not Boston.

The headlines of the Fort Wayne *Journal-Gazette* of March 30, 1907, read, MEDITATED SELF-SLAYING, CHICK STAHL HAD OFTEN TALKED ABOUT SUICIDE, and BASE BALL PLAYER HAD ENTERTAINED DANGEROUS IDEAS ABOUT SELF DESTRUCTION.

None of Chick's close friends in Fort Wayne were surprised at his suicide. "I looked for it when I heard he was worrying about the management of the team," said one city official who had been a friend since childhood. He continued, "About five years ago I heard him tell a barber who was shaving him that it would be a good thing for him to put the razor through his neck to rid him of his troubles." Additional newspaper accounts described periods of "mental depression" and "half-repressed melancholy" of more than a decade's duration.

Did his indiscriminate social behavior drive Stahl to suicide? Was that the dark secret that O'Connell claimed many people in baseball's inner circle knew? I don't think so. I think O'Connell did know the truth, but the truth was not that Stahl was responding to a blackmail threat. It was that he was responding to his own haunted emotions.

I think that had Chick Stahl had been born a century later, a good therapist and simple prescription for an antidepressant might have allowed him to lead a long and productive life.

Jake—Garland (no middle name) Stahl was born in the village of Elkhart, Illinois, on April 13, 1879,[18] to Henry Stahl, an Ohio native of German ancestry who fought in a number of Civil War engagements as a member of the 14th Illinois Infantry, and his wife, Eliza Ebey Stahl.[19] Many early editions of various baseball encyclopedias correctly listed Jake Stahl's birthplace as Elkhart, Illinois, but later editions confused the issue by listing it as Elkhart, Indiana.[20]

The Stahls had six children: three boys and three girls. Jake did have an older brother named Charles S. Stahl who was born in 1875, making him two years younger than the ballplaying Chick Stahl. In 1990, I received a letter from the granddaughter of Charles Stahl, Jake's brother. He had died in 1954,[21] but his granddaughter, who still resided in Elkhart, informed me that her cousin, eighty-year-old Garland "Jake" Stahl, Jr. was alive and well and living in Santa Barbara, California. Several pieces of information in this article came from phone conversations I had with Garland, Jr.

Jake graduated from the University of Illinois with a law degree in 1903.[22] A standout on both the college gridiron and the baseball diamond, where he caught batterymate Carl Lundgren, Stahl had hopes of joining the Chicago Cubs with Lundgren, but instead signed a contract with the Boston Americans for $500 a month.[23]

Stahl's stay in Boston was brief, but by 1905, at the age of twenty-six and with fewer than 200 professional games under his belt, Jake was named manager of the Washington American League club, for which he was the regular first baseman.

On January 24, 1906, Jake married his college sweetheart, Jeanne Mahan, in a Methodist ceremony at the winter home of the bride's parents in Pasadena, California.[24] Jake's new father-in-law, Henry W. Mahan, was a wealthy Chicago banker.

Over the next few years Stahl split his energy between baseball and banking. He was the property of the Chicago White Sox in 1907, but couldn't come to terms with Charlie Comiskey. An educated guess is that Stahl presented Comisky with tougher contract negotiations than, say, Joe Jackson.

The next three years saw him spend about half a season with the New York Highlanders before returning to the Red Sox. His first-born child, a daughter named Adeline, died in St. Louis on May 24, 1909.[25] This was probably why he played in only 127 games that year. In 1910, he led the American League in home runs. But before the 1911 season, he retired from baseball and went into banking full-time.

"The Washington Park National Bank started in business May 1, 1910 with a capitol of $100,000 and deposits of $147,000 at the southwest corner of 63rd and Evans."[26] The resources of the bank, which was in the Woodlawn section of Chicago, had reached just over $8,000,000[27] in the spring of 1921 when bank president Jake Stahl finalized a deal for, "what is expected will be one of the most imposing South Side business improvements outside of the loop—the new nine story home of the Washington Park National bank at the corner of Cottage Grove Avenue and Sixty-third street." The total investment in land and building was estimated at close to $1,000,000.[28]

In the fall of 1911, American League president Ban Johnson orchestrated a deal wherein John I. Taylor, scion of the publishing family that owned the Boston *Globe*, sold the Red Sox to former major league player Jimmy McAleer, American League secretary Robert McRoy, and some unnamed investors, for $148,000, outbidding Ned Hanlon, who had offered $125,000.[29]

McAleer soon announced that Jake Stahl had been signed to a two-year deal to manage the club. Also announced were the newest stockholders. They were C. H. Randall, Henry W. Mahan, and Garland Stahl, all bankers from Chicago.[30]

What more need be said abou 1912 to a true Recd Sox fan? Tris Speaker and Smoky Joe Wood; Hooper, Lewis, and Gardner. Beating the Giants and Christy Mathewson in the World Series. Bob Gibson, Enos Slaughter, and Bill Buckner are all just afterthoughts.

Jake had a good year all the way around. He hit .301, had nine hits in the Series, claimed the title as best manager in baseball, and could boast he bested Connie Mack and John McGraw in the process. Oh yeah, he also took home $35,000 for his efforts.[31]

Stahl came back in 1913 but the Red Sox were injury-prone, the biggest hurt being Wood's broken thumb.

McAleer replaced Stahl in midseason with Bill Carrigan, another future bank president. It's doubtful that Ban Johnson was pleased with McAleer's decision, and McAleer himself was soon out of a job himself.

Jake devoted most of his time after 1913 to the banking business. He satisfied his love for the game by serving as president of the South Side Business Men's Baseball League in Chicago.[32]

As the Roaring Twenties arrived and Babe Ruth was introducing a new style of baseball to the country, Jake Stahl, still in his early forties, was dying from tuberculosis. He headed west with his wife and son to the open-air, desert climates of California, standard medical advice given to tubercular patients of the time.

As several different stories have it, Stahl, up until just a few weeks before his own death, went for daily walks in the desert. He would sometimes provide financial assistance to families he found camping along desert highways on their way to California.[33]

Jake Stahl died in Monrovia, California, on September 18, 1922. His death certificate listed the cause of death as, "Pulmonary Tuberculisis [sic] with Tuberculosis Laryngitis" of two years' duration.[34] The remains were returned to Illinois for interment.[35]

Chick and Jake Stahl were not related by blood. They were, however, related by their physical talent for the game, by their connection with the Red Sox, and by the fate that took them both before their time.

Notes:

1. *The Official Encyclopedia of Baseball*. A. S. Barnes and Company, 1956, pp 499.

2. *The Baseball Encyclopedia*. The Macmillan Company. First Printing. 1969.

3. *Sporting Life*, October 22, 1898.

4. Ibid., March 31, 1906.

5. Avila town officials in 1986 stated that records were available only from 1882.

6. Unidentified clipping in Stahl's HOF file.

7. Fort Wayne *Journal-Gazette*, March 29, 1907.

8. Death certificate issued to author on December 12, 1986 by the Orange County Department of Health, Paoli, Indiana.

9. Unidentified clipping in Stahl's HOF file.

10. Ibid.

11. Fort Wayne *Journal-Gazette*, March, 30, 1907.

12. Ibid., March, 29, 1907.

13. "The Manager's Endgame." Glenn Stout. *Boston Magazine*. May, 1986.

14. *Baseball: The Golden Age*. Oxford University Press. 1971. pp 102.

15. *American Baseball. Volume 2. From The Commissioners to Continental Expansion*. University of Oklahoma Press. 1970. pp 71.

16. Fort Wayne *Journal-Gazette*, January 27, 1902.

17. *Sporting Life*, February 8, 1902.

18. Lincoln *Herald*. April 17, 1879.

19. *History of Logan County, Illinois*. Interstate Publishing Co. Chicago. 1886. pp 688-89.

20. *The Baseball Encyclopedia*. Macmillan. 6th Edition.

21. *The Village of Elkhart*. Elkhart, Illinois. Siltennial History, 1855-1980.

22. 1918 University of Illinois Alumni Directory.

23. Unidentified clipping in Stahl's HOF file.

24. *Sporting Life*, February 3, 1906.

25. Ibid., May, 29, 1909.

26. Unidentified newspaper clipping in Stahl's HOF file.

27. Ibid.

28. Ibid.

29. *Sporting Life*. November 18, 1911.

30. Ibid. *The Sporting News* issue of January 29, 1942 repeated that Stahl was a stockholder.

31. Ibid., November 2, 1912. $10,000 in salary, $4,024.69 in World Series share, and $22,500 for 5 percent stock interest on Boston's $450,000 profit in 1912.

32. Unidentified clipping in Stahl's HOF file.

33. Unidentifed clipping in Stahl's HOF file.

34. Death certificate issued to author on August 21, 1987 by the Registrar-Recorder, Los Angeles County, California.

35. Ibid., Also Lincoln *Evening Star*. September 21, 1922.

A Streetcar Named Obscurity

Jay Berman

Pity the Pasadena Silk Sox.

The team with the unlikely name played only four games in the ill-fated Southern California Trolley League of 1910, losing all of them, before the franchise folded.

Not that anyone else in the six-team league fared much better. Play began on April 3, a Sunday. All games were to have been played on Sundays, a feature that organizers said made it unique in professional baseball. In truth, others had attempted similar schedules and, in the end, it is probably the league's obscurity that defines it better than any other factor.

A month after play began, Pasadena and the Los Angeles Maiers, owned by the local Maier brewery, folded. That left the league with four teams—the Redondo Beach Wharf Rats, Santa Ana Yellow Sox, Long Beach Sand Crabs, and Los Angeles McCormicks.

On June 13, the circuit disbanded, contradicting what Ed Crolic, Santa Ana's manager and the league's secretary, had written in the April 7 *Sporting News*, when he predicted: "The league will play ball all the year around."

The "Trolleyites," as *The Sporting News* called them, were not alone in failure. There were fifty-two leagues in organized baseball in 1910, and thirty-one were rated "D," the lowest classification. Geographically, they ranged from the Connecticut Association down to the Southeastern League in Tennessee, Alabama, and Georgia, all through the Midwest, and as far west as the Washington State League. Five leagues had teams in California.

All the "D" leagues had one thing in common. They were temporarily gone by 1917. Some were victims of the Federal League war, which siphoned players from minor league rosters. Others failed because automobiles and silent movies were giving people options for spending their free time they had never known before. Others, of course, were victims of World War I. Wartime travel restriction finished off a few of the "D" leagues by 1917, but most had gone under by 1914. Ten circuits founded in 1910 failed the same year. Only two completed the season, neither closing early nor shedding insolvent franchises along the way.

But no other league in Organized Baseball history, before or since, played fewer games than the Trolley League. When its final games were completed on June 12, Redondo Beach had a record of 9-2, Santa Ana was 8-3, Long Beach was 4-5, and the McCormicks—named for manager and league president James McCormick—were 2-7. The Maiers were 1-3 when they ceased operation along with 0-4 Pasadena, two days after their games of May 1.

Newspaper stories that appeared before play began were filled with the boosterism typical of that era. The first mention of the league was seen in the weekly Redondo *Reflex* of March 17, with the notice: "All Redondo Beach players who expect to play with the local team in the new Class D League are expected to sign up by next Monday evening."

The weekly Redondo *Breeze* of April 2 virtually ordered its readers to attend the April 10 home opener

Jay Berman *is a retired journalism professor an an original member of the Pacific Coast League Historical Society. He and his wife Irene live in Manhattan Beach, California.*

against the Maiers, promising them "an automobile parade, a brass band, the mayor pitching the first ball...and a red-hot contest." The article also indicated that one civic leader would bring his goat, apparently an added inducement for attending.

Civic leaders "have worked hard and long to bring this class of baseball to Redondo Beach," the story read, "and their efforts should be appreciated by the local fans and a good attendance shown each game." Readers were assured that "Manager (George) Love has the right combination for a pennant-winning aggregation."

Crolic, the Santa Ana manager and league secretary, had promised "the support of the Pacific Coast League" in his April 7 *Sporting News* brief, indicating the league would operate in Los Angeles after the PCL's Angels had finished play for the year.

Redondo Beach, Santa Ana, and the McCormicks won the April 3 games, and Redondo Beach went to 2-0 on April 10, defeating the Maiers, 2-0, with 6-foot-4 Slim Abbott throwing a two-hitter "with the skill of a Mathewson," according to the *Breeze* account of April 16. Losing pitcher Tom Piña had allowed only three hits, but "was a trifle wild at times."

The Santa Ana *Daily Register* of April 11, reporting on a 4-0 win over Long Beach the previous day—only the second game for each team—offered the opinion that "The team is working fine now and should give all the clubs a fight for the pennant."

After three weeks, Redondo Beach and Santa Ana remained undefeated at 3-0. The contests were generally low-scoring. That week's scores included Redondo Beach beating the McCormicks, 4-0, while Santa Ana edged Pasadena, 7-6, and Long Beach shut out the Maiers, 4-0.

Crolic managed another brief article in the April 28 *Sporting News*, assuring readers that the new league had opened "with good crowds in all the cities" and predicting that "there are many good ball players in the league who will be in better company before our first series is over."

The only paper to regularly print full box scores and standings was the Los Angeles *Examiner*, whose coverage of the league far surpassed that of any other paper. The *Examiner*, while concentrating on the major leagues and the Pacific Coast League, with its local teams in Los Angeles and Vernon, still managed to cover the Trolley League each week. The Los Angeles *Times* of 1910 had a fondness for auto racing, bowling and track meets. It covered a Whittier High School baseball game in one Monday edition, but said nothing of Trolley League action of the previous day and apparently dismissed it entirely.

The St. Louis-based *Sporting News* gave the league a few paragraphs nearly every week, both Redondo Beach weeklies did what they could given space and size constraints, and the Santa Ana *Daily Register* covered the Yellow Sox regularly.

Curiously, no newspaper mentioned the demise of the Maiers and Silk Sox. They simply appeared in league standings one week and were gone the next.

Because the teams played weekly, there was no need for pitching depth. A preseason story in the *Breeze* listed Abbott and Stanley—the use of first names was rare—as the entire pitching staff.

Abbott, who had been a local semipro pitcher, tossed a three-hitter in his first game, allowing one run; threw two-hit shutouts in his second and third starts, then carried a shutout into the twelfth inning of his fourth game before losing, 4-0, to Santa Ana on April 24.

A *Sporting News* article of May 5 assured readers that the season was "progressing in fine shape and all teams are playing as good ball as is found in leagues of higher class." It offered the opinion that "the race appears to be between Santa Ana, Redondo Beach and the McCormicks," but, since only one-half game separated those clubs, admitted that "it is a little too early to tell what may happen."

The *Breeze* of May 7, reporting on games of May 1, called Abbott "our mighty and now departed Slim Abbott." He pitched seven innings of two-run, five-hit ball to defeat Pasadena in what would be the losers' final game. On May 21, the *Breeze* indicated Abbott had moved on to another league, but didn't specify which one, saying only, "Advices from Slim Abbott state that he lost his first game, 5-0, but he says he will win sure the next time. The old boy has still got the confidence left anyway."

Meanwhile, the pennant race was coming down to a Redondo Beach–Santa Ana showdown. Both teams were 6-1 after seven weeks of what one *Sporting News* account said was to have been a twenty-game season. As play headed into June, there was no indication in the press that everything was about to end.

The June 6 *Daily Register*, reporting on the previous day's 6-3 win over Long Beach, also noted that Redondo Beach had beaten Los Angeles the same day, "thus leaving the pennant still tied up between Santa Ana and the fishermen." It continued, "Next Sunday, the locals will play Redondo at the beach resort." At the time, both clubs were 8-2.

The following week's coverage marked the first mention that the league was going out of business. The June 13 *Examiner* account came under a headline that read, in part: REDONDO...DEFEATS SANTA ANA IN CLOSING TROLLEY LEAGUE GAME.

The lead paragraph read, "In the deciding game of the Trolley League pennant race that closed here today [June 12], the local team [Redondo Beach] decisively defeated the hitherto invincible Santa Ana aggregation by the score of 8 to 2."

Even though Redondo Beach scored its eight runs

on twelve hits, holding Santa Ana to just two hits, the *Daily Register* coverage claimed Santa Ana would have won had it not been for poor fielding.

"The game marked the poorest fielding exhibition that the locals have put up this season," it commented, suggesting that the losing pitcher would have won "had the locals given him the support that they have in previous games."

Strangely, as though its reporter didn't know the league was going under, the account concludes, "It is now hoped that the boys have their systems cleaned and will be able to put up the same kind of ball that they have been giving the fans all season."

The *Redondo Reflex* of June 16 obviously knew the league was done. Reporting on the win over Santa Ana, it indicated, "This game wound up the present series in the Trolley League. It is understood that all out-of-town players will be released, and the local team will be re-organized on an all-home plan."

In another example of local boosterism, the final paragraph of the account suggests, "There are local fans who insist that if it were possible to break into the Pacific Coast League with the present team, they would make good in that company also."

Since the six-team PCL was rated class "A," the highest minor-league designation of that time, the boast was certainly without merit.

The June 13 *Examiner* story was the first to include a crowd count, reporting, "The largest crowd of the season was on hand to cheer the home team on to victory, nearly 600 fans being in attendance." That might seem an insignificant number, but SABR's Richard Beverage, founder of the Pacific Coast League Historical Society, calls a paid crowd of 600 "pretty good for that time." Of course, if 600 was the largest turnout, others may have been much smaller.

The only other indication that something may have been amiss was buried in a Redondo *Reflex* story of June 6. After an account of the previous Sunday's game, it read:

> On account of increasing expenses in the Trolley League, it has been found necessary to increase the admission charge for the games.
>
> "Hereafter the general admission will be 25 cents, with 10 cents extra for gentlemen in the grandstand. The 25-cent ticket will entitle ladies to seats in the grandstand with no extra charge.

The story did not, however, indicate what the admission cost had been and, since the league went under a week later, the ticket price hike clearly was not enough to turn things around.

On June 13, the day the league disbanded, the *Examiner* ran a brief story separate from its regular coverage. Under the headline TROLLEY LEAGUE MEETING, it reported

> President James McCormick of the Southern California Trolley League will call a meeting of the directors of the league to be held during the coming week at his pool parlors on South Spring Street. The meeting will be called for the purpose of settling the affairs of the league. In the future, the former Trolley League teams will play independent ball.

Santa Ana went on to sweep a series from Covina in what the *Daily Register* called "the Southern California championship," without mention of the late Trolley League, and the circuit—baseball's fastest-failing and certainly one of its least-remembered—was seldom mentioned again by anyone. When the 1911 *Reach Guide* printed a list of leagues that had folded the previous year, the Trolley League wasn't even included among the failures—certainly a measure of true obscurity.

Trotters lost only game they played

By definition, no team will ever play fewer games than the Woonsocket (Rhode island) Trotters, a team that was supposed to play in the Atlantic Association in 1908. The Trotters lost the only game they played, on May 2, and that was by forfeit. The league outlasted the Trolley League by a few games, bit met the same midseason fate. Rick Harris of Cranston, who heads the Rhode Island Historical Baseball Project, believes it failed because it wasn't as strong as competing mill league teams. The Trotters, so called because they were going to play at a fairground's race track, also lost all their preseason exhibition games. In one, against Worcester of the New England League, they not only lost, 11-2, but committed seven errors, allowing their opponents to score nine runs in two innings without a hit.

Then, on May 2, captain Frank Burrell brought his team to the opening game, only to see that fewer than 30 people were in the stands. He told the umpire he wasn't going to put his club on the field for such a small turnout, and took the forfeit loss instead. The league president said he hadn't heard of it, and offered assurances that everything was OK, but a hotel where some of the players had stayed confirmed that they had checked out the day after the game.

Other teams in the league were Pawtucket and Newport, R.I.; Lewiston, Maine; and Attleboro, Mass., which was the second team to fail, on May 18. Pawtucket folded a few days later, and the whole league was gone by the end of the month.

—J.B.

Last Days of the New England League

Charlie Bevis

Bob Pugatch was the last batter to face a pitch in the long, storied history of the New England League. At 4:30 on a Sunday afternoon in Portland, Maine, fifty-one years ago, Pugatch hit an infield fly for the third out in the top of the ninth inning, ending a game in which the Portland Pilots defeated the Springfield Cubs, 11-0, to capture the 1949 New England League title.[1]

"What a way to be remembered!" Pugatch, now retired, recalled from his home in Delray Beach, Florida. "I thought all I had left of my baseball career was my autograph," he joked of his baseball playing days that ended in the Texas League in 1953.[2]

"It was so long ago, I can't remember a thing about the game," Pugatch admitted about that last bat-swing of New England league play. However, he has fond memories of his days playing minor league baseball in an era in which the game was paramount and fan attendance drove the team economics.

"I don't believe I've talked to anyone who understood what it was like to play professional baseball in those years," Pugatch said. "I enjoyed those years and appreciated the fact that I gave it a shot."

Pugatch, along with the other Springfield players on the losing end of that seven-game playoff series with Portland, didn't receive a dime for playing for the league title.

"League President Claude Davidson presented the $1,200 for which the teams played—winner take all—

to Manager Skeeter Newsome, whom the Pilots lugged off the field to his obvious embarrassment," the Portland *Press Herald* reported of the final New England League game.[3]

Springfield shortstop Hank Nasternak had no regrets about being on the losers end of the winner-take-all deal. Actually he pushed for it.

"The winner of the game was supposed to get seventy-five percent and the loser twenty-five percent," Nasternak vividly recollected from his home in Buffalo, New York. "We had a choice to vote 100 percent winner and zero percent loser. I was surprised that a lot of our players voted for the first option. I was very annoyed and spoke up for the 100 percent winner's share. After a little debate, our manager Bob Peterson finally agreed to the winner-take-all. The sad fact about it was we got clobbered in the last game."[4]

The fabric of the league—The New England League was a Class B minor league, four rungs down from the major leagues. Its history dated back to 1877 when "the New England League, the third minor league formed in 1877, was established around a group of amateur and semipro teams that had played during the Civil War."[5]

By August, 1949, though, there were only four teams left in the league, just half of the eight teams that had started the season. The league's future was in jeopardy.

Frank McConvery was the Portland catcher waiting to receive Charley Dyke's final pitch in the championship game on September 18, 1949, which earned Portland the Governors' Cup, symbolic of the New England League title. "I remember winning that game

Charlie Bevis *lives and writes baseball history in Chelmsford, Massachusetts. He is the author of more than thirty published articles and of the 1998 biography,* Mickey Cochrane: The Life of a Baseball Hall of Fame Catcher.

against Springfield for the league championship," McConvery recalled from his Cape Cod residence. But he had his suspicions about the league continuing into 1950. "We knew it was going to fail because attendance was down so low that salaries couldn't be met," McConvery remarked.[6]

Today, the New England economy revolves around service and hi-tech industries. Back in 1947, though, nineteen percent of the region's employment, or 280,000 jobs, was centered in the textile industry. Just two years later in 1949, close to 40,000 textile jobs had disappeared and by 1954 another 75,000 were gone. Competition from southern states with lower production costs, especially labor, drove the decline. A national recession in 1948-1949 expedited the industry's decline as mill owners shut down their outmoded plants.[7]

Two chapter names in one scholarly treatment of the New England textile industry sum it up: "Years of Hope, 1945-1949" and "Crisis Years, 1949-1952."[8]

Since the majority of New England League franchises were located in cities dependent on the textile industry, the league succumbed as well. There were just too many fans now unemployed to sustain the viability of the league.

"The fans were wonderful," remembered McConvery, who was honored by Portland fans at the season-ending team testimonial at Portland's Graymore Hotel. McConvery received a wristwatch "in recognition of his colorful and faithful service" as well as a portable radio.[9] The gesture seemed to spur McConvery, as he hit .400 in the playoffs after batting .273 in the regular season.

"The fans were great," Pugatch agreed. "Personally, I could never get over the fact that people were paying to watch me play."

"The fans in Springfield were always very good to me," Nasternak said. "They were well informed of the game of baseball and appreciated especially the hustle and drive and attitudes of the players. I have very fond memories of Pynchon Park, a very nice ballpark, beautiful atmosphere. I remember Patty the groundskeeper, we always teased him to get that infield in good shape. A very, very nice man."

The beginning of the end—The Providence Grays were the first New England League team to fold in 1949, disbanding on June 21. The league had run the team since June 2, when the Grays failed to meet its payroll.

"Providence became the largest city in the United States not represented in organized baseball at midnight last night," the Providence *Journal* reported on June 22, "when the New England League decided to close out the franchise of the Providence Grays and continue as a seven-club circuit."[10]

Providence had tried to interest the Cleveland Indians or the Philadelphia Athletics into taking on the Grays as a farm team, but was unsuccessful. Playing in Cranston Stadium, outside the Providence city limits, in a neighboring community, was a drawback to the club's fortunes. Perhaps a harbinger of the league's future, Providence's last scheduled game, on June 21 at Portland, was rained out.

Four weeks later on July 19, three more NEL teams succumbed to economic distress: the Fall River Indians, Lynn Tigers, and Manchester Yankees. League President Davidson announced that "a scarcity of paying spectators in cities hit by unemployment forced the collapse of four teams, but that the schedule had been redrawn to take in the four remaining clubs: Nashua, Pawtucket, Portland, and Springfield."[11]

The four remaining teams were all in the top half of the league standings (see the table on the next page), while the disbanded teams all had sub-.500 records.

"Several factors were instrumental in the death knell of organized baseball in this city," wrote Leo Cloutier in the Manchester *Union* about the failure of the Manchester Yankees, who played in a city renowned for the Amoskeag Mills.

> The proximity of this city to major league attractions, the Boston Red Sox and Boston Braves, with a representation of local fans at nearly all the games, did not help attendance at Athletic Field one iota. Television played its part on nights when the Braves and Red Sox entertained clubs. A large number of the 1,500 or more television-set owners in this locality remained in the comforts of their homes to watch the telecasts. Another item which must not be overlooked was the tag of 78 cents for admission to the local bailiwick. It must be remembered that this is a mill town and there aren't too many people who could afford to dish out that kind of cold cash three or four times a week.[12]

"Night baseball in the majors has killed all interest in the minor cities of the New England League," the Lynn *Daily Evening Item* explained the demise of the Lynn franchise.

> Sunday baseball here for the last few years has proven a dud as fans flocked to Fenway Park and Braves Field or went on weekend motor excursions to summer camps or to the many beaches. Against these outside interests, Lynn hasn't a chance to retain organized baseball here and the attendance at Fraser Field has been pitiful to behold.[13]

The league was not prominently featured in many newspaper sports pages in league cities. The Red Sox, the Braves, and local amateur teams were often given higher billing. For example, CYO League baseball and Girls Playground League softball had better status in the "Sports Schedule" of the Fall River *Herald* than the Fall River Indians games.[14]

When he addressed the loss of the league's four weakest teams, Davidson also announced that:

the owners of the four franchises voted a split season, with the first half ending last night and the second half starting today and running to Labor Day. The pennant winner will be picked on the percentage of games won and lost for the total season. For the playoffs, the league will match the three teams with the best percentage showing for the second half.[15]

Second half of the season—Nashua was in first place on the morning of July 20, with a 53-22 record. But with a number of Nashua players advanced to higher-classification teams by the Brooklyn Dodgers organization, Nashua fell to last place in the second half with an 18-30 record, and missed the playoffs.

The Pawtucket Slaters captured first place in the second half with a 31-17 record, clinching with nine games to play. Pawtucket also had the best record for the full season (83-43), led by the hitting of Bob Montag (.428) and the slugging of George Crowe, a future major leaguer. The Portland Pilots (26-22) made the second half standings (see table) look closer than the race actually was, though, by sweeping the four-game season-ending series from Pawtucket, including a season-ending doubleheader victory on Labor Day.

Pawtucket earned a bye for the first round of the playoffs, but the team elected to reject the free pass and play in the first round. Newspapers completely glossed over why Pawtucket passed up the bye, as if it were obvious why the second place team had the bye and first and third place teams were matched in the playoffs.

"The New England League playoffs will open at McCoy Stadium on Wednesday Sept. 7 with the first place Slaters meeting either Springfield or Portland, depending on which team finishes in third place," the Providence *Journal* reported, without commenting on the incongruity. "The second place finisher draws a bye

in the first round, meeting the winner of the first playoff series."[16]

The Portland *Sunday Telegram* offered a dubious explanation when it reported that "Pawtucket could have sat on the sidelines, but preferred the action and the taking of a chance it won't reach the final."[17]

Pawtucket's motive almost certainly was an additional payday at the gate. However, only 721 hardy fans showed up at McCoy Stadium for the first game that Wednesday night. Worse yet, the Slaters blew an 8-2 lead and lost 11-9 to the Springfield Cubs, a team it had defeated seven of the last eight times the teams met. The Slaters, ironically named for the man who started the textile industry in New England, then seemingly packed it in for Game 2 at Springfield. The Cubs scored seven runs in the first inning and cruised to a 10-6 victory to advance to the Governors' Cup series.

The early finish for Pawtucket may have led to a fortuitous major league moment for Slater shortstop Steve Kuczek, who was recalled to the Boston Braves immediately following the loss to Springfield.

Kuczek wound up pinch hitting for Braves second baseman Connie Ryan in the second game of a doubleheader between the Boston and Brooklyn on September 29. Ryan had been ejected from the game for wearing a rain slicker into the on-deck circle, protesting the dreary playing conditions caused by the steady rain and growing darkness.

"I got a double off Don Newcombe in that fiasco of a game," Kuczek recalled of his lone major league appearance, which earned him a lifetime 1.000 batting average. "In addition to Ryan wearing a raincoat to bat, somebody in the dugout had built a bonfire on the steps of the dugout."[18]

Governors' Cup series—Instead of fighting for a chance to play Pawtucket for the New England League title, Portland and Springfield now found themselves battling for the Governors' Cup.

There was a problem for Springfield, though, since baseball was a means to another end for some minor league players. Second baseman Ed McDade had returned to his studies at Notre Dame, after agreeing to stay for the first round of the playoffs. This opened up a spot for Nasternak, who moved in from the outfield to play shortstop for the Governors' Cup series. Billy Klaus, a future major leaguer but then a twenty-year-old who hit .324 for the Cubs, moved from shortstop to

1949 Standings—First Half			
	W	L	Pct.
Nashua	53	22	.707
Pawtucket	52	26	.667
Portland	40	35	.533
Springfield	36	37	.493
Fall River	27	42	.391
Lynn	28	44	.389
Manchester	29	47	.382
Providence	18	30	.375

1949 Standings—Second Half			
	W	L	Pct.
Pawtucket	31	17	.646
Portland	26	22	.542
Springfield	21	27	.438
Nashua	18	30	.375

third base while Lou Macrinotis moved from third to second base.[19]

Portland demolished Springfield, 20-4, in the first game and after defeating its opponent, 7-2, in Game 4 on the road before 2,635 fans at Pynchon Park, took a commanding 3-1 lead in the series.

Springfield had led the league in attendance with 102,387 paying customers in 1949, with Portland number two at 83,100. The two most successful franchises in the league in attracting fans were the farthest from Boston among the eight teams that began the season. More important, the cities were not dependant on the textile industry. Springfield was renowned for firearms manufacture and Portland for shipping, with one of the East Coast's busiest ports. The Pilots were named for the navigating pilot boats that led larger ships into the harbor.

Then in Game 5, Springfield found itself without another education-minded player, center fielder Pugatch; as manager Peterson substituted himself for his tardy outfielder. "I missed that game because I was registering for classes at Boston University and didn't get back in time," Pugatch remembered about his absence that day. "I promised my dad when I signed for $5,000 to play baseball that I'd finish school. It took me seven years or so to finish school. I started playing pro ball and college in 1946. I finished playing ball and college in 1953."

The Pugatch-less Cubs put in a bid for the winner-take-all payoff by defeating the Pilots, 9-0, and then on Saturday, with Pugatch back in the lineup, took Game 6, 4-3, in eleven innings to force a showdown in Game 7.

Symbolic of the league's troubles, the sixth game of the Governors' Cup series at Portland Stadium was delayed to Saturday in order to play a high school football game there on Friday night. The match between Deering and Portland High drew 6,000 fans. The Pilots-Cubs game attracted just 1,800 that Sunday for the seventh and deciding game for the league championship.[20]

Portland thwarted all Springfield comeback thoughts by erupting for eight runs in the first inning of Game 7 to cruise to a 11-0 victory and gleefully split up the $1,200 winner-take-all pot.

League history—"The withdrawal of Fall River, Manchester, and Lynn sounds the death knell of the New England League unless league directors can perform an administrative miracle," Blaine Davis wrote in his Portland *Press Herald* column "Mainely Sports" on July 20, 1949. "If the circuit folds, and only the most optimistic will hold hopes for its survival beyond this season, history will have repeated itself for the fourth time."[21]

Actually, it was more than four. But Davis was right on point for twentieth-century league demises.

The New England League is perhaps best known today for its role in the integration of baseball. The 1946 Nashua Dodgers team included Roy Campanella and Don Newcombe, who both eventually joined Jackie Robinson with the Brooklyn Dodgers.

"The racial barriers of baseball were not broken in Brooklyn, they were broken here in Nashua in 1946," Daniel Webster College president Hannah McCarthy said in celebration of the fiftieth anniversary of the integration of major league baseball in 1947, at ceremonies when Newcombe received an honorary degree.

Newcombe and Campanella had originally been ticketed for the Three-I League before that circuit's president balked. Branch Rickey then called NEL president Davidson and asked about two black men playing in Nashua. "Can they play baseball?" Davidson was said to ask. When assured that they could, he replied, "Then you send them."[22]

The New England League was a loose confederation of teams in its early years when it began play in 1877. It began serious play in 1885, but there were sporadic league stoppages until 1894, when the league's heyday began, with play continuous through the 1915 season. Hall of Famers such as Joe Kelley, Nap Lajoie, Rabbit Maranville, and Wilbert Robinson all got their start in the New England League.

After a brief post-war attempt at restarting the league in 1919, the New England League resumed play in 1926 before disbanding again in 1930, the result of the Great Depression. With some optimism, the New England was revived in 1933, but it lasted just one season.

In the 1946 revival, many franchises abandoned their independent status to affiliate with major league teams in hopes of economic survival. But it was not enough. to spare the New England League from its eventual fate. The failure of the New England League was a precursor to the general decline of the minor leagues. In 1949, forty-two million fans paid to see 464 teams play in fifty-nine leagues. By 1954, attendance at minor league games was down fifty percent to nineteen million and the number of leagues had dropped to thirty-six.[23]

The demise of the textile industry in the late 1940s was predominantly responsible for the New England League's failure, before the "usual suspects" of minor-league decline—television and increasing leisure options—really came into play. No doubt, the league would have probably failed eventually even with a strong New England economy. But in those few post-war years, the league gave players such as Pugatch, Nasternak, McConvery, and Kuczek a chance to play the game in front of appreciative fans as the era of hometown minor league play began to dissolve.

Notes:

1. Portland *Press Herald*, September 19, 1949, and August 10, 1999.

2. Letter to author from Bob Pugatch dated June 4, 1999, and telephone interview on July 21, 1999. Subsequent attributions in the article to Pugatch are from these sources.

3. Portland *Press Herald*, September 19, 1949.

4. Letter to author from Hank Nasternak dated June 21, 1999. Subsequent attributions in the article to Nasternak are from this source.

5. Neil Sullivan, *The Minors* (New York: St. Martin's Press, 1990), p.14.

6. Letter to author from Frank McConvery dated May 28, 1999. Subsequent attributions in the article to McConvery are from this source.

7. R.C. Estall, *New England: A Study in Industrial Adjustment* (New York: Frederick Praeger Publishers, 1966), p. 34.

8. William Hartford, *Where is Our Responsibility? Unions and Economic Change in the New England Textile Industry* (Amherst MA: University of Massachusetts Press, 1996).

9. Portland *Press Herald*, September 7, 1949.

10. Providence *Journal*, June 22, 1949.

11. Manchester *Union*, July 20, 1949.

12. Manchester *Union*, July 20, 1949.

13. Lynn *Daily Evening Item*, July 20, 1949.

14. Fall River *Herald*, July 16, 1949.

15. Lynn *Daily Evening Item*, July 20, 1949.

16. Providence *Journal*, August 31, 1949.

17. Portland *Sunday Telegram*, September 4, 1949.

18. Letter to author from Steve Kuczek dated April 29, 1997.

19. Springfield *Union*, September 7, 1949.

20. Portland *Press Herald*, September 17, 1949, and September 19, 1949.

21. Portland *Press Herald*, July 20, 1949.

22. Manchester *Union Leader*, April 16, 1997.

23. Robert Obojski, *Bush League: A History of Minor League Baseball* (New York: Macmillan Publishing, 1975), p. 27.

Namesakes of a Hall of Fame catcher

We all know Mickey Mantle was named for his father's favorite player, Mickey Cochrane. Many other parents also named their children after Cochrane, especially those with the same surname as the Hall of Fame catcher or the nearly identical version lacking the "e." Some namesakes grew up to experience a degree of renown, while others are just ordinary citizens and baseball fans. Here are a few of their stories.

Mickey Cochrane of Bowling Green, Ohio. *He coached college soccer at Johns Hopkins and Bowling Green, which earned him a spot in the National Soccer Hall of Fame. "My father and grandmother were avid baseball fans. In the Army in 1957, I tried out for the baseball team at Fort Sam Houston in Texas. They asked me 'What's your name?' and I replied, 'Mickey Cochrane.' The quick response was 'Yeah, and I'm Ty Cobb. Get out of here!' I was continually asked throughout my career, particularly in the 1950s and '60s, if I was the player, due to the athletic connection. The soccer field at Bowling Green is named after me. I always wonder what people will think fifty years from now—what's the connection with the Detroit catcher?"*

Mickey Cochran of Zeeland, Michigan. *He currently coaches baseball and basketball at Zeeland High School. "My father was a great baseball fan. Living in Michigan, we live and die with the Tigers. The questions and looks were almost predictable—'Are you related to him?' I've always had people inquire about my name. It has just become a way of life and probably pushed my desire to play baseball. Funny thing is, I played every position but catcher, mainly a pitcher and infielder at college. I think I would have made a pretty good catcher, but I never tried. If I could do it again … who knows?"*

Rev. Mickey Cochran of Chalmette, Louisiana. *"My Dad was a great ball player and he loved the game. Dad and Mom agreed to name their first son after Dad, so when I came along, Dad had an open field, and he named me after the famous baseball catcher. In school, the kids didn't know who Mickey Cochrane was, but their parents would always ask me, 'Do you know who you're named after?' I would tell them the famous catcher. I played outfield and second base in high school. One day the coach said some scouts were coming to our game to see me. I asked him if it was because of my name or my talent, and he laughed. Anyway, my scouting report was good glove, good speed, good name, weak arm."*

Mickey Cochran of Columbus, Ohio. *"My father, Ray 'Lefty' Cochran, was probably the best left-handed pitcher that never made pro ball in the 1940s and '50s. His love for the game gave him the perfect reason to name me after Mickey. Growing up I had little interest in baseball. The old timers who played the game with my dad would usually make a complimentary comment to me about being named after such a great player. It wasn't until my father reached his golden years and became terminally ill did I realize the quality of his baseball stories. During this time, I began to value and honor his baseball career and naming me after Mickey. I then considered it an honor being named after him. When I purchase Mickey Cochrane items at card shows, and the vendor finds out that I have the same name, there is always a favorable comment. Thanks, Dad!"*

And last, but certainly not least, there is the **Mickey Cochran Prize** *awarded annually to a student at Solanco High School in Quarryville, Pennsylvania. The $100 savings bond honors Clair Cochran. She was for many years the postmaster in Quarryville.*

– Charlie Bevis

Bill Frawley and the Mystery Bat

Rob Edelman

If William Frawley were alive today, you could safely bet your collection of 1950s baseball cards that he would consider a membership in SABR. The actor, who died in 1966 and is best-known for playing Fred Mertz on the classic 1950s television comedy *I Love Lucy*, was a rabid baseball fan, consumed by a deep love of the game.

Frawley's baseball fanaticism became evident to me while I was researching the newly published *Meet the Mertzes*, a double biography of Frawley and Vivian Vance, his *I Love Lucy* co-star.

"He was like a sports encyclopedia," noted Don Grady, who appeared with Frawley on *My Three Sons*, the actor's post-*I Love Lucy* sitcom. "If you had a question about sports, you went and talked to Bill."

In fact, the Frawley section of *Meet the Mertzes* is as much a sports book as a stage-and-screen profile. I conducted interviews with as many ballplayers as show business types, and they provided numerous anecdotes regarding Frawley's passion for sports in general and baseball in particular.

When Frawley first came to Hollywood from Broadway in 1933, he insisted that a clause be inserted in his Paramount Pictures contract permitting him time each fall to attend the World Series. A similar provision was added to his *I Love Lucy* contract, signed in 1951. Only here, the stipulation was that he could frequent the Fall Classic when the American League pennant winner

was the New York Yankees.

Back in 1934 and 1935, the Detroit Tigers copped the American League flag. Tigers hurler Elden Auker recalled that Frawley attended both World Series in the company of tough-guy George Raft. Auker added that the two actors were friends of Tigers player-manager Mickey Cochrane. The old pitcher's memory was not tossing a curve ball. A photograph of Frawley and Raft in the stands at a series game recently was up for bidding on eBay, the online auction house.

Another period photo I uncovered while writing *Meet the Mertzes*, this one a Paramount Pictures publicity still, features Frawley proudly showing off a baseball bat to B-film star Arline Judge. This caption appears on the back of the photo:

> MOST TREASURED BAT—Arline Judge is inspecting Bill Frawley's most treasured sport article which she expects to win from Bill as he is wagering it with her on Giants. This bat was given to Bill last year by "Goose" Goslin after he had won the series with it.

"Last year" was 1935. The Tigers faced the Chicago Cubs in the series. The deciding sixth game was won by Detroit, 4-3, as Goslin's ninth-inning single knocked in Cochrane with the tiebreaking run.

However, in *George Raft*, a 1974 biography, Lewis Yablonsky offered up an anecdote regarding the very same bat. Yablonsky wrote that, after smacking the game-winning hit:

> "Goose," a friend and fan of George's,

Rob Edelman *is co-author (with his wife, Audrey Kupferberg) of* Meet the Mertzes *(Renaissance Books). His other books include* Great Baseball Films *(Citadel Press) and* Baseball on the Web *(MIS: Press).*

came over to his box and respectfully presented him with a prize gift—the bat that won the game. "Here's a present for you, Georgie. Take it home with you."

That bat to George was as valuable as any Oscar. Still clutching it, Mack [Raft's friend, Mack Grey] and George jumped into a cab to head for the train station. They had to rush in order to catch a westbound train to California to fill an important movie commitment. George told the driver, "Step on it. Get us there in time and I'll give you an extra ten-spot." The driver went as fast as he could through the jammed traffic near the stadium. A truck pulled out in front of them, almost forcing the cab off the road, and made them miss a green light. When George's cab caught up with the truck at a stop light, George leaned out the window and let the truckdriver know what he thought of him. The truckdriver, as he pulled away, yelled at George and Mack, "Drop dead, you Jew bastards."

This was all George had to hear. George was mad enough to pull the driver out of the truck and beat him up properly, but he didn't have the time. He instructed the cab driver to pull right alongside the truck at the next stop light. The cab driver did as he was told. Just as the light was turning green, George leaned out the window, took careful aim, and threw the bat like a spear at the truckdriver's head. George never found out how hard he hit the man, because the cab driver took off on cue, peeling rubber, for the station. They made their train.

In this 1936 Paramount publicity still, Frawley shows Arline Judge his Goose Goslin bat.

On the way to California, George was filled with remorse, not only because he lost a treasured memento, but also because, once again, he had lost control of his temper.

This anecdote, and the manner in which it contradicts the evidence regarding Frawley and Goslin's bat, illustrates a problem faced by every researcher, biographer, and historian: how does one verify facts?

In this case, it appears that the Yablonsky anecdote is a fiction, and not only because of its fanciful nature. For openers, Frawley's presence with Raft, first mentioned by Auker and then verified by the eBay photo, is not cited by Yablonsky. Then there is the content of the Frawley–Judge photo, with its accompanying caption written at the time the still was released to the media.

What is indisputable, however, is the manner in which Frawley and Raft connected their careers to baseball. One of the stills reproduced in *George Raft* is a Paramount publicity shot of the actor dressed in a New York Giants uniform. Frawley, meanwhile, was a natural for supporting roles in baseball films. He got to wear a Chicago Cubs warm-up jacket on-screen in *Alibi Ike* (1935), playing "Cap," the Cubbies manager, and Yankee pinstripes in *Safe at Home!* (1962), cast as Bronx Bombers coach "Bill Turner." In *The Babe Ruth Story* (1948), he was Jack Dunn, manager of the minor-league Baltimore Orioles. In *It Happened in Flatbush* (1942), *Kill the Umpire* (1950), and *Rhubarb* (1951), he played the Brooklyn Dodgers' business manager, the head of an umpire school, and manager of the fictitious big league Brooklyn Loons.

Off the set, Frawley really lived and breathed the game. In addition to Mickey Cochrane, he was close buddies with countless ballplayers. One was Francis Joseph "Lefty" O'Doul. Even though he passed away in 1969, the San Francisco restaurant that bears O'Doul's name still is in existence. While attending the SABR national convention in San Francisco in 1998, I made a visit to the eatery. Hanging over the bar, directly to the left of the entrance and amid the dozens of baseball photos that give the saloon its flavor, is a large head-shot of Frawley, circa *I Love Lucy*. It is inscribed, "Best on earth to my pal Frank from his pal Bill Frawley."

Another Frawley friend was Joe DiMaggio. The actor might have scripted the scene in "Lucy Is Enceinte," the classic *I Love Lucy* episode in which Lucy Ricardo tells husband Ricky that she is pregnant. In the sequence, Fred enters with a ball, bat, glove, and New York Yankees cap. He hands the latter three to Lucy, "for my godson." Regarding the baseball, he adds, "And wait'll you see the name on this. That's the name of the best ballplayer the Yankees ever had."

"Uh, Spalding," Lucy blurts out, after glancing at it. "C'mon honey, turn it around," Fred instructs. "Oh, DiMaggio," Lucy declares. "You betcha," Fred responds, taking a mock batting stance. "Ol' Joltin' Joe himself."

On October 3, 1954, the actor appeared on Ed Sullivan's *Toast of the Town* television show. At the end of a brief chat, Sullivan told Frawley, "Dusty Rhodes is waiting off in the wings, [so you can] continue going on with that World Series discussion." Rhodes's pinch-hitting exploits had just helped the New York Giants beat the Cleveland Indians in the Fall Classic. Later on in the show, after being introduced on camera, Rhodes quipped, regarding *I Love Lucy*, "That's one show I don't think I'd like to pinch hit for."

Chuck Stevens, former major league first baseman and another Frawley pal, reported that the actor attended "probably ten or fifteen or twenty" annual dinners sponsored by his organization, the Association of Professional Baseball Players, which offers assistance to ailing and financially troubled ballplayers. "He would sit at the head table, and he would entertain," Stevens said. "Five-hundred baseball people would be there."

At these affairs, Frawley would be seated beside Joe DiMaggio and Lefty O'Doul or some other big-name ballplayers, and would amuse those on hand with picturesque, baseball-related anecdotes.

One easily can imagine Frawley doing the same at a SABR convention—and offering up his own brand of truth on the plight of the Goslin bat.

Chuck Stevens

Frawley is pictured at far right at a 1952 dinner sponsored by the Association of Professional Baseball Players. Directly to his right are his pals Lefty O'Doul, Joe DiMaggio, Babe Herman, Beans Reardon, and Hollis "Sloppy" Thurston.

Nelly Kelly's Waltz

Edward R. Ward

Is there any American who has not sung or hummed "Take Me Out to the Ball Game"? The song is known well and sung constantly. This piece mentions two notes (pun intended) about the song given to us by Jack Norworth, who crafted the words, and Albert von Tilzer, who composed the music.

First, most people may not know the words that precede the singing of the phrase, "Take Me Out to the Ball Game." The words are:

Nelly Kelly loved baseball games,
Knew the players, knew all their names.
You could see her there ev'ry day,
Shout "Hur-ray" when they'd play.
Her boyfriend by the name of Joe
Said to Coney Isle, dear, let's go.
Then Nelly started to fret and pout
And to him I heard her shout:
Take me out to the ball game.

A second verse is also unknown to millions:

Nelly Kelly was sure some fan.
She would root just like any man.
Told the umpire he was wrong,
All along, good and strong.
When the score was just two to two
Nelly Kelly knew what to do.
Just to cheer up the boys she knew,

She made the gang sing this song:
Take me out to the ball game.

An alternate lyric is:

Katie Casey was baseball mad,
Had the fever and had it bad;
Just to root for the hometown crew,
Ev'ry sou, Katie blew.
On a Saturday, her young beau,
Called to see if she'd like to go,
To see a show but Miss Kate said, "No,"
I'll tell you what you can do:
Take me out to the ball game.

Second, "Take Me," is a "spirited waltz," believe it or not, written in 3/4 time. The song is manageable for both the beginner and the experienced singer. "Take Me" is not a "fight song." It is not the "take charge" music played when a hockey team hits the ice. Football may be a martial march, and basketball may be jazz, but baseball is more gently rhythmic. The waltz is a perfect invitation to some conversation and seventh-inning stretching at a ball game.

Some may note that "Take Me" is sometimes not sung at certain ballparks along the banks of the Mississippi during the seventh-inning stretch. "Meet Me in St. Louis, Louis" has been heard instead. For what it's worth, "Meet Me" is to be sung "moderately," also in 3/4 time. Its words were written by Andrew B. Sterling, the music by Kenny Mills.

Let's take it from the top: "Nelly Kelly loved baseball games, knew the players, knew all their names...."

Edward R. Ward *is a Catholic priest (Carmelite Order) living in Bogota, New Jersey. He was raised in Illinois on the Chicago White Sox.*

Utica Indoor Baseball 1897-1902

Scott Fiesthumel

An 1898 newspaper photo of "the Old Utica Indoor Base-Ball Team"

By the late nineteenth century, baseball was the most popular sport in America. It was so popular that some players looked for a way to play year-round. This led to the "invention" of an indoor baseball game that could be played in the winter. The game invented in Chicago by George Hancock in 1887 is the forefather of modern softball. Ordinary baseball uniforms were worn, with the exception of the shoes, which were rubber soled rather than spiked. The game could be played on any hard floor surface, as long as it was at least forty by sixty feet. Each side of the diamond was twenty-seven feet. From home to second base was thirty-eight and a half feet. The balls were seventeen to eighteen inches in circumference (present day softballs are twelve inches) and weighed about eight ounces. Bats were no longer than two and a half feet long and an inch and three-eighths in diameter. The bases were white canvas, a foot and a half square and usually filled with sand.

It took about ten years for indoor baseball to join other winter sports (curling, bowling, hockey, and eventually basketball) in the Mohawk Valley. In March, 1897, the hardwood floor of Utica's National Guard

Armory was the site of several baseball games. One of the first organized contests took place between the Utica YMCA and the National Guard's 44th Separate Company (also known as the Utica Citizens Corps).

The Utica *Daily Press* described it as a "lively game," played with a ball "larger and several degrees softer" than an official baseball. The diamond "is more like a sheet of plate glass than a field of greensward. The bases have the unpardonable tendency to slide themselves when the runner throws himself upon them with some force." Spectators crowded the balcony and "set up a howl of satisfaction at the result," a 15-14 win for the YMCA.

Scott Fiesthumel *is researching and writing about all types of baseball in Utica, and plays indoor baseball's descendant, beer league softball.*

The YMCA would play a three game series against both the 44th and 28th Separate Companies. Each of the games began at 8 PM and admission was ten cents. Attendance was 200-300 per game. The Y took the three games from the 44th by scores of 15-11, 9-5, and 18-14. It also swept the 28th, 4-3, 19-4, and 26-18 to go undefeated and win the unofficial city championship.

The success of the relatively few games played in the spring of 1897 led to the formation of a league for the winter of 1897-98. In November, the executive committee of the Oneida County Indoor Base Ball League met. The committee decided each team would appoint an umpire and official scorer, adopted "Spalding's rules" for league games, and set admission at fifteen cents. To accommodate teams from Herkimer County, the league would soon become the Mohawk Valley Indoor Baseball League.

The four league teams would be the YMCA, the 28th Separate Co., the Arcanums (the Arcanum Club was a "social and sporting" club in Utica), and the 31st Separate Co. of Mohawk. These teams would play about one league game a week. There were also independent teams like the Chesterfields, the Genesees, and the 44th Separate Co.

The league's first games were played on December 8, a doubleheader at the Utica Armory. The YMCA beat the 28th, 8-6, and the Arcanums beat the 31st, 22-17, before a paid crowd of 231. On January 19, 1898 the Utica *Daily Press* reported, "Lewis of the Arcanums sent the ball into the gallery for the first time this year in a match game." A week later, the Arcanum team fielded a team that included the finest centerfielder in the National League, Mike Griffin, a native Utican who lived there during the off-season, who had hit .318 and scored 136 runs in 134 games for Brooklyn in 1897.

In February 1898, the 28th beat the Genesees, who had future major leaguer Willie Duggleby pitching for them. The 28th then lost to the Chesterfields at Sink's Opera House in Rome. By the end of the month, the YMCA was once again the league leader and would remain so. On March 3, the Utica Elks traveled west to play the Syracuse Elks. Griffin played for Utica and received a loud ovation from the crowd of 1,000 when he stepped to the plate. Syracuse won, 14-12.

During the next two seasons, there was no organized league, though over the winter of 1898-99 teams from Utica, Little Falls, and Mohawk did compete regularly. Crowds numbered up to 500, and dances were often held after the games. In 1899-1900, the 28th, Uticas, Clippers, and International Heater Company competed. On March 29, 1900, The Uticas beat the 28th, 21-3. The Utica *Daily Press* called it the first time that local teams had met on a forty-five-foot diamond instead of the thirty-foot one they had been playing on. They also used a fourteen-inch ball rather than the normal eighteen-inch one. In April the Utica Elks

hosted their brother Elks in Syracuse before 400 fans. Utica won, 7-1, but the game was marred by the broken ankle suffered by Syracuse player Earl Persse.

League play resumed for the winter of 1900-01 in the form of the Utica City League. The Uticas, Clippers, and the 28th were joined by the Thistles, among whose players were future major leaguers Lee Fairbanks and Jimmy Dygert (who would go 20-9 for the Philadelphia A's in 1907). Complete boxscores appeared in the Utica *Daily Press* for the first time, giving a good picture of the indoor game.

Games were fast-paced, often high scoring affairs. The short basepaths lead to many (sometimes *very* many) stolen bases. A New Years Eve doubleheader on December 31, 1900 saw the 28th beat the Thistles, 18-4, in 1 hour, 5 minutes, and the Uticas beat the Clippers, 4-3, in an hour. There were 28 stolen bases in the first game, six in the second. On January 23, 1901, the four teams combined for 39 stolen bases in two games. A month later, the 28th beat the Clippers, 21-16, in a 1 hour, 45 minute game that had 33 steals. The second game that night saw the Uticas defeat the Thistles, 7-4, in a game that took only 47 minutes.

The final game of the season at the beginning of April brought the Syracues Elks to Utica. The Elks , had become one of the best indoor baseball teams in the state, and drew 800-2,000 fans to their games in Syracuse. About fifty Syracuse players and fans entrained for Utica on board "The Empire" for the game in Utica. The Elks beat an "all-star" team of Uticans, 8-3, before about 300 fans.

There was nor formal league in the Utica area the following winter (1901-1902), but a few of the teams (including the 28th and the Uticas) competed against each other. In January of 1902, one of the best teams in the state, St. Peters Lyceum of Troy traveled to the Utica armory to play the 28th Separate Co. team. Troy pitcher Kavanaugh walked twelve of the home team, and the 28th won, 13-5, before 500 fans. Two weeks later, the 28th traveled to Troy for a New Year's Eve rematch. The 28th lost the game, possibly because a seventeen-inch ball was used rather than the twelve-inch ball the team had become used to.

The game also led to what the Utica *Sunday Tribune* called, "a Base Ball War… Among Indoor Devotees". It seems the Troy team had advertised the game as being against the "All-Uticas" and the team known as the Uticas didn't appreciate it. The players on the 28th explained that they had no control over what Troy wanted to call the team and said the Uticas wouldn't have complained if the 28th had won the game. The 28th prevailed after a challenge was issued to play a series of games to decide the champion of Oneida County.

The indoor game continued to be played in the Mohawk Valley, although not with the same level of interest as there was after its introduction to the area.

Willard Hershberger and the Legacy of Suicide

Brian J. Wigley, Dr. Frank B. Ashley, and Dr. Arnold LeUnes

Mention the Cincinnati Reds to today's baseball fans and most will immediately recall the Big Red Machine and the championship seasons of the 1970s. A few historically minded fans might conjure up visions of the 1919 Reds and their tainted World Championship. Few will remember the championship team of 1940. Manager Bill "Deacon" McKechnie's squad, which included Ernie Lombardi, Bucky Walters, and Paul Derringer was a great team during an erra of great baseball. However, below the surface of victories and celebrations looms one of the most bizarre and tragic stories in the history of America's pastime.

Willard Hershberger, the Reds second-string catcher remains the only player to take his own life during the baseball season. On August 3, 1940, in Boston's Copley Hotel, "Hershy" meticulously laid towels on the bathroom floor, knelt before the bathtub and with a safety razor belonging to his Reds roommate, opened his throat, ending a life of depression and melancholy.

Early career—Born on May 28, 1910, in Lemoncove, California, Willard Hershberger's greatest passion was sports. At Fullerton Union High School, Forty miles southeast of Los Angeles, where his family had moved when his father got a job in the oil fields of Shell Oil, Willard was the only junior to qualify for the Lettermans' Club, an exclusive group of athletes with at least five varsity letters. The 1928 Fullerton High

School yearbook labeled Hershberger "the boy with the golden toe" referring to his football achievements, and "the greatest little catcher to ever put on the Fullerton uniform."

Hershberger's professional baseball career began in the minor leagues, where he played for four teams in as many years. Sent by the Yankees to Erie of the Central League in 1932, Hershberger hit .339 and was considered the league's premier catcher, easily making the All Star team. Batting .304 in 1933 for NYP League champion Binghamton,Willard was voted "most popular player" by the fans. Three seasons later with the great Newark Bears, Hershberger was named the "International League Catcher of the Year."

A Cincinnati *Post* story dated August 8, 1939, describes Hershberger as the only man to play baseball on the Atlantic Coast on one day and the Pacific Coast the next. Traded from the Bears to Oakland of the Pacific Coast League, "Little Hershey" (5 feet, 10-1/2 inches, 167 pounds) played a game for Newark, caught a night plane, then suited up and played for the Oakland squad the following afternoon. Sold to the Reds during the winter of 1937 for $25,000 and minor league players, Hershberger first appeared in the majors on April 19, 1938.

During his short time in the big leagues, Hershberger established himself as a solid catcher and consistent threat with the bat. Appearing in 63 games during the 1939 season, "Bill," as he was called in the majors, hit .345, and earned a reputation as a deft contact hitter, dangerous with runners in scoring position. Hershberger would likely have been the number-one receiver for almost any other team in the league. In a

Brian J. Wigley *is a doctoral student in Sport Managment at Texas A&M University.* **Frank B. Ashley** *is Associate Dean of Undergraduate Education and chair of the Sport Management division at Texas A&M, and* **Arnold LeUnes** *is a professor in the Department of Psychology at Texas A&M.*

statistical comparison of all catchers with at least 100 at-bats in 1939, Hershberger ranks second in batting average for both the National and American Leagues (Table 1). Hershberger's average of .13 runs scored per at-bat ranks him third in the National League, ahead of Lombardi, and thirteenth in the majors.

Table 1 1939 : Catcher statistics

American League

Team	Player	G	AB	R	H	HR	RBI	BB	SO	AVE
NY	Bill Dickey	128	480	98	145	24	105	77	37	0.302
NY	Buddy Rosar	35	105	18	29	0	12	13	10	0.276
BOS	Johnny Peacock	92	274	33	76	0	36	29	11	0.277
BOS	Gene Desautels	76	226	26	55	0	21	33	13	0.243
CLE	Rollie Hemsley	107	395	58	104	2	36	26	26	0.263
CLE	Frankie Pytlak	63	183	20	49	0	14	20	5	0.268
CHI	Mike Tresh	119	352	49	91	0	38	64	30	0.259
CHI	Norm Schlueter	34	56	5	13	0	8	1	11	0.232
DET	Birdie Tebbetts	106	341	37	89	4	53	25	20	0.261
DET	Rudy York	102	329	66	101	20	68	412	50	0.307
WASH	Rick Ferrell	87	274	32	77	0	31	41	12	0.281
WASH	Tony Giuliani	54	172	20	43	0	18	4		70.250.
PHIL	Frankie Hayes	124	431	66	122	20	83	40	55	0.283
PHIL	Earle Brucker	62	172	18	50	3	31	24	16	0.291
STL	Joe Glenn	88	286	29	78	4	29	31	40	0.273
STL	Sam Harshaney	42	145	15	35	0	15	9	8	0.241

National League

Team	Player	G	AB	R	H	HR	RBI	BB	SO	AVE
CIN	Ernie Lombardi	130	450	43	129	20	85	35	19	0.287
CIN	W. Hershberger	63	174	23	60	0	32	9	4	0.345
STL	Mickey Owen	131	344	32	89	3	35	43	28	0.259
STL	Don Padgett	92	233	38	93	5	53	18	11	0.399
BKL	Babe Phelps	98	323	3	92	6	42	24	24	0.285
BKL	Al Todd	86	245	28	68	5	32	13	16	0.278
CHI	Gabby Hartnett	97	306	36	85	12	59	37	32	0.278
CHI	Gus Mancuso	80	251	17	58	2	17	24	19	0.231
NY	Harry Danning	135	520	79	163	16	74	35	42	0.313
NY	Ken O'Dea	52	97	7	17	3	11	10	16	0.175
PIT	Ray Berres	81	231	22	53	0	16	11	25	0.229
PIT	Ray Mueller	86	180	14	42	2	18	14	22	0.233
BOS	Al Lopez	131	412	32	104	8	49	40	45	0.252
BOS	Phil Masi	46	114	14	29	1	14	9	15	0.254
PHIL	Spud Davis	87	202	10	16	0	23	24	20	0.307
PHIL	Wally Millies	84	205	12	48	0	12	9	5	0.234

Statistics averaged per at-bat, minimum 100 AB's (Neft, 200-203)

Gabe Paul, the Reds' publicist and traveling secretary, and later the general manager of various teams, sums up Hershberger's offensive skills as follows, "As good a hitter as I ever saw at getting a man in from third with less than two outs, Hershberger would find a way to get a man home. A hell of a ballplayer". Hershberger struck out only four times in 174 at-bats, an average of once every 43.5 times per plate appearance, the lowest strikeout-per-at-bat ratio of all major league catchers in 1939.

Reds management had enough faith in Hershberger's abilities to look at the possibility of trading Lombardi. During the winter meetings at the Congress Hotel in Chicago between the '37 and '38 season, Paul called various newspapermen together and said, "We've just traded Ernie Lombardi to the Cubs, or at least Bill Mckechnie thinks he has. He is waiting now for confirmation." P.K. Wrigley, president of the Cubs, never okayed the deal, which had been swung by manager Charlie Grimm and scout Clarence Rowland. The Cincinnati organization's willingness to consider such a roster move is significant for two reasons. First, it demonstrates its confidence in Hershberger, and second, had this trade had been carried out, Hershberger would have been exposed immediately to the pressures of playing every day—suggested by some as the primary reason for his suicide.

Hershberger's quiet personality and sensitive nature led many to believe that he was susceptible to the pressures of the game. He was content to back Lombardi and remain out of the spotlight. Hershberger seemed to be troubled for much of his professional career. Lew Riggs, the Reds' backup third baseman and Hershberger's roommate, recalled peculiarities in Hershberg's behavior… "I'd find him seated in a chair by the window staring out into the darkness." Hershberger was also perceived to be a hypochondriac. It was widely known that he never traveled without a large briefcase filled with bottles of pills. He visited team trainer Doc Rohde more than any other player, often suspecting he was suffering from various ailments. His mother Maude said later that she noticed a change in Willard's personality when he returned home during the off-season after his first year in the major leagues. "I'd find him up late at night, sitting in the dark by the window smoking cigarettes."

Hershberger also exhibited signs of paranoia. Teammates recalled that Hershy was, "riddled by hallucinations that the world was against him, and that several of the players were his secret enemies." During the New York series just before his death, Hershberger turned to Morrie Arnovich seated next to him on the bench and blurted out, "There's a lot of fellows on this club who are down on me." Arnovich attempted to convince him otherwise, but he "lapsed into silence."

Despite his withdrawn and idiosyncratic behavior, he was a popular players with Cincinnati fans, ranking second only to Lombardi in a 1940 poll of female fans.

The picture of Hershberger painted by his major league peers varies greatly from information provided by high school friends. Hershberger attended Union High School in Fullerton, California, long considered the athletic mecca of southern California. The list of outstanding athletes to hone their skills at Fullerton includes two members of the Baseball Hall of Fame, Arky

Willard "Bill" Hershberger

Vaughan—Hershberger's best friend—and Walter "Big Train" Johnson, winner of 416 games in 21 years in the major leagues. Voted junior-class president, Hershberger was a very popular student and leader at Fullerton. His disposition was perceived as very healthy and optimistic. Blanche McKee Maloy, Hershberger's cousin, described young Willard as "a very lovable human being, very happy and well-adjusted until...that terrible thing happened to his father."

Father's suicide—The life of Willard Hershberger changed forever at 2:30 AM on November 21, 1928. Willard was as passionate about hunting as he was about sports, and on this afternoon he inadvertently left his shotgun leaning against the downstairs stair case. It was with this gun that his father took his life. The Fullerton *Daily News* described the tragic event as follows:

Claude E, Hershberger, 54, of 222 N. Yale Ave., father of Willard Hershberger, prominant high school athlete, committed suicide in his home ...today by shooting himself with a shotgun.

The decedent had been despondent for several weeks it was believed, brooding over financial worries brought on by changes in personnel of the oil company for which he was employed and which were said to have left him in an inferior position to that which he had formerly held.

Retiring to the bathroom of his home, Hershberger is said by police to have pointed a shotgun at his breast while seated on the edge of the bath tub. The trigger was pushed by means of a cane. Death was believed to be instantaneous.

Willard was upstairs in his bedroom at the time and was the first to reach his father. His sister Lois soon followed. The two siblings embraced, but never discussed the event. Willard blamed himself for not returning the shotgun to the gun case and never adjusted to his fathers death. Florence Dysinger, a physical education teacher at the high school, said that Lois came to talk to her the next day and expressed concern for Willard. She claimed that Willard was, "terribly shocked, something snapped. It didn't go away. It ate into him. It changed his life." She also stated that, "Willard never took a bath in a tub again, only showers."

Indicators of a worsening of his condition began to appear in the early summer of 1940. Hershberger threatened on numerous occasions to leave of baseball altogether. Manager Bill McKechnie reported that on two occasions Willard mentioned to fellow players that he was planning to kill himself. Hershberger bought a savings bond, placed it in a safe at the Kemper Hotel and told his roommate to see to it that his mother got the money "if anything should happen to me."

Ernie Lombardi injured his ankle on July 23 during a game at Brooklyn. This thrust Hershberger into the starting role and may have marked the beginning of the end for him. Catching the second game of the doubleheader that day, Willard had four hits, including a double, and two RBIs. After this game, however, his production dropped. Entering the road trip batting an impressive .353, Hershberger's average had dipped to .309 by the time the team played in Boston.

During the road trip, on July 31, Hershberger blamed himself for the Reds' final-inning loss to the New York Giants. This may have been the straw that broke the camel's back. The New York *Times* offered this description:

Four times in a row Bucky Walters was one strike away from winning. Four times he failed. He had a 3-2 count on Bob Seeds and lost him by issuing a pass. He reached the same tally on Burgess Whitehead and Whitey slashed a home run just inside the right field foul line. He did it again before Mel Ott walked. Then up stepped Harry the Horse Danning. Bucky was taking no chances. He whisked in two strikes, took aim and fired again. The Horse swung from his heels and the ball sailed through the mild night air into the upper left field balcony.

After the game Willard became despondent, claiming that the loss was his fault because he had called for the wrong pitch on the 3-2 count to Danning.

Two days later, on August 2, in a game versus Boston, Hershberger went 0 for 5 at the plate as the Reds lost their third straight. Hershberger continued to blame himself for the losses. During the game he failed to field a bunt that rolled slowly in front of home plate. McKechnie asked him if something was wrong. Hershberger replied, "You bet there's something wrong. I'll tell you about it after the game." After the contest, MeKechnie and Hershberger had a long conversation at the team's hotel, during which Hershberger broke down and openly wept, saying that his father had killed himself when he was young and he would do the same thing. He admitted that, "I was gonna kill myself this morning when we got off the train. I went to the drugstore and bought a big bottle of iodine. I was gonna drink that, but then I thought there was a better way to do it." The two men went to dinner and carried on their conversation until almost midnight. McKechnie later stated that Hershberger discussed the nature of his problems that evening under the condition of confidentiality. True to his word, McKechnie would say only that the nature of the problem was personal, and not related to baseball. At the end of the evening, Hershberger convinced his manager that his spirits were lifted and that he would be at the ballpark ready to play the next day.

Hershberger ate breakfast the following morning with Lou Smith, a writer for the Cincinnati *Enquirer*. Smith later reported that Hershberger appeared to be in good spirits. Later in the afternoon, when Willard failed to show up for batting practice, McKechnie asked Gabe Paul to call Hershberger's room at the Copley. Hershberger took the call and said that he was not feeling well. Paul told him that McKechnie was worried about him and that he could come to the ball park and watch the game from the stands in street clothes. Hershberger agreed and said that he would be right out.

When he had not arrived at the ballpark after the first game of the doubleheader, McKechnie dispatched Dan Cohen, a Cincinnati shoe store owner who often traveled with the team, to the Copley to look for him. Finding the hotel room locked, and getting no response from repeated knocks, Cohen finally convinced a hotel employee to open the door. Hershberger's body was discovered lying over the edge of the bathtub.

Aftermath and questions—Upon learning of Hershberger's death during the second game, McKechnie left the bench and instructed coach Hank

Gowdy not to tell the players the tragic news. After the final out, McKechnie joined his team in the clubhouse. "All right, now be quiet," the manager said. "Willard Hershberger has just destroyed himself."[17]

Gathering the team together that evening in the hotel, McKechnie told the players some of the details of his conversation with Willard the previous night. He related Hershberger's tale of his father's suicide and his plans to do the same. The emotionally drained manager said that he sincerely believed that he had convinced the young catcher not to take his life. He told the team only that Hershberger's problems were personal and not related to baseball. Honor-bound to the dead catcher, McKechnie swore he would never reveal the details of the conversation.

The team vowed to win the World Series in honor of their fallen teammate and to vote his mother a full share of the championship bonus. Lombardi's injury and the absence of Hershberger forced forty-year-old coach Jimmy Wilson to catch six of the seven World Series games. Wilson became an unlikely hero of the team's race to the world championship. Playing though tremendous pain caused by old legs and hands turned soft by years of retirement, Wilson hit .353 with six singles in 17 trips to the plate. The Reds defeated Detroit to become world champions. True to their word, the team presented Maude Hershberger with a World Series Champion's bonus pay: $5,803.62.

Tragically, Hershberger's death is not the end of the bizarre tale. Dan Cohen followed in his friend's footsteps and committed suicide in 1961. Just four years after leaving baseball, Ernie Lombardi himself fell into a deep depression. Visiting a relative while in transit to a treatment center in 1953, Lombardi excused himself, went to the restroom and cut his throat with a straight razor. Surviving this incident, Lombardi died in 1977 and was elected into baseball's Hall of Fame in 1986.

Numerous theories have been proposed as to the reasons for Hershberger's suicide. Some historians have pointed to the fact that his death occurred just days after he assumed the role of everyday catcher. Perhaps the pressures of the game weighed too heavily on him. Others believe that the memory of finding his father just moments after his suicide haunted him.

Further examination of the Hershberger family reveals that not only did Claude Hershberger precede his son in suicide, but two male cousins of the elder Hershberger also ended their own lives. This troubling family history leads others to believe that Hershberger viewed suicide as an acceptable end to life's troubles.

Perhaps Bill McKechnie, after his long conversation with Hershberger the night before the tragedy, had the best idea of Willard's motivation. But he kept his promise and took his knowledge with him to his grave on October 29, 1965.

Look For Hershberger To Shine, read the Fullerton *News Telegram* headline of March 2, 1940, reflecting the belief held by those who had followed the catcher's career. His future appeared very bright, indeed. Perhaps Hershberger himself attempted to forewarn the world of the darkness to come. Glancing at page 28 of the 1929 Pleiades yearbook, one sees a group of optimistic young high school seniors looking forward to the future. All looking forward, straight into the camera, as if to proclaim to the world that they were ready to take on the any challenges. One student however looks away, Willard M. Hershberger, stares off intensely, away from the camera, away from the expectations. Hershberger, just a few months after hearing the shotgun blast and discovering the body of his father, seems to understand what the others do not. He has seen and understands his legacy.

Sources:

Allen, L. 1948. The Cincinnati Reds, G. P. Putnam's Sons, New York, pp. 278-280.

Barbour, J. 1987. The death of Willard Hershberger. *The National Pastime*, 06(1) Winter 87, 62-66.

Barbour, J. 1988. On the death of Willard Hershberger. *The Journal of Sport Literature*,. Spring 88, 55-64.

"Catcher Hershberger recalled by Yankees." *Fullerton NewsTelegram*, September 6, 1935 p.6.

Grayson, F. "Hershberger's Mental Condition of Long Duration, Friends Declare." Cincinnati *Times Star.* August 8, 1940. A1, A4.

"Hershberger One of Finest Young Catchers, Story Says." Fullerton *News Telegram*, February 13, 1934. p.8.

"Hershberger Banquet Set." Fullerton *News Telegram* . October 17, 1939, p. 2.

"Hershberger Rites Will Be Held At Three Rivers." Fullerton *News Telegram*, August 5, 1940, p. 1.

"Look For Hershberger To Shine." Fullerton *News Telegram.* March 2, 1940, p.A1.

Nack, W. 1991. The Razor's Edge. *Sports Illustrated*, 74(17) May 6, 1991. 52-56,58,60,62.

Neft, D. & R. Cohen. 1985. *The Sports Encyclopedia:Baseball*—6th Edition, St. Martins Press, New York, 1985. p. 200-203.

Light, J. F. 1997. *The Cultural Encyclopedia of Baseball*. McFarland & Company Publishers Inc. 708.

Pleiades, The. 1928. Union High School, Fullerton California, pp.118, 127.

Pleiades, The. 1928. Union High School, Fullerton California, pp. 49,65,115.

Quinn, J. "On the Pennant Path." Cincinnati *Post*, August 1, 1939. B4.

"Redleg Catch Ends Life."Cincinnati *Enquirer*, August 4, 1940. pp. A1,A8.

Simpson, D. 1984. "No player, only pilot of '39-40 Reds to shrine." *Baseball Research Journal*, 64-66.

"'Slug's' Suicide Left Reds Numb." Cincinnati *Enquirer,* September 2, 1988. p. A2.

Smith, Lou. "Throat is cut by player." Cincinnati *Enquirer.* August 3, 1940. p. A1.

"Stars Obtain Hershberger." Fullerton *News Telegram,*, Janurary 6, 1934, p.6

"Tears Are Shed as Redlegs Pay Tribute." Cincinnati *Times Star,* August 8, 1940. pp.A1, A8.

"Dutch" and the Game

James C. Roberts

Last summer I noticed a short obituary reporting that Billy Jurges had died at age ninety. Jurges' passing attracted little notice, even in the sports press. He had been a good, but not great, player for the New York Giants and Chicago Cubs during the thirties and forties, and had managed the Boston Red Sox during parts of 1959 and 1960. For me, though, Jurges was a household name because I had heard Ronald Reagan mention it often. From 1932 to 1937 "Dutch" Reagan had been a sportscaster for radio station WHO in Des Moines, Iowa, broadcasting Cubs games in the era of re-creation.

As Reagan explained it in his autobiography, *An American Life*:

> I was doing the games by telegraphic report. Well, just picture that the fellow sat on the other side of a window with a little slit underneath, the headphones on, getting the Morse Code from the ball park, and he typed out the play. And the paper would come through to me saying something like, "S1C." that means strike one on the corner. But you're not going to sell Wheaties yelling "S1C!" So I would say, "So-and-so comes out of the windup, here comes the pitch…and it's a called strike breaking over the outside corner to a batter that likes the ball a little higher.

James C. Roberts *is president of Radio America, a national news/talk network. He is completing a book of baseball essays whic is scheduled for publication in the spring of next year.*

An event during this period provided Reagan with the grist for a story that he has told more often than any other. (In July, 1985, at a White House reception for supporters of my Radio America Network, he thanked me for giving him the opportunity to get back into radio and used that as a pretext for telling the Jurges story yet again.)

As Reagan described it (again in his autobiography):

> One day I saw Curley—the teletype operator—start to type, so I started another ball toward the plate. Then I saw him shaking his head, and I thought it was a miraculous play. But when the slip came through it said, "The wire's gone dead." Well, with those other five or six fellows out there doing the same game, I knew that if I said, "We will pause for a brief interlude of transcribed music until they get the wire fixed," everybody'd switch to other stations.
>
> Then I remembered the one thing that doesn't get in the scorebook—foul balls—and knew I was on my own. I looked at Curly on the other side of the window, and he was helpless. It was the Cardinals and Cubs, and Dizzy Dean was pitching. I made Dean use the resin bag and shake off a couple signs to take up time, Then he threw another one, and another. Bill Jurges was at bat, and when he hit a foul, I described kids in a fight over it. Then he fouled one to the left that just missed being a home run.
>
> About six minutes and forty-five seconds

later, I'd set a world record for someone standing at the plate—except that no one keeps such records. I was beginning to sweat, when Curly sat up straight and started typing. When he handed me the slip, I started to giggle, and I could hardly get it out. It said, "Jurges popped out on the first ball pitched."

(When I mentioned this story to Reagan during a meeting in 1992 he chuckled and noted proudly that the incident had made it into Ripley's "Believe It or Not.")

For Reagan the teletype story was just one of many baseball-related jokes and anecdotes that he told throughout his career on the "rubber chicken circuit." It also reflects a lifelong enthusiasm and affection for the national pastime.

What I am today—"How could I not love baseball?" Reagan said on many occasions, "It made me what I am today." This will no doubt surprise many who associate Reagan with football. And it is true that Reagan played football rather than baseball in high school and college, and his best known movie role was that of Notre Dame football player George Gipp in *Knute Rockne: All American*, a role that gave him the well-known nickname "the Gipper."

His choice of football was dictated in part by his nearsightedness. As Reagan recalled, "I never cared for baseball because I was ball-shy at batting. When I stood at the plate, the ball appeared out of nowhere about two feet in front of me. I was always the last chosen for a side in any game. Then I discovered football: no little invisible ball—just another guy to grab or knock down."

But indeed, as Reagan said, it was baseball that was to make him famous. In 1932, young "Dutch" Reagan, fresh out of Eureka College, Illinois, decided that the burgeoning medium of radio offered him the best opportunity for Depression-era success. He was a quick study and had a certain stage presence thanks to his acting experience in college plays, but he had no radio experience.

After being repeatedly rebuffed by the Chicago stations he visited, he took the advice of a program director who suggested that he try a station in a smaller market. In Davenport, Iowa, program manager Peter MacArthur told him that he couldn't hire Reagan because the young man had no experience. Dutch angrily asked how he could gain experience if no one would hire him.

As he headed for the door, Reagan, to his surprise, heard MacArthur ask him to come back.

"Could you announce a football game?" MacArthur asked.

Reagan said he would give it a try and, stepping up to a microphone for the first time in his life, he re-told a half of a football game he had played in as if he were watching it. Impressed by the young man's raw talent, MacArthur offered him a job on the spot.

It was Reagan's first big break. Quickly proving himself an adept announcer, he was transferred in early 1937 to a sister station, WHO, in Des Moines. Although Des Moines was a small city, WHO had a powerful, 50,000-watt signal. Reagan thus quickly became a regional celebrity. Former *Time* magazine correspondent Hugh Sidey recalls growing up in Iowa listening to Reagan and being impressed by how good he was.

Col. Barney Oldfield, later to become Reagan's publicist, was also a radio personality at the time, working at a station in Lincoln, Nebraska. He remembers that "Reagan had a reputation as being one of the best broadcasters in the Midwest."

In 1936, *The Sporting News* conducted a write-in poll, asking its readers, "Who is your favorite baseball broadcaster?" Of those announcers not in major league cities, Reagan finished fourth. Assessing his talents, the publication called him "an Iowa air ace" with "a through knowledge of the game, a gift for narrative and a pleasant voice."

One of Reagan's fans was Jim Zabel, who would eventually succeed him at WHO. Zabel, then living in Davenport, listened to Reagan regularly and recalls that he "had a natural glibness about him and a great voice and a great quickness of mind." As an announcer, "he was very colorful, very good at describing the purple shadows coming across the field—that kind of thing." Powerful testimony to Reagan's prowess as an announcer, Zabel says, is the fact that many people preferred listening to his re-creations of Cubs games to the live broadcasts coming from Wrigley Field.

Pictures of Reagan during this time convey the image of a young star. One of the more famous photos shows a dapper young Dutch Reagan smoking a pipe with an accompanying inscription, "yours for Kentucky winners and Kentucky Club—Dutch Reagan."

In later years, Zabel interviewed Reagan eighteen times, and he notes that the conversation always seemed to drift back to his happy days in Des Moines and to baseball. "He could remember going to Wrigley Field and how much he liked that and what a colorful place it was," Zabel recalls. "He hated the fact that they were getting rid of all the old baseball parks at the time. He liked baseball the way it was with all its mystical lore."

Zabel is convinced that many of the skills that made Reagan a leading actor and later a successful president—the ability to set a scene, to tell a story convincingly, to project the full scale of emotions—were honed during his days recreating baseball games at WHO.

In one of the later interviews, Zabel asked Reagan

what would have happened to him if he hadn't gone to Hollywood. Reagan's answer, he says, was that he was very happy in Des Moines and that he guessed that he would have stayed there for several years and then, when the opportunity arose, he would have gone to Chicago and auditioned to be the Cubs' announcer. That, of course, was not to be. Reagan did go to Hollywood and the rest, as they say, is history.

Playing baseball—In the spring of 1937, Reagan got his second big break. He had persuaded the WHO management to let him accompany the Cubs to spring training on Catalina Island, twenty-six miles offshore from Los Angeles. In Los Angeles he ran into Joy Hodges, a film agent for Warner Brothers whom he had known in Des Moines. Joy arranged for a screen test, and soon after his return to Des Moines, Reagan received a telegram advising him that he had passed the screen test and that a $200-a-week contract was on the way. Reagan soon became a leading star, appearing in more than fifty films.

In 1952, toward the end of his movie career, Reagan was tapped to play the role of pitcher Grover Cleveland Alexander in *The Winning Team*. Calling the experience "the happiest chore I've had since *Knute Rockne: All American*," Reagan immersed himself in learning the craft of pitching by working with the great Cleveland Indians pitcher, Bob Lemon, who was hired as his advisor and as an extra on the film. Reagan's daughter, Maureen, recalls that her father, working overtime at home, developed the irritating practice of throwing pebbles at her feet by the swimming pool as he developed his pitching form.

Reagan was then dating his future wife, Nancy Davis. One day, Reagan recalled, "She came out on the set, and I said, 'How would you like to have a baseball autographed by all these great ballplayers?' Oh, she thought that would be great. I started out, looked back, and there were tears in her eyes, and she was standing there. And I said, 'What?' And she said, 'Can't I go get them?'"

In addition to Lemon, a number of major leaguers—Gene Mauch, Hank Sauer, and Peanuts Lowrey among them—worked as advisors on the film and Nancy, herself an avid baseball fan, frequently accompanied Reagan to the set to see them.

Bob Lemon recalls, "He was very graceful and easy to teach. I had this little quirk in my own motion where I did a little leap after I released the ball, so I would be in position to field a ball back to me. By the time they started shooting the movie, Reagan was doing exactly the same thing."

Reagan developed a real respect, affection and sympathy for Alexander, or "Alex" as he called him, expressing regret that Alexander had developed a reputation as a drunk. He noted that one reason the

pitcher drank was that he was an epileptic and was so ashamed of his affliction that he preferred to explain his seizures as drunkenness.

In the movie, Alex is knocked out by a ball hitting him between he eyes as he tried to steal second base. This event, based on one actually involving Dizzy Dean, was prefigured for Reagan by a serious injury he did suffer three years earlier in June, 1949, when he was on a celebrity softball team playing the Pacific Coast League Hollywood Stars. Johnny Grant, then a deejay for KMPC, was the announcer.

As Grant, now "honorary mayor" of Hollywood, recalls, "The game was a benefit for the City of Hope hospital and was played on the old Wrigley Field in downtown Los Angeles. Bob Hope was pitcher, Donald O'Conner played second base, and Janet Leigh was one of the cheerleaders. Either Henry or George Tobias was playing first base."

Bill Demarest was the umpire and had called two balls and a strike on Reagan, Grant says, adding, "Then Reagan bunted and tried to beat out the bunt by sliding into first base." Instead, he slid hard into the first baseman and, as Reagan recalls, "my leg broke like a wet cigar."

"You could hear the pop of the leg all the way to the stands," Grant recalls "and the game was stopped while Reagan was carried off the field and taken to the hospital."

Reagan's son, Michael, remembers that when he visited his father in the hospital he told him, "Well, I hope that at least you were safe." His father replied, "You know, I don't know if I was or not." Reagan remained in the hospital for two months while the leg, which had been broken in four places, healed.

A letter to Feller—Cleveland Indians pitching ace Bob Feller recalls receiving a letter from Reagan during that time. As Feller tells the story in his autobiography, *Now Pitching:Bob Feller*, Reagan explained that in the hospital he had made the acquaintance of a ten-year-old boy whose father, a World War II hero, had become mentally unhinged and shot himself and the boy's mother. The boy was in the hospital for a lengthy period of psychological treatment and Reagan had taken an interest in him, Feller writes, "and they became even closer when they discovered that they both loved baseball."

Reagan, who had interviewed Feller at WHO, wrote, "He is an ardent fan and it seemed to be his one real interest. Of course, I became head man when I tossed your name around as someone I knew personally." The boy had a birthday coming up, Reagan explained, and he asked Feller if he could send him a baseball autographed by the Indians players.

Reagan closed the letter saying, "You'd contribute a lot toward pulling this little guy out of a dark world he's making for himself. I know this is an imposition, Bob, and I would hesitate to bother you if I didn't believe it could do a lot to really help a nice little kid who can very easily end up going haywire."

"By that time" Feller wrote, "the old sports announcer from Station WHO in Des Moines, who interviewed me on his radio show while I was still a high school pitcher, had become a successful movie star. I was impressed with the sincerity of his request—how he said he hoped I would remember him, even though he was famous now, and how genuine he was in his interest in the boy's recovery.

"I sent Reagan a ball autographed by the whole team."

Years later, in 1981, Feller was chatting with Reagan at the White House and mentioned the letter to him. "We talked about baseball and Iowa—and about that autographed baseball for the little boy more than thirty years before. I told him I remembered it well and that I even kept the letter over the years.

"He couldn't believe it. There wasn't anything in 1949 to believe it was a letter from a future President, but that wasn't why I kept it anyhow. I kept it because of what Ronald Reagan did, taking the time to write out a two-page letter in longhand to help a kid he hardly knew. That seemed to me to be a special act of human kindness, and the memories of deeds like that are worth preserving. That's why I kept the letter.

"The President asked me to send him a copy, which I was pleased to do as soon as I got back to Cleveland. After only a few days I got another letter from Reagan, only this one was on White House stationary instead of a hospital's. He told me:

> Thank you again for sending the baseball more than 30 years ago. I'll confess I'm more than a little overwhelmed that you kept the letter.
>
> I'll sign this one the same way. I remember in '49 I did it in case you didn't remember me. Now I'll do it for "Auld Lang Syne."
>
> Again, thanks and best regards.
>> Ronald Reagan
>> "Dutch"

Politics and nostalgia—Barney Oldfield recalls that "Reagan followed baseball when he was in Hollywood and he talked about it a lot and he never forgot it." As governor from 1967 to 1975, Reagan continued to follow the sport. Following his two terms as governor, Reagan hit the "rubber chicken circuit" as a highly paid lecturer, and baseball stories and jokes were a staple of his repertoire. I recall his speech to the Conservative Political Action Conference in Washington, DC in February, 1977, and Reagan telling of the young married couple with a new baby:

The wife asked her husband to change the baby's diaper, but he begged off saying he didn't know how. Well, the man was an avid baseball player and so she said to him, "Look, pretend that the diaper is a baseball diamond. Fold second base until it touches home plate and lay the baby's bottom where the pitcher's mound would be. Now bring first base, third base and home plate together and fasten with a safety pin." Then she said, "Oh, one more thing: if it starts to rain, the game isn't called. You just start all over again."

In February, shortly after his inauguration as President, he spoke to another CPAC gathering and told this apocryphal story:

> You know, one day the great baseball manager Frankie Frisch sent a rookie out to play center field. The rookie promptly dropped the first fly ball that was hit to him. On the next play he let a grounder go between his feet and then threw the ball to the wrong base. Frankie stormed out of the dugout, took his glove away from him and said, "I'll show you how to play this position." And the next batter slammed a line drive right over second base. Frankie came on it, missed it completely, fell down when he tried to chase it, threw down his glove, and yelled at the rookie, "You've got center field so screwed up nobody can play it!"

A month later, on March 27, the new President had a special treat when he spoke to a White House luncheon for members of the Baseball Hall of Fame. The President was seated between Duke Snider and Willie Mays and he chatted with the likes of Joe DiMaggio, Warren Spahn, and Harmon Killebrew. At the podium, the President told the old timers, "Nostalgia bubbles within me and I might have to be dragged away."

Speaking off the cuff, he told a story "that has been confirmed for me by Waite Hoyt."

> Those of you who played when the Dodgers were in Brooklyn know that Brooklynese have a tendency to refer to someone by the name of Earl as "oil" But if they want a quart of oil in the car, they say, "Give me a quart of earl." And Waite was sliding into second. And he twisted his ankle. And instead of getting up, he was lying there, and there was a deep hush over the whole ball park. And then a Brooklyn voice was heard above all that silence and said, "Gee, Hurt is hoit."

Back to the ballpark—Days later, Reagan was almost killed by a bullet fired by would-be assassin John Hinkley. Maureen Reagan writes in her book, *First Father, First Daughter*, that as he lay severely weakened in the hospital, "One of the ongoing dialogues that day was between Dad and his ever-present doctors concerning the President's scheduled commitment to throw out the first baseball of the major-league season in Cincinnati the following Wednesday. Dad's always been a big baseball fan, and he said he had waited all his life to be invited to throw out the first ball on opening day; this was his first opening day as President, and he didn't want to miss it."

Reagan didn't throw out the first pitch that year, but he did so in Baltimore to open the 1982 and 1986 seasons. Mike Deaver, then deputy chief of staff, recalls one trip to Baltimore with a chuckle.

"When we arrived," he says, "they escorted Reagan to the pitcher's mound where he began to chat with players and Orioles officials. As they talked, I noticed that they kept moving slowly toward home plate. "When they were about half way there," Deaver remembers, "someone said to Reagan, 'I think this is about right, Mr. President.'"

Reagan politely declined, Deaver recalls, and said, "I think I can do it from the mound." The President then "walked back to the pitcher's mound and fired a ball right across the plate. The crowd went wild." As Deaver sees it, "This was just one example of people always, always, underestimating Reagan."

Late in 1981, Reagan's long-time association with the Cubs surfaced in a New York *Times* item that chagrined the new President. A *Times* reporter noted with incredulity that Reagan had declined to join the Emil Verban Society, a Washington, D.C.-based Cubs fan club. Shortly thereafter, Society president Bruce Ladd received an urgent call from Mike Deaver, who made it plain that the invitation had disappeared in the White House correspondence bureaucracy and that *of course* the President would join. Not long after, an astonished Ladd received a call from the President himself who apologized profusely for the snafu and began immediately reminiscing about his days with the Cubs.

"He named every player on the Cubs 1935 pennant-winning team including their positions," says a still amazed Ladd, adding, "Alzheimer's or not, it's clear to me that his Cubs experience is permanently imprinted on his mind."

In 1987, Reagan was awarded the Ernie Banks Position Award by the Emil Verban Society and, although he couldn't attend the luncheon he send a special video tape with remarks recorded for the group.

He also attended a World Series game in Baltimore in 1983 and on September 30, 1988, he threw out the ceremonial first pitch at Wrigley Field and did an inning and a half of play-by-play with Cubs announcer Harry Caray. "You know in a few months, I'm going to be out of work and I thought I might as well audition," he told Harry.

Caray commented later, "You could tell he was an old radio guy. He never looked at the monitor once." The President who had begun his career as a Cubs announcer had come full circle.

After he left the White House, Reagan returned once to join Caray in the booth, and he joined Vin Scully for some play-by-play during the 1989 All Star Game.

Michael Reagan says, "You can't believe the amount of baseball stuff that people have given him—balls, bats, gloves—all kinds of memorabilia. He could open up a store." Much of this material is on display at the Reagan Library in Simi Valley, California.

If Reagan is remembered, as many believe, as one of our most successful modern-day presidents, perhaps the reason for his success is, as political commentator David Broder suggests, his long-suffering experience as a Cubs fan. Broder wrote in 1981:

"For four years, Ronald Reagan broadcast games of the Cubs and in the process became that rarest of nature's noblemen, a Cub fan. Nothing before or since those four years has prepared him more fully to face with fortitude the travails of the Oval Office. As a Cub fan, he learned that virtue will not necessarily prevail over chicanery, that swift failure follows closely on the heels of even the most modest success, that the world mocks those who are pure in heart, but slow of foot, but—(and here's the famous Reagan optimism)—that the bitterest disappointment will soon yield to the hope and promise of a new season."

A Hardy Pinch-Hitting Average

Bill Deane

Most die-hard baseball fans know that Carroll Hardy is the only man to bat for Ted Williams. Terrible Ted, in the final days of his Hall of Fame career, fouled a ball off his foot in the first inning of a game on September 20, 1960. After he limped off the field, Hardy came in to replace him and lined into a double play.

Few people know, however, that Hardy's pinch-hit résumé goes well beyond this claim to trivia immortality. Besides Williams, Hardy batted for another Hall of Famer, a two-time Most Valuable Player, a World Series MVP, a Rookie of the Year, a Cy Young Award-winner, and the subject of a major motion picture. All in an otherwise forgettable big league career that saw him make only 71 pinch-hitting appearances with a .190 batting average in that role. "I guess," Hardy once said, "I'm in the twilight of a very mediocre career."

Hardy was a three-sport star at the University of Colorado. There, he was called "Preacher," for his fanatical devotion to training rules and conditioning. Besides baseball, Hardy excelled in track and field, long-jumping 24'2" and running the 100-yard dash in ten-flat. Football was his best sport, however. In his final college game, Hardy ran for 238 yards and three touchdowns in an upset win over Kansas State.

Hardy signed with the Cleveland Indians in 1955, then cut short his baseball season to play with the San Francisco 49ers. He was reportedly the first man to sign pro baseball and football contracts in the same year. Hardy had a fine rookie season in the NFL, teaming up with quarterback Y.A. Tittle to average 28 yards per reception. Besides catching passes, Hardy served

the team as a punter and defensive halfback.

In March, 1956, Indians' G.M. Hank Greenberg told Hardy to choose between the two sports. It wasn't a difficult decision: he preferred baseball, and didn't like the physical demands of football. After a year in military service, Hardy resumed only his pro baseball career, and made it to the majors in 1958. On April 15, he walked in his big league debut while pinch hitting for Cal McLish. Hardy became good friends with teammate and fellow Dakotan Roger Maris, the future single-season home run champ and two-time MVP. While batting for Maris on May 18 of that year, Hardy hit his first big league homer, a three-run, game-winning shot in the eleventh inning. It was his only hit in six pinch at-bats that year.

After reaching on a bunt single in his first pinch-hit appearance of 1959, Hardy went 0-for-11 in that role the rest of the season. Among those he batted for were Herb Score and Jimmy Piersall.

Hardy was dealt to the Red Sox in 1960, giving him the opportunity to bat for Williams, among others. Hardy was 2-for-7 as a pinch hitter in 1960, and 4-for-15 (not 3-for-14, as shown in *The Baseball Encyclopedia*) in 1961. Three of his '61 appearances were in place of rookie Carl Yastrzemski (as with the Maris substitution, it was simply a matter of percentages: the righthanded-hitting Hardy replacing an unproven left-handed swinger against a lefty pitcher). Hardy collected two hits, including a three-run double on July 14, while batting for the future Hall of Famer. He would get only one more major league pinch hit over the next six years.

Hardy played fairly regularly in 1962, going 0-for-7 as

Bill Deane *served eight years as Senior Research Associate for the National Baseball Library.*

a pinch hitter. He was then traded to Houston for Dick Williams, and went 0-for-4 in the pinch in 1963. Hardy was sent down to the minors in 1964, but was called up when the Colts demoted Rusty Staub in July. He batted for former World Series MVP Don Larsen that month, then broke his 0-for-17 pinch-slump with a single on August 26. He finished the '64 season with a 1-for-5 record coming off the bench.

After three more seasons in the minors, Hardy resurfaced with the Twins in the final month of the 1967 season. He went 3-for-7 as a pinch hitter, including a two-run homer and a single in place of future Cy Young Award-winner Jim Perry. Hardy made his last big league appearance on September 27 of that year, pop-ping out for Jim Merritt. After managing St. Cloud to the 1968 Northern League pennant, Hardy returned to the Twins in September to get the fourteen days he lacked for a big league pension. He did not play for Minnesota that year, and retired from baseball after the season. His eight-year major league average was .225, including 12-for-63 as a pinch hitter.

Hardy returned to his football roots. He had become a scout for the Denver Broncos, and he continued in that role until 1987, by which time he was the team's Director of Pro Personnel. He then became a Kansas City Chiefs' scout, working out of Steamboat Springs, Colorado.

Carroll Hardy's Pinch-hitting Record

Researched and Compiled by Bill Deane, with Assistance from David W. Smith/Retrosheet

Yr.	Date	In.	Batted for	Result	Comments
1958:	4/15	7	Cal McLish	Base on balls	ML debut (Cleveland)
	5/13	5	Cal McLish	Strikeout looking	
	5/16	2	Don Ferrarese	Base on balls	Stayed in at CF, 0-3
	5/18 (1)	11	Roger Maris	3-run homer	Won game
	6/27	7	Woodie Held	Fly out	Stayed in at CF
	6/29 (1)	8	Billy Moran	Pop out	
	7/11	9	Morrie Martin	Strikeout	
	7/12	3	Don Ferrarese	Strikeout	
1959:	4/17	7	Russ Nixon	Bunt single	Stayed in at CF, 1-1
	4/24	6	Johnny Briggs	Pop out	
	4/26 (1)	5	Al Cicotte	Strikeout	
	4/26 (2)	9	Herb Score	Foul out	
	5/1	10	Russ Nixon	Force out	
	5/3 (1)	7	Jimmy Piersall	Ground out	Stayed in at CF
	5/10 (2)	7	Woodie Held	Ground out	Stayed in at CF
	5/23	8	Russ Nixon	Strikeout looking	
	6/2	9	Mudcat Grant	Base on balls, run	
	6/3	6	Herb Score	Ground out	
	6/7 (2)	5	Mudcat Grant	Ground out	
	6/9	9	Al Cicotte	Pop out	
	6/13	6	Mike Garcia	Ground out	
1960:	5/13	5	Wynn Hawkins	Ground out	
	6/28	7	Tom Sturdivant	Double, run	(Boston)
	7/4 (1)	4	Tom Sturdivant	Base on balls	
	7/6	8	Mike Fornieles	Strikeout	
	8/26	8	Tom Sturdivant	Base on balls, run	
	9/16	9	Mike Fornieles	Strikeout	
	9/20	1	Ted Williams	Line into DP	Stayed in at LF, 1-3
	9/24	8	Frank Sullivan	Single	
	9/27	9	Jerry Casale	Force out, run	
1961:	4/11	7	Tracy Stallard	Base on balls	
	4/18	6	Billy Muffett	Fly out	
	4/22	7	Ike Delock	Single	
	4/29	7	Billy Muffett	Ground out	
	5/8	7	Gary Geiger	Double, RBI	Stayed in at CF
	5/14 (2)	5	Tracy Stallard	Strikeout	
	5/31	8	C. Yastrzemski	Single, run	Stayed in at LF, 0-1
	6/6	7	C. Yastrzemski	Fly out	Stayed in at LF
	6/9 (2)	9	Don Buddin	Ground out	
	6/28	7	Gary Geiger	Fielder's choice	Stayed in at CF, 0-1
	7/1	6	Tracy Stallard	Line out	
	7/2	10	Dave Hillman	Strikeout	
	7/14	7	C. Yastrzemski	3-run double	Stayed in at LF, 1-1
	9/5	7	Mike Fornieles	Fly out	
	9/16	6	Gary Geiger	Ground out	Stayed in at CF, 0-1
	9/26	7	Gary Geiger	Ground out	Stayed in at CF, 0-1
1962:	5/13	8	Mike Fornieles	Pop out	
	7/3	8	Gary Geiger	Fly out	Stayed in at CF
	7/4 (1)	9	Gary Geiger	Pop out	
	7/22	7	Galen Cisco	Pop out	
	7/25 (2)	8	Mike Fornieles	Strikeout	
	8/22	9	Hal Kolstad	Strikeout	
	9/13	9	Arnie Earley	Strikeout	
1963:	4/9	3	Dick Farrell	Fielder's choice	(Houston)
	4/21 (1)	9	Chris Zachary	Ground out	
	4/27	8	Ken Johnson	Strikeout	
	5/2	7	R. Kemmerer	Base on balls	
	5/8	8	H. Woodeshick	Fly out	
1964:	7/9	7	Don Larsen	Fielder's choice	
	7/10	8	John Bateman	Ground out	
	7/11	9	Gordon Jones	Strikeout	
	8/26	6	Gordon Jones	Single, run	
	9/16	4	Gordon Jones	Pop out	
1967:	9/5	8	S. Valdespino	Single	(Minnesota) Stayed in at LF
	9/6	9	Al Worthington	Strikeout	
	9/8 (2)	8	Ron Kline	Base on balls	
	9/12	8	Rich Reese	Reached on error	
	9/17	8	Mudcat Grant	Ground out	
	9/23	5	Jim Perry	2-run homer	
	9/25	3	Jim Perry	Single	
	9/27	9	Jim Merritt	Pop out	ML finale

Totals: 71 G, 63 AB, 8 R, 12 H, 3 2B, 2 HR, 9 RBI, 8 BB, 15 SO, .190 AVG, .282 OBP, .333 SLG.

Throwbacks

Mike Ward

"We must *get it done!"*
—Motto of the Erie-Buffalo Baseball Club.

As the last grainy specks of day's light are absorbed into evening's uncertain darkness, the venerable Erie-Buffalo Baseball Club takes the field at the well-groomed Sports Complex in Welland, Ontario. The familiar sounds, smells, and pregame chatter are rejuvenating. Emerging from the dugout, the players take their positions at a fast trot. With tufts of graying hair (or what's left of it) protruding from underneath their custom-stitched caps, it seems almost as wishful and quietly inspiring as the surreal "Kick the Can" episode of *The Twilight Zone.* It's time to play ball!

But soon Erie-Buffalo's giddy enthusiasm is transformed into grim-faced reality. After building an early 15-2 lead against the Chiefs, their long-time Canadian rivals, Erie-Buffalo manages to hold-on for a 15-13 victory, ending a frustrating three-game losing skein. The win is met with less than the usual back slapping and "way-to-go" plaudits. For some players, the incessant war to stave off the physical deterioration of getting old may be nearing the final battle. At the very least, it appears to be looming more clearly with each passing game. Fiery Mike Myers, who plays first base and serves as team statistician, is overheard later, muttering something unprintable about a dubious team record being set: six (or was it seven) errors.

Mike Ward *is a freelance writer and has been a broadcast news journalist for over 20 years. A lifetime baseball loyalist, he lives in Rochester, New York. E-B's website,* www.eriebuffalo.com, *includes schedules, directions to ballparks, game recaps, league standings, other relevant information, and a merchandise catalogue.*

The hard truth is that the errors weren't mental errors or those committed by the over-exuberant hustle of youth. They were the kind of natural errors that occur when the intense physical demands of playing baseball can no longer be met. For example, chasing down a soft fly ball is less an effort to make a fine running catch than to get the ball back to the infield before an opposing runner can take an extra base on an age-weakened throwing arm.

To compensate, this gritty lot of mostly middle-aged ballplayers relies on fundamental play, perseverance, and "all-for-one" support. It doesn't seem to matter that half the players are in their early fifties. They keep competing—and mostly winning—against teams of skilled players half their age or younger. The fact that Erie-Buffalo has maintained virtually the same roster for over a decade—longer than any other amateur baseball team in western New York—is even more compelling.

Some have called the Erie-Buffalo Baseball Club "throwbacks." That's accurate. They're serious players, not just a bunch of old-timers getting together for a tour down memory lane and a few beers. More than anything, "E-B" compares to the amateur and semipro teams of the rugged barnstorming era of the early to mid-1900s. The biggest difference is that unlike barnstormers from a bygone era, E-B doesn't get paid for its time or travels. Interestingly, Myers' dad Marvin, a Brooklyn Dodger prospect, was one of only two non-major leaguers chosen to barnstorm across the country with the renowned Max Lanier All Stars in the late forties. In those days, barnstorming from town to town was a productive way for players to supplement their salaries and keep in shape for the coming season. Lanier, who pitched for the St. Louis Cardinals, added Myers to the team because of his versatility and fiery play. It's no coincidence that his son's intensity and devotion to the game has been so influential with his Erie-Buffalo teammates.

The Erie-Buffalo old-timers play with the same grit and hustle they learned in their childhoods thirty and forty years ago. They can no longer play ball on the local sandlots from dawn until dusk, but three or four days a week, E-B players rush gleefully to the ballpark after days spent as responsible adults, working at careers that range from managing a manufacturing facility to helping people with their finances.

Defying nagging aches, frustrating injuries that take longer to heal, and even career-threatening surgeries, they seem to draw strength from each other to keep playing. "There's an unspoken bond between the guys not to let each other down," says catcher Len Previte, a seven-year Erie-Buffalo veteran who himself is facing lower back surgery before the 2000 season. Enduring a relentless 80-plus game schedule that takes them from the Buffalo area to hallowed Doubleday Field in Cooperstown to the Major Senior Baseball League (MSBL) World Series in Arizona each year, the bond among E-B teammates is as firm as epoxy, and their love for the game is equally strong. "We're loosey-goosey at times," says Previte, "but we've played together so long we know when it's time to strap it up and go to work."

Outfielder Ed Warnke, the only E-B player to grow up outside the Buffalo area, was raised on the tough sandlots of Brooklyn before playing two seasons in the Independent Cape Cod League alongside prospects who eventually played in the major leagues. Facing years of minor-league travel to get his shot, Warnke decided to complete his college degree at Niagara University near Buffalo, where he married and settled.

Warnke offers another explanation for the team's unity: "Some [people] have a sort of need to compete that's beating inside. Everyone on this team feels that need, and playing baseball—as long as we can be competitive—is what keeps us going." The forty-six-year-old white-haired slugger joined Erie-Buffalo in 1994 after he got fed up with his former team's passionless approach to the game.

Pitcher Bob Ward has been the team's workhorse since it was formed in 1988. Ward can no longer overpower hitters, but relies instead on guts, guile, and a wicked changeup. The holder of Erie-Buffalo's record for most victories (123) and innings pitched, he has fought back from three major surgeries resulting from the constant wear and tear of E-B's spring-fall schedule. In 1994, cartilage removal and ligament repair were required on his right knee. Two years later he had similar surgery on his left knee. Since then he has also

undergone risky surgery on his pitching shoulder that could have left his arm permanently damaged. Why would he go to these extremes at his age? "It's hard to answer that," Ward says after a long pause. "I guess I just wanted to keep playing ball." Like Warnke, he believes that the competitive aspects of the game he and his E-B teammates grew up loving to play is really what drives him. "Let me put it this way" he contends. "Some say it's denial—that we're avoiding the reality." But, he asserts, "Why quit when I'm enjoying it so much? Besides, it's pretty obvious that the people who put us down are envious—they wish they could still play too."

Beginnings and longevity—As much as Ward defines the team's persevering spirit and durability, E-B coach Ralph Proulx personifies team leadership. More than anyone, he is responsible for galvanizing the Erie-Buffalo Baseball Club and leading the resurgence of western New York's Municipal League (MUNY) during a time when local amateur leagues were collapsing faster than a cheap umbrella in a stiff wind. Before Proulx's emergence as league president in the late 1980s, it was not unusual to see players wandering onto the field carelessly attired in soiled jeans or sweatpants. Opposing pitchers would peer in for the sign in the classic pose, with Nike jogging shoes farcically straddling the rubber. At first it was laughable, but it fast became intolerable to Proulx, who was determined to cleanse the league of slovenly indifference. "Yeah, it was funny" he explains, "but here we were dressed in quality unies, taking pride in the team and ourselves and then you realize you're trying to get some kid in a Tommy Hilfiger tee-shirt out!" It didn't take him long to institute change. "It was one of my first rules," Proulx says. "All teams are required to wear uniforms or you don't play." Now, twin brothers Pete and Paul Englert design the team's custom-stitched uniforms each year. Professionally tailored, the uniforms are the definitive standard for the league's vastly improved dress code.

At the time, interest and excitement for amateur baseball in Buffalo, as in towns all over the Northeast, were being swallowed up by the proliferation of beery "tavern" leagues playing slo-pitch softball. People were turning their backs on a sport that had been as integral to Buffalo's heritage as the Great Lakes, railroads, steel mills, and sturdy blue-collar neighborhoods. "I couldn't believe what was happening to this great game that was such a huge part of my childhood and this city," Proulx recalls incredulously. Unwilling to accept the situation, he was intent on turning things around.

As co-owner of ESI Technologies in Buffalo, a top manufacturer of industrial software, Proulx has used his business savvy to deal with player shortages, weed-ravaged diamonds and community apathy.

Orchestrating the consolidation of several leagues that were fragmenting or had ceased operations altogether, he pooled players from MUNY A, MUNY AA, and Buffalo's failed Major Senior Baseball League (MSBL) franchise, forming a united MUNY AA league. The consolidation included a firm policy on rules and conduct, and much-needed solidarity between players, coaches, and league officials. A partnership was also established with nearby Canadian leagues to create expanded schedules and take advantage of the natural rivalry with teams just across the Niagara River.

The team's only coach, Proulx put the original Erie-Buffalo roster together, inserting himself at second base, his brother Jim, known as "Perx," at third, Jim Galbo or Ward (when he didn't pitch) at shortstop, and Myers at first. In the outfield were Bob Kirbis, along with the Englert twins, remembered by some as members of the Warlocks, a popular local rock band during the late sixties and seventies. The catcher was Glenn "Short-hop" Hauptman, nicknamed for his uncanny ability to get his body in front of pitched balls that didn't quite make it the full 60 feet six inches to home plate. By the early nineties, pitcher Steve Pepi, outfielder Dan Ingersoll, Warnke, and Previte had joined the team. Pepi had a small role in the popular baseball movie, *The Natural*, starring Robert Redford. The movie was partly shot at Buffalo's old "rock pile," War Memorial Stadium. Pepi appeared in two scenes. One was sliding into second base and the other after Redford's character, Roy Hobbs, had knocked the lights out with a fantasy-shot home run. Remarkably, only Hauptman has moved on, leaving after the 1998 season. He is preparing to join the Senior Professional Bowler's tour this spring.

"They're a fascinating group," says rival coach John Dunn of the St. James Zeniths. "They seem to transcend age with how they conduct themselves." He refers to Erie-Buffalo's vigorous execution of the game's fundamentals as a "hammer and tongs and screw your belly into the ground" style. "I tell my play-ers to emulate them and play with the same quality and intensity."

Terry Soldwisch, who coaches Home Run Derby, agrees. "First and foremost I try to run my team like theirs. E-B does everything first class from their uniforms to their equipment. They treat the game and each other with such great respect." More important, Soldwisch also credits Erie-Buffalo with giving the league credibility, making it easier to recruit younger players. "There's an aura about them—it's like playing against a pro team," he says. "My guys see how the game was meant to be played and want to follow their example."

Despite the years of hard work and spirited play, Erie-Buffalo has gone mostly unnoticed in its hometown. Word spreads slowly in a town where interest in a once-cherished pastime has shriveled. Bleachers sit mostly empty during games, but the few that attend are staunchly loyal. Long time Erie-Buffalo fan Ray Jezerio of Kaisertown remembers when fans and passersby would line both baselines of Buffalo ballparks, cheering for their favorite team. "People don't know what they're missing," he says. "These guys play harder and smarter than paid players do," Jezerio adds emphatically. He and his wife Carol have maintained their loyalty to Erie-Buffalo even though their two sons play for Wiechec's, the reigning MUNY AA champion.

It's hard to say how much longer E-B's original mambers will continue to "barnstorm." But what is their legacy has also become their future. The bittersweet ending at the Welland Sports Complex last July produced a natural irony that cannot be ignored. As E-B's lead was slipping away, Proulx brought in Ward to relieve the tiring Pepi. Methodical and poised, Ward got the job done, earning a much-appreciated save. The first to greet him afterward was his Uncle Bob, who proudly clasped the hand of his eighteen-year-old nephew and escorted him off the field. The torch had been passed to Erie Buffalo's first second-generation player.

Ninth Man Out

Rick Swaine

Eight Men Out! The Black Sox! Shoeless Joe! What baseball fan isn't familiar with the saga of the infamous Chicago White Sox team that threw the 1919 World Series to the Cincinnati Reds?

Even the most casual fan knows about legendary left fielder Shoeless Joe Jackson. But it takes a student of the game to name the other conspirators who were banned from organized baseball for life along with Jackson. Of course, there's star third baseman Buck Weaver. He took no money and played his best, but had, in the words of Commissioner Kenesaw Mountain Landis, "guilty knowledge" of the fix. Then there's Chick Gandil, the rough and tumble first baseman and acknowledged ringleader of the gang. And Eddie Cicotte, the veteran hurler who received $10,000 for throwing the first game of the Series and later retired Moonlight Graham in *Field of Dreams*.

Those are the easy ones—now it starts to get tricky. Let's see, there's pitcher Lefty Williams, who lost three games in the Series. And Swede Risberg, the rifle-armed shortstop, another of the ringleaders. And Happy Felsch, the naive, good natured, power-hitting center fielder who just seemed to be along for the ride. The eighth man, Fred McMullen, is a tough one. He was a utility infielder who rarely played, but overheard the others discussing the plot and weaseled his way in.

The ninth man out? Everyone knows there were only eight Sox players suspended in the closing days of the 1920 season and subsequently barred from the game for life. In fact, *Eight Men Out* is the title of the best-known book (subsequently a movie) on the subject.

But there was a ninth major league player banned from the game for his role in the 1919 Series. He didn't play in the Series. He wasn't even a member of the White Sox, but his career in organized baseball was closed with the same finality as the others.

No, the ninth man wasn't the notorious Hal Chase. Chase was certainly involved and, in fact, was indicted in the scandal. It wasn't Benny Kauff, either. His name came up in the hearings, but he was suspended from baseball for stealing cars, not fixing games. It wasn't Bill Burns. The professional gambler and former Sox pitcher played a role in the fix, but had been out of the majors for eight years. Nor was it Ivy Olson, or Johnny Rawlings, or Jean Dubuc, other players whose names came up in the investigation. How about White Sox pitcher Dickie Kerr, the hero of the Series who won two games while many of his teammates were laying down behind him? Kerr did get suspended from organized ball—allegedly for barnstorming against the banished players. But, that was after the 1921 season and he was eventually reinstated. He was a hero of the scandal, not a villain.

The ninth man was twenty-six-year-old infielder Joe Gedeon, a member of the St. Louis Browns.

Who's Joe Gedeon? Why is he rarely mentioned in most accounts of the scandal? Was he just another forgettable character on the fringes of the great conspiracy?

Good player, bad company—Actually, Gedeon was a valuable ballplayer, the Browns' regular second baseman and a potential star. His testimony was key to

Rick Swaine *is a C.P.A. and sometime writer who lives in Tallahassee, Florida.*

the legal proceedings against the Black Sox and his subsequent expulsion was considered unfair by many.

Gedeon seemed to have a knack for getting in with the wrong crowd. He was friends with several of the conspirators, especially Risberg, who also hailed from Northern California. He had played with Risberg, Williams, and McMullen in the Pacific Coast league, and had been a Washington Senators teammate of Gandil. He was also on excellent terms with certain representatives of the St. Louis gambling community. Gedeon attended the Series both in Chicago and Cincinnati. He traveled with the Sox and hung out with his buddies. Not surprisingly he heard about the fix and placed a few "sporting" bets.

Rumors of a fix had started circulating even before the 1919 Series began and reached a crescendo when the heavily favored Sox lost in a suspicious manner. Shortly thereafter, White Sox owner Charles Comiskey offered a $20,000 reward for information regarding the alleged conspiracy.

Many baseball historians consider Comiskey's offer nothing more than a grandstand play. Gedeon, however, rose to the bait and traveled to Chicago to meet with him. He apparently confirmed that games had indeed been fixed and named several prominent St. Louis gamblers who were involved. Comiskey refused to pay Gedeon, dismissing his information as useless. A year later, a grand jury would take a different view.

The Cook County Grand Jury was convened on September 7, 1920, to investigate the possible fixing of a Chicago Cubs game played a week earlier. However, the jury's focus quickly shifted to the 1919 World Series and the eight White Sox players. As evidence mounted, the players grew jittery. Cicotte, followed by Jackson and Williams, confessed their involvement. The eight Sox players were indefinitely suspended from organized baseball. At the time of the suspension, the Sox stood a half-game behind the Cleveland Indians with three games left on the schedule—ironically enough, against Gedeon's Browns.

During the last weeks of the season, while the controversial hearings raged, Gedeon had been a nervous wreck. According to a November 4, 1920, *Sporting News* article he "trembled in constant fear and dread, lost twenty pounds, and played ball like a man dumb and dazed." The added pressure of playing the last three games against the Sox, with the conspicuous absence of the suspended players, undoubtably took a toll.

Shortly after the season ended with the Sox in second place, Gedeon's name surfaced in the continuing investigation and he voluntarily journeyed from his California home to appear before the grand jury in Illinois. According to his testimony, he and Chase (who managed to dodge the proceedings) placed bets on the Reds on a tip from one of the indicted players, presumably Risberg. On the stand, Gedeon also revealed the names of several St. Louis gamblers involved in the fix. He may, in fact, have been responsible for their involvement. Upon receiving the tip, Joe asked some local gambling acquaintances for assistance in getting money down on the Reds, unintentionally passing the inside information on to the gambling community. Gedeon testified that he pocketed between $600 and $700 from his bets. Asked to explain his relatively paltry winnings, he said his conscience began to bother him. His later admission that he didn't have much seed money is probably closer to the mark.

After his appearance, it was announced that Gedeon was exonerated from complicity in the throwing of games in the Series, but had materially strengthened the case against some of the men already indicted.

Outside the courtroom, Gedeon told the press that he feared he was through with baseball. He was right. According to a brief notation in the 1922 *Reach Guide*, Gedeon was permanently disqualified by Commissioner Landis on November 3, 1921, for having "guilty knowledge" of the conspiracy. It was hardly necessary. The Browns had dropped him from their roster immediately after his grand jury appearance. He wasn't even included on their reserve list for the 1921 season, although the Sox reserve list included all eight of the banned players.

Effect on the Browns—Gedeon's role in the Black Sox scandal may not have altered the course of baseball history, but his banishment from the game may have greatly affected the future of the St. Louis Browns franchise. In the early twenties, the Browns were solid contenders and the favored team in St. Louis. They finished fourth in 1920, with young superstar George Sisler hitting .400 at first base, and Kenny Williams, Baby Doll Jacobson, and Jack Tobin all topping .300 in the outfield. Gedeon teamed with shortstop Wally Gerber to form a classy double play combination. The next season, without Gedeon, they finished third. Seven players tried their hand at second with rookie Marty McManus, a converted third baseman, finally settling in as the regular. In summarizing the 1921 season the *Reach Guide* noted the Browns season-long infield weakness due to Gedeon's absence.

In 1922, the New York Yankees, led by slugging phenom Babe Ruth, captured their second straight pennant. Yet the Browns fought them down to the wire, winning 93 games. When the dust settled, a single game separated the two clubs. McManus was solid at bat for the Browns, but led the league in errors at second base. Meanwhile a host of prospects and suspects mishandled the hot corner. It wouldn't be much of a stretch to conclude that with Gedeon at second and McManus at his natural third base post, the Browns might have made up that game on the Yankees and brought the pennant to the city of St. Louis.

Instead, the first St. Louis pennant of the twentieth century went to the rival Cardinals when they won the flag in 1926. They also captured the heart of the city and became a National League power. Meanwhile, the Browns drifted into the depths of the American League standings and seemed to become permanently relegated to second-class status. Even a 1944 wartime pennant couldn't revive the struggling Browns franchise (the Cards beat them in the World Series) and they finally fled to Baltimore in 1954.

Would Gedeon have made the difference? The record indicates he could have. At the time of his suspension, he was just reaching his prime. Joe was acquired by the Browns prior to the 1918 season and settled in as their regular second baseman. He hit only .213 in his first year with them, but improved more than 40 points to .254 in 1919. He jumped another 38 points in 1920 to finish with a solid .292 average, and scored 95 runs in 153 games.

Just in from the Coast—Gedeon was only nineteen when he first reached the majors with Washington in 1913. When he didn't get much playing time with the Senators he was returned to the Pacific Coast League. Gedeon was comfortable in the Coast League and was often quoted as saying he would just as soon stay on the coast where it was warm. In fact, his strong affinity for temperate climates almost ended his major league career before it started. When Joe was due to arrive for his first major league training camp, Washington manager Clark Griffith, mindful of the youth and inexperience of his new recruit, dispatched coach Germany Schaefer to meet him at the train station. Griffith's club was training in Charlottesville, Virginia, and a midnight blizzard had blown in. Young Gedeon, who was seeing snow for the first time, adamantly refused to disembark. "I ain't getting off in a blizzard for nobody!" he shouted at the shivering Schaefer from the Pullman. He returned a week later when the snow melted. Normally a raw rookie would be unceremoniously booted out of camp for this, but Gedeon was apparently such a prodigy that he was forgiven.

After an outstanding season with Salt Lake City in 1915, he signed with the outlaw Federal League for $7,000, a tremendous sum in those days for an unproven player. When the Federal League folded, his contract was sold to the Yankees. But his career didn't begin to blossom until he was traded to the Browns.

The redheaded Gedeon was a rangy, 6-foot, 167-pound, righthanded hitter with good speed and an excellent glove. He had a history of terrorizing pitchers early in the year, but tailing off as the season progressed. Joe apparently had a well-developed sense of humor. An often-told story involves an encounter between fireballer Walter Johnson and Gedeon, when he was with the Yankees. After a called strike by umpire Billy Evans, Gedeon asked where the pitch was. Sensing a dispute, the suspicious arbitrator asked why he wanted to know. "I never saw it. I had to close my eyes," Joe admitted meekly.

His hometown paper, the Sacramento *Bee*, provided this synopsis of his brief career: "Joe was never a batter of high average but he offset that by being a mighty smart batsman. Most of the time in his major league career he was second in the hitting order and was regarded as one of the best in the tricky business of hit and run. Gedeon was a wonderful defensive player. His fielding at second base brought him the rating as one of the greatest keystone artists in the majors."

Unfair treatment?—A good argument could be made that Gedeon was treaty unfairly. After all, he didn't play in the Series and there's no proof that he had anything to do with plotting the affair. In fact, he insisted that he didn't even know about the fix before the Series started. Gedeon's "guilty knowledge" doesn't appear to be any greater than that of several other players on the fringe of the scandal, including some of the "clean" Sox. What set Gedeon apart was that he cooperated with the grand jury and apparently told the truth.

The Sporting News bade farewell to Gedeon with these remarks. "There are other Joe Gedeons— ballplayers who are as culpable as the former second baseman of the Browns, but they are not bowed in shame…When we look at them or recall their names as they have appeared on the suspected list, we can but think: Gedeon, bad as you appear, you are a credit to baseball beside those you have left behind."

Unlike the banished Black Sox, Gedeon quickly dropped out of sight. He continued to play in independent West Coast leagues, and resurfaced briefly when other players were threatened with banishment from organized baseball for playing against him. Otherwise, he lived in obscurity in the Sacramento area until moving to San Francisco in the late thirties.

He preceded all of the banished Sox to the grave, suffering a slow death from cirrhosis of the liver at the age of forty-seven in 1941. His occupation was listed as retired saloon keeper. Brief obituaries in the New York *Times* and the San Francisco *Examiner* referred to him as an ex-ballplayer, but failed to mention his role in the scandal that cost him his career.

A Celebrity Allegory

Larry Bowman

Few baseball players in the late nineteenth century captured public admiration to the degree that John Montgomery Ward did in the New York of the late 1880s. A great pitcher who became a great shortstop, Ward combined pugnacity, flair, and daring on the field with polish and sophistication off of it. He earned two degrees from Columbia, reputedly spoke several languages, wrote several articles about baseball, lived in fashionable downtown Manhattan, and counted many famous people among his friends. At a time when most ballplayers were viewed as rude and crude, Ward projected the image of a cultured young man distinguished by his prowess in the highly competitive, rough-and-tumble world of professional baseball. Ward was both an overachiever and a natural leader. Boys idolized him, grown men admired him, and women were intrigued by his verve and dash. Ward lived the sort of life that was everyone's dream. He was the toast of New York baseball and the darling of the city's cranks.[1]

In 1890, Ward was the subject of an allegorical tale published in one of the more influential magazines of his day. *The Cosmopolitan* published Sydney Cowell's "The Enchanted Baseball: A Fairy Story of Modern Times."[2] The tale reads partly as a satire on Ward's accomplishments as enumerated in the press and partly as a fond commentary on his golden career. It is interesting to learn that a magazine like *The Cosmopolitan* would expect its readers to recognize John Montgomery Ward in Cowell's tale and to chuckle at her description of his alter ego:[3]

Algernon de Witt Caramel was a highly accomplished young gentleman. He conversed in all the modern languages, and had mastered Greek, Latin, and Hebrew with the utmost ease. His voice was an exquisite tenor, and his paintings far excelled those of any living artist. In appearance he was a veritable Adonis. He was, moreover, a graceful dancer, a fearless swimmer, a daring equestrian, a brilliant conversationalist, and was acknowledged to be, by all odds, the best-dressed man in town. These various and attractive attributes had placed him in a very prominent and enviable position, but he had yet to win another title, one that was to make him world famous; in fact, the greatest celebrity of his age. Who lives who has not heard of Algernon De Witt Caramel, the Champion Short-Stop of America?[4]

The fairy tale opens in the Polo Grounds in 1889 where the wondrous "Brobdingnagians" of the metropolis (the National League's New York Giants) are about to do battle with the Bridegrooms from the City of Churches (the American Association's championship team from Brooklyn) for the fame and glory of claiming the title as the best baseball team in the world.[5] As the god-like Caramel takes the field to prepare for the oncoming contest, he is greeted warmly by his admirers and lovingly watched by his fiancee, Miss Violet Veronica Van Sittart, a woman of peerless beauty and accomplishment (one who certainly fits the description of the New York actress Helen Dauvray to whom Ward was married).

Larry Bowman *lives in Denton, Texas.*

All, however, is not well in the Polo Grounds that fateful day. Among the visiting Bridegrooms stands the evil Rudolph Von Hostetter, who jealously watches Caramel accept the plaudits of the crowd. Von Hostetter, who unavailingly pursued Miss Sittart before the shortstop came into her life, hates Caramel.

No single player on the Brooklyn's roster seems analogous to Von Hostetter. He is simply created for the sake of the tale. A player of some renown himself, he harbors a malevolent plan to defeat and discredit Caramel. He carries in his pocket an enchanted baseball, for which he paid a magician on Green Street five dollars, and he plans to use the doctored ball at an opportune moment during the contest.

A titanic struggle between the Brobdingnagians and the Bridegrooms ensues. When the game enters the bottom of the ninth, the Brobdingnagians lead, 2-1. As their infielders toss the ball around (they obviously made the rare choice, possible in those days, of batting first), an errant throw sends the ball rolling to Von Hostetter's feet. He deftly exchanges spheres, putting the enchanted ball in play.

The "nimble" Timotheus (Tim Keefe, the workhorse of the Giants pitching staff in the 1880s and briefly brother-in-law to Ward)[6] is pitching for the Brobdingnagians, and to the pleasure of his catcher, Duck Owing (Buck Ewing, the Giants' great catcher), he promptly retires the first two hitters he faces. Then the malevolent Rudolph Von Hostetter takes his place in the batter's box. The sky is blue, birds chirp, newsboys sell their papers on the streets, children at play run and shout with innocent glee, the fans in the Polo Grounds are enraptured by the spectacle before them, and no one except Von Hostetter suspects that an extraordinary event is about to take place.

Gallant Timotheus sets to work. Von Hostetter patiently takes pitches until he has a full count. Von Hostetter heaves the next pitch in toward Caramel. The shortstop moves confidently to intercept the ball, but it grazes his fingertips and streaks toward the left field fence. Simultaneously, Caramel feels an electric shock course through his body as he pursues the baseball, which bounces once and leaps over the fence.

The shortstop continues his hot pursuit and suddenly realizes that he, too, is in flight. Down the street toward Central Park they speed, past startled women and children, sometimes reaching a velocity of eighty miles per hour! Down Fifth Avenue toward the Battery, past the Battery, and over the blue waters of the harbor they go. Eventually, Caramel realizes that he is at sea, still pursuing the baseball.

By this time, he has become accustomed to his altered state and thinks nothing of the fact that he flies above the waters with ease. In the distance he spots a plume of smoke from a regal steamship of the White Star Line. He and the accelerating baseball soon quickly overtake the ship as they race eastward across the Atlantic. Two elderly gentlemen on deck are enjoying a cocktail when Caramel and the baseball arc past. Both immediately pledge that they will forswear alcohol forever.

Finally, Caramel spots the twinkling lights of villages, and he realizes that his flight has taken him to Europe. The magical baseball crashes into the wall of a castle frowning down from a mighty cliff. It rebounds, and Caramel catches it and puts it in his pocket.

Caramel stands gazing at the massive portals of the castle, which silently swing open. He enters and discovers a glittering court populated by regally attired knights and lovely ladies. To one side, Caramel spies a beautiful young woman. Caramel notices one peculiarity about the members of the prince's court: everyone is exquisitely handsome, but all wear golden goggles over their eyes.

As he advances, he is challenged by the man in charge, Prince Otto Von Blitzenburg, to identify himself. Caramel responds, "I am an American. My name is Caramel, and I am the champion Short-Stop of the world."[7] His words create a visible stir. Von Blitzenburg immediately welcomes the champion Short-Stop to his court, and introduces Caramel to the beautiful young woman, his daughter Aldegonda.

Caramel is smitten by Aldegonda. As their relationship ripens over the next three months, she often asks him to give her the baseball. The champion Short-Stop finally declares he will give it to her as a wedding present. Not long after, Prince Von Blitzenburg declares that the two shall be wed at midnight on the morrow.

Returning to his apartment after Von Blitzenburg's announcement, Caramel experiences another astonishing event. In a brilliant burst of light, a sprightly figure appears and identifies itself:

> I am here to save you from the evil spells of a
> vile band of enchanters who plan your eternal
> destruction. Know that I am the fairy Iolanthe.
> I loved your mother well; indeed, you are my
> godson, boy![8]

Iolanthe warns her godson that he is the victim of a cruel spell; that she had posed as the magician who sold Von Hostetter the enchanted baseball; and that he is in mortal peril. She further advises Caramel to look into the eyes of Aldegonda when she is not wearing her golden goggles.

Caramel points out that Aldegonda always wears the golden goggles. How, he queries, is he to see the damsel's unfiltered eyes? Iolanthe replies that Aldegonda often does not wear them on her evening strolls about the castle grounds. She also instructs

Caramel to fling the baseball into Von Blitzenburg's face at an opportune moment. Then the fairy departs.

At that moment, Aldegonda appears without her goggles. Caramel has an unobstructed view into her eyes. The champion Short-Stop is shocked. In her left eye he sees a tiger rending the flesh of a lamb, and in the right orb he observes a foul fiend with talons outstretched to grasp him.

Caramel, fortified by Iolanthe's timely warning, remains calm and bides his time. The next day, while standing before Prince Von Blitzenburg, he follows Iolanthe's advice and throws the enchanted baseball into the prince's face. The prince's goggles shatter, peals of thunder ring out, lightning flashes, and the entire castle and all its denizens sink into the earth.

As a dismayed Caramel attempts to understand what has occurred, he feels a nudge from the enchanted baseball and observes it departing in westward flight. He follows the baseball on its return journey, and soon finds himself in left field at the Polo Grounds with the ball nestled in his hand. Von Hostetter is rounding third base on his way to score the critical run. Caramel launches the ball to Duck Owing as Von Hostetter arrives at home plate, and Owing tags him out. The day is saved. The Brogdingnagians are champions of the world. Cowell's tale ends with the declaration:

"There is little more to add. Three weeks after the events recorded above our hero was united to his charming Violet Veronica. As Caramel's professional earnings represent a yearly income of several millions, the young couple is doing very nicely indeed."[9]

Beauty, fidelity, and decency prevail. Other than Von Hostetter and his evil ilk, the champion Short-Stop of the world has disappointed no one.

Serious folklorists are not likely to spend much effort studying Cowell's simple fairy tale. It is not particularly challenging or original. But from one point of view it is significant. Baseball players were becoming popular heroes in the 1880s, and the tale is certainly an example of hero-worship carried to an unusual level. Several years ago, Dale A Somers observed that the 1880s were a time when enthusiasm "for recreation on a great scale developed rapidly as the United States shifted from a rural-agrarian to an urban-industrial society."[10]

As America underwent dramatic change in the 1880s and adapted to rising tides of immigrants and alterations in city cultures nationwide, baseball players, who earlier were perceived as coarse and itinerant rascals, now reached a new level of acceptability in popular culture. The more successful and polished became folk-heroes, and as a result, a few players became the objects of hero-worship perhaps well beyond their due.

Notes:

1. Mark Alvarez, "John Montgomery Ward," in Frederick Ivor-Campbell, Robert L. Tiemann, and Mark Rucker, *Baseball's First Stars* (Cleveland: The Society for American Baseball Research, 1996), 167. Cited hereafter as Alvarez, "Ward." For a detailed discussion of Ward's rise to prominence as pitcher with the Providence Grays, his move to New York, and his eventual emergence as the premier shortstop and superstar of his era, read David Steven's *Baseball Radical For All Seasons: A Biography of John Montgomery Ward* (Lanham, Maryland: Scarecrow Press, 1998), passim.

2. Sydney Cowell was an actress who graced the New York stage until she retired in 1903 owing to poor health. Miss Cowell was born in England in 1846 to a famous family of performers, migrated to the United States in 1871, appeared in a number of productions in New York City, and died in 1925. The New York *Times*, April 22, 1903. Phyllis Hartnoll, ed., *The Oxford Companion to the Theatre* (New York: Oxford University Press, 1983), 190. Raymond D. Gill, ed., *Notable Names in the American Theatre* (Clifton, New Jersey: James T. White & Company, 1976), 373.

3. Sydney Cowell, "The Enchanted Baseball: A Fairy Story of Modern Times," *The Cosmopolitan* (April, 1890): 659-68. Cited hereafter as Cowell, "The Enchanted Baseball." Note that Cowell, or her editor, proved inconsistent with the player's name. The paragraph begins spelling his name Algernon de Witt Caramel and concludes spelling "de Witt" as De Witt."

4. Ibid., 659.

5. In 1889, the Giants won their second consecutive World Championship when they defeated the Brooklyn Bridegrooms six games to three in the first New York-Brooklyn series which, of course, rose to legendary dimensions in the post-World War II years. For a brief account of the games and box scores, see Jerry Lansch, *Forgotten Championships: Postseason Baseball, 1882-1981* (Jefferson, North Carolina: McFarland & Company, Inc., 1989), 34-40. Also see John C. Tattersall, *The Early World Series* (Havertown, Pennsylvania: Privately printed, 1976), 57-75.

6. In August, 1889, not too long before the championship series between New York and Brooklyn, Tim Keefe married Clara Helms, who was the widowed sister of Helen Dauvray, Ward's wife. New York *Daily Tribune*, August 23, 1889, 3. *The Sporting News*, August 28, 1889, 7.

7. "The Enchanted Baseball," 665.

8. Ibid., 666. Cowell took the fairy Iolanthe from the popular Gilbert and Sullivan opera that opened in London in 1882, and played to audiences all over the world by 1890. See Hesketh Pearson, *Gilbert: His Life and Strife* (London: Methuen & Co., Ltd., 1957), 115. For the script of Iolanthe, see Deems Taylor, ed., *Plays and Poems of W. S. Gilbert* (New York: Random House, 1932), 235-87.

9. "The Enchanted Baseball," 668.

10. Dale A. Somers, "The Leisure Revolution: Recreation in the American City, 1920-1920," *Journal of Popular Culture* V (Summer, 1971): 126. Somers' article sheds a good deal of light on the rise in popularity of sports in late nineteenth-century America, and the concomitant glorification of professional athletes such as Ward.

George Sisler

Paul Warburton

When baseball enthusiasts of today discuss the great first basemen of the old days, sluggers Lou Gehrig, Jimmie Foxx, and Hank Greenberg are most often mentioned. There was a guy named George Sisler, however, who deserves to be included in the same company. The emphasis in today's game is on power. Sisler could not match the Herculean power of Gehrig, Foxx, or Greenberg, but what he lacked in clout he made up for in other ways. A time-travel visit back to his 1922 season reveals just how magnificent "the Picture Player's" talents were at the zenith of his career.

Ty Cobb, who was not one to deal out compliments to his rivals, called Sisler "the nearest thing to a perfect ballplayer." In 1922, Sisler ran off a 41-game hitting streak, slashed a league-leading 246 hits in 142 games, and also paced the American League in runs scored (134), stolen bases (51), triples (18), assists (125), and batting average (an incredible .420). He also drove in 105 runs, placed third in the league in doubles (42). All this, and he struck out only 14 times.

Unfortunately, the 1922 season was the last showcase for the real Sisler. After the season, severe sinusitis infected his optic nerves and for a while he saw double. An operation followed. Sisler missed the entire 1923 season and his eyes never regained their former acuity. He came back in 1924, but was never the same ballplayer again.

Sisler recalled his bout with sinusitis: "All season long [1923], I suffered. I felt sorry for the fans, for my teammates, for everyone except myself. I planned to get back into uniform for 1924. I just had to meet a ball with a good swing again, and then run. The doctors all said I'd never play again, but when you're desperate, when you're fighting for something that actually keeps you alive—well, the human will is all you need." Sisler did manage to hit .320 in 4,112 at bats from 1924 to 1930 and wound up with a .340 lifetime mark. But the baseball world never got a chance to witness the kind of career that could have been for "t,he Sizzler."

Branch Rickey, a shrewd judge of baseball talent and Sisler's first manager with the St. Louis Browns, described his former first baseman: "I'd say he was the smartest hitter who ever lived. On the bases he ran with the judgment of Pee Wee Reese and with vastly greater speed. In the field he was the picture player, the acme of grace and fluency." On another occasion Rickey offered: "My, but he was lightning fast and graceful—effortless. His reflexes were unbelievable. His movements were so fast that you simply couldn't keep up with what he was doing. You knew what had happened only when you saw the ball streak through the air."

Sisler graduated from the University of Michigan, where he was coached by Rickey, with a degree in engineering. He starred as a .400-hitting pitcher. In May, 1911, he struck out 20 batters in a seven-inning intrasquad game. He entered the major leagues with the lowly Browns in 1915 as a pitcher. That year his four victories included 2-1 and 1-0 wins over Walter Johnson. Sisler could pitch. He posted a career 2.35 ERA in 111 innings. But like Babe Ruth, his hitting was too phenomenal to be restricted to a pitcher's sched-

Paul Warburton *is a former center in hockey and outfielder in baseball and softball who now tries his luck at USTA tennis and USTTA table tennis.*

George Sisler, "the Picture Player," demonstrates his grip.

ule. He was switched to first base where he hit .337 from 1916 to 1919 while swiping an average of 37 bases a season.

Baseball history shows that the years just before 1920, when Sisler got 28 percent of his at-bats, were among the toughest of the century for hitters. In 1920, the "trick" pitches were outlawed and umpires were told to throw discolored balls out of play. Hitting performances improved dramatically.

Sisler's hitting exploded in 1920. He knocked out 257 hits (still the major league record) while batting .407. Ruth led the majors in home runs but Sisler's combination of doubles (49), triples (18), and homers (19) helped him top the Babe in total bases, 399 to 388. The Yankees had purchased Ruth from the Red Sox for $100,000 after 1919. After 1920 they offered the Browns $200,000 for Sisler.

In 1921, Sisler "slumped" to .371 with 216 hits in 138 games, but in 1922 he and his Browns tore the cover off the ball while battling the Yankees down to the wire for the pennant. St. Louis topped the Yanks in runs, hits, doubles, triples, homers, stolen bases, batting average (.313 to .287), and pitching ERA (3.38 to 3.39).

The great season—The Yanks were without Ruth and Bob Meusel for the first month of the season. Commissioner Landis had suspended them for participating in an illegal barnstorming tour. The Yanks managed to keep pace with the Browns until their two big hitters returned. The pinstripers' secret to success was their airtight defense, which committed 44 fewer errors than the Browns and made them extra tough in tight ballgames.

The 1922 season started for the Browns in Chicago on April 12 with their ace Urban Shocker outpitching Red Faber, 3-2. Sisler's first-inning double keyed a two-run rally. The next day Sisler rapped an apparent two-out bases-loaded single against the Chisox, but teammate Frank Ellerbe missed second base, thereby wiping out a hit and two RBIs for George. St. Louis won anyway, 4-2, and completed a sweep two days later, 14-0, with Sisler contributing four of the 21 Browns' hits.

On April 19, St. Louis routed Cleveland, 15-1, with 20 more hits. Sisler singled twice, doubled, tripled and stole three bases, including home. Back in St. Louis on April 22, Sisler singled three times in front of three homers by Ken Williams as the Browns beat Chicago, 10-7. Williams would become baseball's original 30-30 man, leading the league with 39 homers and stealing 37 bases. On May 1, Sisler socked a pair of singles and a triple as the Browns hammered Cleveland, 13-2. St. Louis was leading the league at 12-5, one game ahead of New York.

On May 4, Sisler's three singles pushed his average up to a league-leading .442, but Detroit topped the

Browns, 6-5, on Harry Heilmann's ninth-inning three-run homer. The Sizzler enjoyed a big series in Philadelphia in mid-May, racking up 11 hits in 15 at-bats, including three homers and a double, but Connie Mack's weak A's won two of the three contests. The mini-slump left the Browns a half-game behind Miller Huggins' Yanks in a pennant race whose lead would flip-flop back and forth between the two teams all summer.

The Browns made their first visit to the Polo Grounds on May 20 and scored seven runs after two were out in the ninth inning to beat the Yankees, 8-2. Sisler stroked three more singles, but Baby Doll Jacobson's grand slam was the big blow. The game marked Ruth and Meusel's return from their suspensions, but they both went hitless in four at-bats. New York rebounded to win the next two games, 6-5 and 4-3, in ten and thirteen innings. The Browns won the final game, 11-3, with Sisler contributing a single, a home run, and a stolen base. Ruth managed a home run and a double in 16 at-bats in the series as over 102,000 fans showed up for the four games to see his return. Sisler had six singles, a double and a homer in 19 at-bats and swiped four bases. He left New York hitting .439. Cobb and Bing Miller were also over .400, at .402.

On Memorial Day, the Browns split two with the Tigers in St. Louis, losing the morning game, 6-5, before winning the afternoon tilt, 2-1, in sixteen innings. Sisler's work for the day included five singles and a triple in ten at-bats. As June opened George beat the Chisox with an RBI single in the twelfth inning, 4-3. He put together his seventh four-hit game of the year the following day as the Browns trounced the Pale Hose, 12-4. He enjoyed yet another four-hit day on June 9 as the Browns humbled the Red Sox, 8-1. He would finish the season with thirteen four-hit games. His closest rival in the batting race, Cobb, would knock out a record four five-hit games in 1922 on his way to a .401 season.

Other attributes—Sisler's value to the Browns transcended his hitting and baserunning offensive stats. He was commonly regarded by experts as the best fielding first baseman of his era. His career total of 1,535 assists is the all-time record. But sometimes stats don't tell the whole story. Sisler's fielding plays sometimes bordered on the impossible. In a game against Boston in 1916, the Red Sox had runners on first and third with no outs. The next batter lifted a routine fly to Burt Shotton in left field. Conceding the run, Shotton threw to Sisler to get the runner returning to first. After making the putout there, Sisler whirled and fired to Hank Severeid at the plate for a triple play. Early in 1922 against Washington, Sisler anticipated a squeeze bunt by Roger Peckinpaugh. Racing in with the pitch, he fielded the ball, brush-tagged Peckinpaugh, then threw out Joe Judge at the plate. Two outs on a squeeze bunt grounder are not the norm, but that was George.

The Yankees arrived in St. Louis with a bang on June 10, tagging the Browns, 14-5. Ruth's three hits included his sixth homer. Shocker gave New York's Carl Mays a taste of his own medicine by firing three fast balls close to Mays' head. The next day 30,000 fans somehow squeezed into Sportsman's Park, which had a seating capacity of 17,000. *The Sporting News* reported that the crowd would have been twice that figure if there had been room. The Yanks sent the overflow crowd home disappointed, winning, 8-4. But the Browns regrouped to win the third and fourth games by 7-1 and 13-4 scores. Sisler went 9 for 18 in the series, with two triples.

On June 14, Sisler belted a grand slam to help beat the Senators, 7-6. He was not regarded as a power hitter but with the batting surge of the 1920s his line drives started finding the gaps between outfielders more often for extra-base hits. In addition he used his blazing speed to turn singles into doubles and doubles into triples. He stood just under six feet, packing a streamlined 170 pounds into his frame. Admitting that he patterned his hitting style after Cobb, Sisler choked his 42-ounce bat and preferred the place-hitting science rather than trying to slug away. In the three years from 1920 to 1922, before his eyes were damaged, Sisler ripped 719 hits in 1,799 at bats for a .400 batting average.

The Yanks went into a tailspin in mid-June and lost eight straight. Cobb's Tigers got hot and won 22 of 26 before Ty's star pupil, Heilmann, was forced out of action with a back injury. By June 25, the Browns led the league at 40-28 with the Yanks 1-1/2 games back and the Tigers in third place four games out. Sisler was still on top in the batting race at .429.

The hits kept coming as George went 6 for 9 in a doubleheader in Boston on July 7 with two doubles and a triple. *The Sporting News* reported that he played for two weeks in July with a dislocated thumb which bothered his gripping of the bat. Nevertheless, he was on a pace to make 275 hits.

Cobb made his run at Sisler in July and early August. On July 20, Sisler's lead over Cobb shrank to four points at .413 to .409. The Yanks invaded St. Louis and took three of four games to regain first place. More bad news followed when Sisler was spiked below the knee while sliding into first base against the Red Sox on July 29. He missed six games. In his first at-bat back he lined into a triple play against the A's. But he followed that up with a single and triple as the Browns beat the Mackmen, 4-1. Nonetheless, by August 10 Cobb had overtaken Sisler, .410 to .409.

Ruth was also starting to warm up as he beat the White Sox with a dramatic three-run homer in the ninth-inning at the Polo Grounds on August 20. The

Bambino would finish the year at .315 with 35 homers in 406 at-bats. One pitcher the Babe couldn't solve, however, was Browns rookie Hub Pruett, who fanned Ruth nine of the first 12 times he faced him. Pruett explained: "No trick to it, just bend a slow one in on him and he'll miss it by a mile."

Sisler regained the batting lead from Cobb (.416 to .401) by spraying 10 hits in 15 at-bats as the Browns swept three straight in Boston from August 22 to August 24. The St. Louis bats cooled off at the Polo Grounds, though, as the Yanks took three of four to forge ahead again by 1-1/2 games. Sisler cooled off in Manhattan, too, managing just five singles in the series.

On Labor Day, the Browns blitzed the Indians, 10-3 and 12-1, as Sisler made seven hits in nine at-bats including three doubles and a triple, swiped a base and scored seven times. *The Sporting News* described the chaotic scene at Sportsman's Park on the holiday: "Thousands of fans, unable to get in the park in the ordinary way, because of a shortage of entrance gates, broke down the fences, uprooted turnstiles and went in like a raging flood. One estimate is that 5,000 milling bugs overcame the slim force of ticket sellers and takers and forced their ways into the stands and onto the field." The city was baseball mad!

Down to the wire—The Browns retook first place for the last time the next day with a 10-9 conquest of Cleveland. Williams clubbed a grand slam and Sisler socked two singles and stole three bases. The Sizzler had now hit in 35 straight games and was challenging Cobb's 1911 modern-day record of 40. That night thousands packed the biggest theater in St. Louis where the Browns players were given gold watches and asked to make speeches. The huge crowd would not let Sisler leave the building until he had made a speech.

Sisler was at the peak of his career. In the August 30 issue of *Outlook*, Christy Mathewson said: "Now there is Sisler of the St. Louis team—he is every bit as valuable as Ruth, some people think more valuable. But he has another temperament. When he makes a great hit or a great play and the crowd is ready to idolize him, he modestly touches his cap and fades out of sight."

The Sporting News quoted a writer in the Yankees' home town, New York, as saying this about the Browns' superstar: "If there is anything he cannot do in the national pastime I would like to see it. Whether it is hitting the ball, playing first base, sliding into a bag or beating out a throw, it makes no difference. He can do one just as well as the other. I rate him the greatest player we ever had in the baseball sport."

Sisler raised his hitting streak to 38 games with two singles and a triple as the Browns slaughtered Cobb's Tigers, 16-0, on September 9. Two days later against the Bengals, Sisler tied the score, 4-4, with a two-out ninth-inning triple and scored the winning run on a Marty McManus single. The game proved to be disastrous to the Browns' pennant chances, however. In the seventh inning Cobb grounded to short and Wally Gerber made a wide throw. Sisler stretched so far to catch the ball that he fell forward on his right shoulder. Nothing was made of the play at the time and Sisler helped win the game with his triple in the ninth inning. But the next day he failed to appear for the game until the second inning. His shoulder had caused such pain during the night that sleep was impossible, and he had spent the morning consulting specialists.

The team physician, Dr. Robert Hyland, explained the injury to the St. Louis press: "Sisler is suffering from a severe and extremely painful strain of the deltoid muscle of the right shoulder. Movement of the arm caused him so much misery that I immobilized the arm and shoulder in tape and have ordered him to keep it so for a week."

Hyland added: "I feel that Sisler will be very fortunate to completely recover before the close of the season, though he doubtless will try to play. For one week it is certain he ought not to attempt anything on the ball field, but I guess he will try to get into the Yankees series despite my advice."

Sisler missed the next four games, but was in the line-up when the Yankees arrived in town. On September 16, the Yanks beat the Browns, 2-1. Sisler extended his streak to 40 games with a double, but also hit into a double play with two runners on base. St. Louis fans had waited in line from the night before until noon on game day to buy tickets. Someone in the overflow crowd hurled a pop bottle that struck Yankee centerfielder Whitey Witt in the head in the ninth inning. The bottle knocked Witt out cold and he was carried from the field.

In remembering the race, Sisler later said that the "Pop Bottle Incident" seemed to take some of the heart out of the Browns. They managed to win the second game, 5-1, behind Pruett, and Sisler ran his streak to a record 41 games with a sixth-inning single. The rubber game, however, saw the Yanks win, 3-2, as Witt came back with bandages on his head to drive in the tying and winning runs with a ninth-inning single. Sisler's streak was ended by "Bullet Joe" Bush at 41. He had hit

.460 during the streak.

The Sporting News said of Sisler's attempt to play in the series: "His right arm hung almost lifeless at his side and he could neither field nor hit up to form." In the next game, a 4-3 loss to Washington, he pinch hit and struck out on three pitches from Walter Johnson. He missed the following two games before returning to slap a single in the Browns' 11-5 win over the A's on September 22. The A's then beat the Browns, 6-5, pushing St. Louis 4-1/2 games back. To tie for the pennant the Browns had to win their last four games while the Yanks lost their last five.

It almost happened. St. Louis beat Philadelphia, 7-4, on September 24, while Cleveland shut out the Yanks, 3-0. Sisler smacked three singles, stole two bases, and forced two errors leading to extra bases. The Browns were idle on September 28, but the tail-end Red Sox beat New York, 3-1. On September 29, the Browns topped Chicago, 3-2, and Boston beat New York again, 1-0. The Browns were two games out with two to play.

The Browns outscored Chicago, 11-7, on September 30, as Sisler singled, doubled, and banged a homer into the rightfield bleachers. In Boston, Red Sox manager Hugh Duffy chose to pitch Alex Ferguson instead of Herb Pennock against the Yanks. He was widely criticized for this later. Ferguson gave up three first-inning runs before being relieved by Pennock, who pitched shutout ball the last eight innings. The damage had been done, however, as Waite Hoyt pitched New York to the pennant, 3-1.

St. Louis won its meaningless final game, 2-1, and the Yankees lost, 6-1, making the final New York margin of victory a single game. Many St. Louis fans looked forward to the 1923 season with optimism, but Sisler's eye problems ruined what should have been an interesting next few years in Brownieville. Sisler and the Browns deserved better. Today their fabulous 1922 season is hardly remembered. With home runs flying out of stadiums in record numbers, modern fans have also forgotten Sisler and his all-around greatness. Tell them to call me the next time someone peppers the field with 257 hits in a season or bats .420 while leading the league in stolen bases and fielding his position better than anyone in the game. I want to know how much money he signs for in his next contract.

Rube Marquard's Lucky Charm

Gabriel Schechter

When he was with us, we won. When he wasn't, we didn't."

The speaker was ninety-two-year-old Hall of Famer Rube Marquard, and he was talking about Charles "Victory" Faust, the eccentric good-luck charm of the 1911 New York Giants.

Charley Faust was a Kansas farmer, a hayseed who foisted himself on John McGraw and the Giants in late July of 1911. He became their mascot, jinx-killer, star of pre-game practice, and victim of endless pranks. In addition to being invincible as a mascot, Faust provided the comic relief that balanced McGraw's harshness and helped the players to relax and play winning baseball. As a reward, McGraw let Faust pitch in two games in the final week of the season, before he was outmascotted in the World Series. In 1912, Faust's presence helped the Giants to an amazing 54-11 start before he returned to Kansas in July.

Marquard was only twenty-four in 1911 and was around Faust only a few months, yet in the last year of his life still credited Faust's legendary jinxing power with helping the Giants win the first of three straight pennants. Or maybe he was thinking of himself. Without Faust, Marquard might not be in the Hall of Fame.

When the 1911 season began, Marquard was widely ridiculed by Giants fans and the press as "the $11,000 Lemon." Manager John McGraw had paid that unprecedented sum to Indianapolis in 1908 for 28-game-winner Marquard (dubbed "Rube" because he reminded people of Rube Waddell), only to see him lose a crucial start late in that heated pennant race. In the two seasons following that nightmarish debut as a scared twenty-one-year-old, Marquard won only 9 games and lost 17.

A lanky lefty known for blazing speed and erratic blowups, Marquard began slowly in 1911, leaving fans skeptical. By the end of June, he had only five wins and found himself in the starting rotation only after the June demise of Bugs Raymond left McGraw with only five pitchers.

In July, Marquard came into his own even as the Giants dropped to third place. He doubled his win total by the time they hit St. Louis to end the month. That's where Charley Faust showed up, and the Giants, particularly Marquard, caught fire. He didn't look back until Faust was gone. By then, Marquard was halfway to Cooperstown, having achieved a record that still stands.

The numbers are right there. From Faust's arrival until he left the team for good midway through the 1912 season, Marquard was 33-3—and Faust was absent for two of the losses. Subtract that uncanny eleven-month stretch from Marquard's lifetime totals of 201-177, and he emerges as a sub-.500 pitcher.

Detractors of Marquard's Hall of Fame credentials point out that he was dominant only from 1911 through 1913, when he compiled a 73-28 mark, and that he earned immortality primarily for the feat of beginning the 1912 season with 19 straight wins. Did Victory Faust just happen to witness Marquard's rise to brilliance, or was there some connection? Is it coincidence

Gabriel Schechter's *book,* Victory Faust: The Rube Who Saved McGraw's Giants, *is available to SABR members for $16 postpaid from Charles April Publications at P.O. Box 754, Los Gatos, California 95031-0754. It is also available at Amazon.com.*

that Marquard won number 19 just before Faust returned to his native Kansas, and that he suffered three losses the next week?

For an answer, let's examine Marquard's fortunes in 1911, with and without Faust. Faust's influence was immediate. The day after he arrived, Marquard shut out the Cardinals on four hits. Two days later, he came back to go the route in a 3-2 win. One New York newspaper said Faust was there, but a St. Louis paper makes a stronger case that he wasn't, so we'll give the full credit to Marquard.

McGraw gave Faust the slip leaving St. Louis, so he missed the rest of the road trip, which saw Marquard lose at Pittsburgh and win at Chicago. He stood at 13-5 for the season when the Giants returned to the Polo Grounds and found

Charles "Victory" Faust

Collection of Thomas S. Busch

Faust waiting for them. Marquard's next start was the best of his career so far. He went 12 innings to outduel Phillies rookie ace Grover Cleveland Alexander, fanning 13 and allowing only two unearned runs.

Marquard faltered in his next start, lasting less than an inning in a 5-4 Giants win. Faust, unable to secure a contract from McGraw, abandoned the team for several days, missing Marquard's 3-2 win over the Cubs. But Faust rejoined the Giants to launch a nine-game win streak highlighted by Marquard's phenomenal pitching.

On August 24, Marquard held the Pirates to two hits and struck out 11, winning, 2-1. He topped himself on August 28 against the Cardinals, yielding only one hit, a seventh-inning single by Rube Ellis. Still, he walked two men, so there was room for improvement when he faced the Phillies on September 1. He did improve, as a fifth-inning single by Fred Luderus was the Phillies' only baserunner.

Both one-hitters were 2-0 wins, so Marquard got as little support as he needed. In the three games, he allowed only four hits and two walks, striking out 30. Neither Sandy Koufax nor Nolan Ryan ever had a trio of starts like that, and it vaulted Marquard ahead of Christy Mathewson as the ace of the New York staff.

The day Marquard one-hit the Phillies, Victory Faust began rehearsing a vaudeville act. An engagement at the Manhattan Theater was the fruit of his sudden celebrity. He opened on Labor Day while the Giants hosted last-place Boston in a doubleheader. Faust watched Mathewson win the morning opener but was busy ducking fruits and vegetables on the Manhattan stage when Marquard and his fastball went to work that afternoon.

A huge crowd of 30,000 cheered Marquard on, and he showed no letdown in form. Through seven innings, he was coasting with a 5-0 lead, three hits allowed, and 12 strikeouts. Then, as if suddenly noticing that Faust was neither stationed at his good-luck perch in the dugout nor warming up in the bullpen, he fell apart, the spell broken. Five runs in the eighth inning tied the score, and Boston drilled five more hits in the tenth, beating the stunned Marquard, who still felt he had good stuff.

Mathewson also lost while Faust was in vaudeville, and only two off-days spared the team from further damage. On Friday, September 8, Faust insisted on going to the Polo Grounds, accompanied by the Manhattan's manager, Billy Gane, to pull the Giants out of their slump. Marquard got the starting assignment and won 3-2.

"The real reason of the Giants' success," wrote Heywood Broun in the New York *Morning Telegraph*, "lay not in the staunch arm of Marquard, nor the ready bat of Fred Merkle, but in the presence of Charlie Faust." The Giants got three early runs, and Marquard took his usual low-hit shutout into the seventh inning.

However, it was show-time at the Manhattan, and Faust had to leave. As Broun noted, "no sooner had he left the field than the tide of battle turned…Whether it was really on account of the departure of Faust or some other cause, Marquard was in grave danger in the seventh." Brooklyn reached him for two runs and threatened again in the eighth, but Marquard held on to win.

The close call convinced Faust that the Giants needed his services for the pennant drive, so he abandoned his vaudeville gig to rejoin them. McGraw was persuaded to take Faust along on the final 22-game road trip. They were proved right early: the Giants won the first ten games on the trip.

Marquard won three of those games, beating Boston (for his twentieth win) and the Pirates before shutting out the Cardinals again on September 20. Two days later, he relieved in the St. Louis finale, replacing Red Ames in the bottom of the ninth and giving up a two-run single that tied the game.

The Giants scored in the tenth, but Marquard got in trouble in his half. A walk, a single, a sacrifice, and another walk filled the bases. Here the story was picked up by Sid Mercer of the New York *Globe*.

> Out in centrefield Matty and Charley Faust were warming up together. "Charley," said Matty, "you better hike to the bench. You know you were not there the other day when we almost lost in the ninth inning." Faust looked at Matty a moment, and just then Marquard passed Bliss to load the bases, with one out.
>
> Without another word the "Kansas Cyclone" tore out across the green and sped madly toward the grand stand. He cut across left field like Casey Jones going down hill and a moment later steamed into the coop puffing, but bringing much good cheer. "I'm here, boys," he panted. "Now, Rube, go get 'em."Those Giants seated on the bench, and McGraw was among them, hailed the coming of the Kansas rube with cries of joy and relief.

As the dugout enthusiasm swelled, Marquard responded by getting the last two outs and the win. "If the Rube had not been game," Mercer concluded, "and if Faust had not been there choking the jinx to death this paean of joy would never have been written." Mathewson told the same story (in *Pitching in a Pinch*, written that winter with ghostwriter Jack Wheeler), calling it "as nice a piece of pinch mascoting as I ever saw."

Marquard started in Cincinnati two days later, but Faust wasn't there. Apple pie was Faust's good-luck charm, the source of his jinxing powers (like Popeye's spinach), and he had bad luck in Cincinnati, wandering the streets in search of even one slice of pie. By the time he got to the ballpark, Marquard was gone, tagged for five runs in five innings. Faust's arrival did spare Marquard the loss, as the Giants tied the game before Hooks Wiltse lost it in relief.

Faust didn't see Marquard lose a game until the series opener in Chicago, when the Cubs ripped Rube for six early runs and Faust couldn't rally the Giants.

Marquard reportedly had a lame arm, caused by that August hot stretch where he fanned 67 batters in six starts.

Or was it Faust's fault? McGraw had announced that if the Giants clinched the pennant in Chicago (by winning the first two of four games), he would let Faust—who had pestered McGraw about pitching in a real game—start the finale. This was Faust's chance to fulfill the mission that had impelled him to join the Giants: to pitch them to the pennant. With so much at stake, was Faust's jinxing effort more selfish, less focused on Marquard, just when Marquard needed him most?

In any case, that loss wiped out Faust's chance; instead, Marquard started the finale, and he shut out the Cubs on six hits. That was his last serious start of the season, since the Giants clinched the pennant days later. His only other appearance was a tune-up effort on October 7—which happened to be the date of Faust's debut as a major-league pitcher.

Marquard went five innings and left with a 2-2 tie. Reliever Louis Drucke surrendered the lead, and Faust pitched the final inning of a 5-2 loss, giving up one run. He had realized his dream, and the Giants were headed for the World Series.

That's where Faust's jinxing power was neutralized by the Philadelphia Athletics of Connie Mack, who employed a hunchback dwarf, Louis Van Zelst, as his good-luck mascot. Faust even witnessed another loss by Marquard, 3-1, in Game 2, as the Giants lost in six games.

How much better was Marquard when Faust was there to watch and cheer him on? Much much better. Without Faust (after July), Marquard was 4-2 with a 3.11 ERA in 55 innings. With Faust, he was 10-1 with a 1.89 ERA in 90 innings.

As for Marquard's 19 in a row to start 1912 (under today's rules, it would have been 20), it is impossible to say how many Faust witnessed. He was with the Giants for most of their home games and part of the road trip that saw him part from the team in early July. However many wins he saw (6 to 10), he never saw Marquard lose in 1912, and only twice in 1911. While he was a part of the team, Marquard ran off 33 wins. After Faust was exiled back to Kansas, kicking and screaming, Marquard went 7-11 the rest of 1912.

Maybe it was coincidence, just as it is coincidence that Marquard and Faust shared the same birthday, October 9, two days after Faust's debut (Faust turned thirty-one, Marquard twenty-five). Maybe we should wonder instead how good Marquard could have been if Faust had lasted.

"When he was there, we won. If he wasn't, we didn't."

That's all Marquard knew in 1979—and all he needed to know in 1911.

Minor League Player

Ross Horning

In the summer of 1942, I was having a good year. I was the second baseman for Rex Stucker's Sioux Falls Canaries in the Northern League. Having finished a two-week home stay, we were in Duluth for the beginning of a two-week road trip. Being the visiting team, we had taken infield practice first. The home team, the Duluth Dukes, were on the field.

Along the first base side, I was playing pepper with some other Sioux Falls players. A young man, wearing a sharp business suit, suddenly appeared. He said to me, "What size uniform do you want?" I responded, "Why? I already have one." He came back with, "You have just been sold to us."

Out of the blue, I had to change sides. I left the Canary first base side, went into the Duluth dressing room, changed uniforms, and came out on the Duluth third base side.

Several of the Sioux Falls' players hollered at me, "What are you doing over there?" I replied, "How do I know what I am doing over here."

The game started. Now, being the home team, we batted last. Pitching against me for Sioux Falls was my good friend and fine pitcher, James "Bud" Younger. I played third that night for Duluth, not second, as I had for Sioux Falls. I made two great defensive plays at third and got three base hits. The biggest reason I was able to get three hits that night was that the Sioux Falls catcher and manager, Tony Koenig, told me every

pitch that Jim was throwing. After the game, Tony said, "I just wanted you to have a good night with your new team."

But for basic economic reasons I did not want to play for Duluth. I had just paid my own expenses for two weeks in Sioux Falls, and was looking forward to the two-week road trip on which the team would pay my expenses. With Duluth, it was another two-week homestand where I would have to pay my own keep.

I argued with the Duluth management for nearly two hours. Finally, they told me sharply that if I didn't play for them, I wouldn't play for another team the rest of my life.

That is the *reality* of the "Reserve Clause."

A fundamental question arose in my mind. Where, in the American free enterprise system, did any employer get the right to inform any employee that if he or she did not agree to work for that employer, he or she would be barred for life from working for anyone else in that profession?

What exactly is this Reserve Clause, which gave such one-sided power to an employer over the destiny of professional baseball players?

The late St. Louis Cardinal outfielder, Curt Flood, famously expressed his objections to the Reserve Clause in a case he took to the Supreme Court. He lost, but it is largely because of Curt Flood that major league players eventually gained the right to sign contracts for a stated time period, and to be free agents afterward.

In 1951, long before the Flood case, I testified before the House Judiciary Committee's Sub-Committee on Monopoly Power. The Reserve Clause, of course, ap-

Ross Horning, Ph.D., *took his degree at George Washington University and was a Fulbright Scholar to India. He is a professor of history at Creighton University. As "Bumps" Horning, he played in the St. Louis Cardinals and the Chicago Cubs systems. He was the Northern League's All-Star second baseman in 1946.*

plied to both major and minor league players at the time.

In "Bumps" Horning's August 7, 1951, testimony before the Sub-Committee, a copy of the Uniform Players Contract, approved by the National Association of Professional Baseball Leagues, was submitted as an exhibit and published on pages 366-371 of the testimony.[1]

The contract states:

> RENEWAL—8 (a) Each year, on or before March 1 (or if Sunday, then the succeeding business day) next following the playing season covered by this contract, by written notice to the Player, the Club or any assignee thereof, may renew this contract for the term of that year, except that the salary rate shall be such as the parties may agree upon.[2]

In actual practice, this meant that whenever a player signed a contract with a professional baseball team within organized baseball, he "belonged" to that organization for as long as that team wished to keep him. He could not, at the end of a season, arrange to play for another team that might want his services.

As long as the organization sent him a contract by March 1 of the following season, a player's services were "reserved" for the coming season. He could, of course, simply retire from baseball or decide to sit out a year. But this did him no good. If he decided to return, he still belonged to the team that held his contract.

The Uniform Players Contract stated, "Except that the salary shall be such as the parties may agree upon."[3] This was profoundly misleading. Since the player was not free to play for any other team, the club was free to send him any contract it wished. It was either play for what was offered or don't play at all.

While the player was under contract for life to the club, he could be fired at any moment. The Uniform Players Contract states:

> TERMINATION: 5 (b) This contract may be terminated at any time by the Club or by any assignee by giving official release notice to the player.[4]

I once played on a team that had twelve shortstops in one summer. Every time you saw a person with a suitcase, you wondered, "Who's next?"

While the player had to agree to a lifetime binding contract, the Club, also under the Uniform Players Contract, had to write a binding contract to that effect. The Uniform Players Contract stated:

> No club shall make a contract different from

the Uniform Contract, and *no club shall make a contract containing a non-reserve clause*, except permission be first secured from the President of the National Association.[5] [Italics added.]

The Reserve Clause operated in many ways. My testimony includes the stories of my friends Arnold "Red" Anderson and James "Bud" Younger.

Red Anderson played for the Washington Senators, the club that later became the Minnesota Twins. Owner Clark Griffith sent Anderson down to Chattanooga. Red didn't want to go. Instead of reporting to Chattanooga, he went off to play for the semipro Sioux City, Iowa team.[6]

Rex Stucker, who owned the minor league Sioux Falls Canaries in the Northern League, and who was a friend of Anderson, inquired of Clark Griffith "that as long as Red did not want to play for Chattanooga and was playing for the semipro team, Sioux City, would Mr. Griffith permit Red to play for Sioux Falls?"

Mr. Griffith emphatically answered in the negative. He said, "that if Red wished to play baseball, he would play for Chattanooga or no one."[7] Stucker's hands were tied.

In 1948, James "Bud" Younger belonged to the New York Giants system and was sent on option to Quebec City, which was not a member of their farm system. The following year, Quebec wanted to buy Younger's contract. Younger, for his part, wanted to keep playing for Quebec, and appreciated the fact that they were willing to pay him more than the Giants. New York said no. They wanted to send the pitcher to one of their own farm teams.[8] Neither Younger nor Quebec had any recourse.

Life in the minors today—This sort of thing is ancient history in the major leagues. Marvin Miller, Curt Flood, Peter Seitz, Andy Messersmith, and Dave McNally, and the Players' Union have seen to that.

But what is the situation of the minor league player? Not all that much different than it was in 1951, it turns out. The clauses dealing with renewal and reservation have not changed significantly, although the exact language and location of the two clauses in the contract have changed from time to time in the various revisions of the standard Minor League Uniform Player Contract.[9]

Instead of the former Lifetime Minor League contract, the latest revised Minor League Uniform Player Contract, March, 1995, now includes a time limit of seven years. Section VI, Paragraph A:

> Unless a different term of this Minor League Uniform Player Contract is set forth in Addendum A, Club hereby employs Player to render, and Player agrees to render skilled services as

a Minor League Player *in seven (7) separate championship* playing seasons...”[10]

In addition to signing a seven year contract, the player also is under contract twelve months of each year for seven years. Paragraph B of Section VI reads:

“This Minor League Uniform Contract obligates Player to *perform professional services on a calendar year basis, regardless of the fact that salary payments* are to be made only during the actual championship playing season.”[11][Italics added.]

Furthermore:

Player understands and agrees that his duties and obligations under this Minor League Uniform Player Contract continue in full force and effect throughout the calendar year, including the Club's championship season, Club's training season, Club's exhibition games, Club's instructional, post season-training or any winter league games, any official play-off series, any other official post-season series in which Club shall be required to participate, any other game or games in the receipts of which Player may be entitled to a share, and any remaining portions of the calendar year. *player's duties and obligations shall continue in full force and effect until October 15 of the calendar year of the last championship playing season covered by this minor league uniform player contract.*[12][Italics added.]

What does all of this mean in relation to the old Minor League Uniform Contract? While there is now a time limit of seven years instead of the life-time service as common in the days of my testimony, the situation is actually more severe than it was under the old contract procedure.

Now, the phrase that “obligates Player to perform professional services on a calendar year basis” means that, if the club wishes to do so, it can prevent a player from returning to college at the end of the season, by holding instructional sessions, postseason training, and winter league competition. Under the old contract procedure, when the season was over, the player could do what he wanted. He could wait until he received notice by the club before March 1 that his services had been “reserved” for the coming season.

Under the 1995 contract, there is no need to send a player a “reserve” clause letter by March 1. He is under a year-round contract for seven years.

Under Section XIX, Paragraph B of the 1995 contract, if, in the judgment of the club, the player does not show sufficient skill or competitive ability to qualify or to continue as a professional baseball player, his contract can be immediately terminated.[13]

This termination clause is similar to the contract of forty years ago. Then as now, if a major league player is released in the middle of the season, he got his salary for the season. If a minor league player is released, his salary immediately stops.

The 1995 contract can be viewed as a successful minor league counterattack by major league teams against the success of Curt Flood's opposition to the reserve clause for major league players. With its seven year limit instead of a lifetime binding feature, it gives the illusion of progress, but it is even more stringent concerning the contract I testified about before the Sub-Committee on Monopoly Power.

Under the 1995 Minor League Uniform Contract, a player is:

(1) Signed for a solid seven-year period.

(2) Under contract twelve months a year for a seven-year period until October 15 of the final year. The club can demand that he attend instructional programs, play in winter leagues. Under the old contract, when the season was over, the player could either find a job or return to college until he received his letter of “Reserve” notice. Now, if the club desires, it can prevent a minor league player from going to work in the off-season or from going to college.

(3) Not free to play for another team during the seven year period, though he can be dismissed at any time without any further compensation.

(4) As before, exposed to being sold during the seven year period to another organization without any share of the compensation acquired through the sale of his contract.

Whose advantage?—What is the future of the 1995 Minor League Uniform Contract? It has replaced the old Reserve Clause system, but major league teams like it. They don't have to send out a reserve letter by March 1 the following year. They control the player all year for seven years.

On the other side, major league players have a good deal and are not too interested in minor league players. The Players' Union represents only major league players. By and large, minor league players accept the situation as being a natural part of professional baseball. As a result, the 1995 Minor League Uniform Contract will likely be the standard contract for many years to come.

In 1947, I played for the Chicago Cubs farm team in Hutchinson, Kansas. Dick (Dickie) Kerr, who had been a “clean” hero for the Chicago White Sox in the 1919 Black Sox Scandal, was our manager.

Two weeks before the end of the season, I walked out on the front porch of the hotel and found Mrs. Kerr crying. After decades of honorable participation in both minor and major league baseball, and having been highly lauded for not having participated in the Black Sox scandal, her husband had been fired. She thought the Hutchinson players were responsible, but we liked Dick Kerr. We, the players, petitioned the head office in Chicago to retain him as our manager, but we were told in no uncertain terms that it was none of our business. Kerr was gone, and we all had a lesson in the inevitable brutality of baseball—a wonderful, enjoyable sport that is also very cruel.

The firing of Dick Kerr reinforced my determination to continue my education.

I think that's still the best path for today's minor leaguers. Most won't have big careers in the majors, and they should prepare for that while still enjoying the terrific experience of playing baseball for money with and against other excellent players.

They should understand that from a contractual point of view, the deck is stacked against them. As wonderful as the game itself is, and as much as they all love it, baseball to the organization is a business, not a sport. While minor leaguers play the very best they can and work hard to improve themselves, they should use professional baseball to their own advantage.

Notes:

1. "The Reserve Clause," Subcommittee on Monopoly Power, Committee on the Judiciary, House of Representatives, 82nd Congress, Testimony of "Bumps" Horning, August 7, 1951, pp. 366-371.

2. Ibid, p. 369.

3. Ibid, p. 369.

4. Ibid, p. 368.

5. Ibid, p. 366.

6. Ibid, p. 393.

7. Ibid, p. 393.

8. Ibid, p. 392.

9. Letter, August 21, 1998, Ben J. Hayes, General Counsel, National Association of Professional Baseball Leagues, Inc., to Dr. Ross C. Horning.

10. Minor League Uniform Player Contract, March, 1995, Section VI, Paragraph A., p. 1.

11. Ibid, Section VI, Paragraph B., p. 2.

12. Ibid, Section VI, Paragraph B., p. 2.

13. Ibid, Section XIX, Paragraph B, Line 4, p. 5.

Tilly Walker

Marky Billson

Greatest athlete from Washington County, Tennessee, in the last half of the twentieth century? Easy. Steve Spurrier. I give you two words of proof: Heisman Trophy.

Greatest athlete from Washington County in the first half of the twentieth century? A tougher read, but it's also just as clear cut. Clarence "Tilly" Walker, a Limestone native who was one of baseball's first big-time home run hitters.

Need proof? From 1920 through 1922, Tilly Walker, also nicknamed "Red" for his hair, would belt 77 home runs, second only to Babe Ruth in terms of major league home-run hitting supremacy. Earlier, the two players tied for the American League home run lead in 1918. In the second game of the 1916 World Series, when both Ruth and Walker starred for the Boston Red Sox, Tilly hit third in manager Bill Carrigan's lineup. Pitcher Ruth was still batting ninth.

But there is more to Walker than just starring in a bygone era of baseball. Walker is remembered by those who knew him as a colorful character who also served for fourteen years as a highway patrolman.

Although several old baseball magazines list Walker's place of birth as Denver, Colorado, and his date of birth as late as 1890, it is now accepted Clarence was born to W.A. and Florence Desler Walker on September 4, 1887, in Telford, south Washington County. The state of Tennessee keeps birth records

only as far back as 1900. His father, who like his son always stood straight and never lost his hair, worked as a blacksmith, and while you could call Tilly country, he wasn't a bumpkin. He became a telegraph operator, continuing that profession in the off-seasons of his early professional baseball career, and attended Washington College Academy in 1908.

It was at WCA that Walker became a baseball player. Legend has it the 5-foot-11 righthander simply tried out for the team, despite little ball playing experience, and proved to be a natural. From WCA he moved on to the University of Tennessee, then a spot on a Carolina Association team in Spartanburg, South Carolina, in 1910. Walker's rookie year was unspectacular, but upon returning to Spartanburg in 1911 his career rocketed. He hit .390 and stole 18 bases in just 35 games, and on June 11 was sold to the Washington Senators for $700.

Despite the presence of Hall of Fame pitcher Walter Johnson, the 1911 Washingtons were far from a great club, finishing seventh in an eight-team league with a 64-90 record. Walker was immediately inserted as the Nats' starting left fielder and hit a respectable .278 while getting good write-ups in the press. However, it did little to impress Washington owner Clark Griffith, and when the Senators contended for the American League pennant in '12, Walker sat on the bench. By August 25, he was released to Kansas City, then a top minor league team in the American Association, along with pitcher Hippo Vaughn, best known for no-hitting the New York Giants in 1917, while Fred Toney was no-hitting Vaughn's Chicago Cubs in the same game. The Nats received two forgettable players who failed to help them down the stretch.

Marky Billson, *28, is far too complex to define in a short listing, but is the last play-by-play announcer the Johnson City Cardinals had. He was introduced to baseball in 1979 growing up down the street from Willie Stargell's home in Pittsburgh. A SABR member since 1992, this is his first articles What do you want to say?*

Tilly Walker

Stardom—The talent Griffith failed to see shone in Missouri, where Walker hit over .300 in the parts of two seasons he played for the Blues. In the off-season of 1912, Walker's rights were bought by the St. Louis Browns, and he joined the last-place Browns in late August of 1913.

Walker achieved stardom in 1914. Under new manager Branch Rickey, Walker took the American League by storm. He led the circuit in hitting until July 26, peaking at .357 on June 10. Walker's feats earned him a feature article in September's *Baseball Magazine*. Written by F.C. Lane, the top baseball writer of the day, it was entitled "Why the Browns Are Winning." In actuality, the 1914 Browns were far from a great team,

but their fifth-place finish was the franchise's highest in six years and Tilly paced his club and ranked amongst the league leaders in batting average (. 298), home runs (6), triples (16), and runs batted in (78).

In 1915, Tilly was moved to center field to take advantage of his legendary throwing arm. In 1914-15, he racked up an incredible 57 outfield assists, tops in the American League. But he fell out of favor with the new Browns manager, Fielder Jones, who felt Walker wasn't a team player. Meanwhile, the world champion Boston Red Sox were involved in a salary dispute with Tris Speaker. With their eye on replacing Speaker in the outfield, Boston acquired Walker for $3,500 on April 8, 1916. Four days later, after Speaker won an exhibition game in Brooklyn with a ninth-inning homer off Rube Marquard, the Boxox dealt him to Cleveland in what was then considered the biggest deal in baseball history. The Indians sent Boston $55,000, $10,000 of which eventually went to Speaker, plus eventual 227-game winner Sad Sam Jones, and third baseman Freddie Thomas, who would start in the 1918 World Series. Walker's defensive prowess and bat made him a suitable replacement for Speaker in 1916, and for the only time in his major league career Tilly found himself on a championship caliber club.

Perhaps even more than home runs, Walker's throwing arm stands the test of time in baseball legend. In a throwing exhibition at a 1917 charity all-star game in Boston, Walker heaved a ball 384 ft. 6 inches, second only to Joe Jackson's peg of 396 ft. 8 inches. SABR's Cappy Gagnon in *The Baseball Research Journal* of 1995 ranked Walker's arm second only to Speaker's among 1900-1920 outfielders who played in over 1,000 games.

Tilly's batting numbers donn't stand out in 1916. He hit .266 with three homers. But the league hit only .249, and those three homers tied Babe Ruth's to lead the world champion Sox. In the World Series against Brooklyn, Walker played in three games, all Boston wins, platooning with lefty Chick Shorten in center. Tilly had two hits, scoring a run while knocking in another in Boston's 6-5 first-game win.

In the second game, Walker had a key impact in the Sox' 2-1, fourteen-inning win, still the longest game in Series history. After misplaying Hy Myers' fly ball into asn inside-the-park home run in the first inning, Walker threw out a runner at third in the next frame to prevent a run. This play was the springboard to Babe Ruth's most cherished record: his 29-2/3 consecutive shutout World Series innings, which lasted until Whitey Ford broke it in 1961. All in all, Walker hit .273 in the series, and Boston defeated Brooklyn four games to one to capture their second consecutive world championship.

To Philadelphia—After the 1917 season, Tilly was shipped with two other players to the Philadelphia Athletics in an trade for first baseman Stuffy McInnis, the last remnant of manager Connie Mack's famed "$100,000 Infield." It was the end of Walker's days of playing for pennant contenders.

Shibe Park was a tough park for an outfielder, with its deep power alleys and a center field fence that seemed to be located in Valley Forge. But Walker's defense continued to excel, and in a season shortened to 128 games due to World War I, he tied Ruth for the majors' home-run lead. He soon caught the fancy of Philadelphia fans with little else to cheer. Tales of Walker's batting grip and eyesight, along with his arm and bat, soon filled Philadelphia's newspapers. It was all they had to write about. The Mackmen were 36-104

in 1919, 48-106 in 1920, and 53-100 in 1921, their seventh consecutive last-place finish.

Playing second fiddle to Ruth, Walker's 10 homers ranked second in the league in 1919, and his 17 was good enough for third in '20. In 1921, perhaps his finest all-around season, he hit 23 homers (fourth in the AL), with a .304 batting average and 101 RBIs for the junior circuit's weakest scoring team. He led the American League in assists for a record fourth time in 1920, a record that would stand for forty-nine years.

In 1921, while the A's were in spring training at Lake Charles, Louisiana, Tilly met Fannella Pomeroy, whom he married on November 30. They had a son two daughters. Bill Walker served in the Air Force, and Virginia and Nella married and moved off to Bellaire, Texas.

Tilly's career high 37 dingers did not win him the American League home run crown in 1922, but it helped Philadelphia to avoid finishing in the cellar. Attendance increased by 80,000 and by the end of the season, Walker's 116 lifetime home runs placed him seventh on the major leagues' all-time list.

But in 1923, Mack surprisingly benched his slugging star. Newspaper accounts said the legendary manager thought Walker was losing his speed afield. Mack theorized the home run was going out of style, what with changes made at Shibe Park and the vast new Yankee Stadium. Tilly spent his last year in the majors on the bench of a sixth-place team, batting .275 with two home runs in 109 at-bats, many of them coming as a pinch-hitter.

In fact, Walker may have drunk himself out of the big leagues. Alcoholism ran in his family, and the image of the hard-drinking, hard-living ballplayer fit the code of the day. His drinking eventually cost him his marriage.

Back home—Walker's baseball career ended in the minor leagues with stops in Minneapolis, Baltimore, Toronto, Mobile, and Greenville, South Carolina. In the majors, he owned two imposing records: most career home runs by an American League right-handed hitter, and most years leading AL outfielders in assists (4). The first mark was short-lived, of course, but the assists record, which he shared with Speaker, lasted until 1969, when Carl Yastrzemski led the AL in that category for the fifth time.

Walker's last season as a player was 1928. He then returned home to Limestone, where he became something of a local legend and character.

"I knew Tilly Walker well," remembered Johnny Mitchell. Walker once got a tryout for Mitchell and two other local boys with the Appalachian League's Greeneville, Tennessee, franchise prior to World War II. "He was some kind of a man with kids." Walker was often seen playing catch with kids in the street, teaching them proper technique, and taking groups of kids to Greeneville to watch the Burley Cubs play. "If someone would stop him and tell him the kids' parents would have to be with them to attend the game, Tilly would tell the usher they all were his!"

"You should have seen his curve ball," remembered Lyle Broyles, who played catch with Walker during this period. "It could drop six or seven feet."

Mitchell also remembered a time when Walker learned of an orphaned family in the depression, and bought clothes and shoes for all five boys and a girl.

A skilled golfer and marksman, Walker was offered a job with the Daisy rifle company as a sharpshooter. "He was the best shot in the country, no question," said Mitchell. "He could put six pump shells in the air, and every time, six birds would come down."

In 1939 Walker joined the Appalachian League as an umpire. Clyde Kluttz, who would go on to a successful major-league career as a catcher, wagered that Tilly couldn't any longer throw a ball the length of the Johnson City field. "It took Tilly two throws from home plate," Mitchell says. "The first only went over third, and, boy, did the crowd let him have it. But the second went right over the fence in left field at Cardinal Park."

Walker went from umpiring to managing the Appy League's Erwin Mountaineers, a new team in 1940. Underfinanced, the team did not have much talent, but Walker remained adamant about his team's prospects. "I guarantee we will not finish in last," Walker told reporters prior to opening day.

In a way, he was right. Tilly was fired a month into the season with a 9-21 record, placing Erwin seventh in an eight-team league. The Mountaineers, under two subsequent managers, finished 27-88, hopelessly in last place, and dropped out of the league at the end of the season.

Walker was appointed to the Tennessee Highway Patrol in 1943, due to his celebrity and staunch Democratic party politics. He operated out of Kingsport, and was "well known on 11W and Hawkins County," according to retired trooper Leroy Watts. But instead of chasing moonshiners, Tilly mostly patrolled school zones. Legend has it he would sometimes arrest drunk drivers after he had taken a nip or two himself in his patrol car. Retired moonshine driver Cecil "Pappy" Correll even recalled being pulled over with a load of liquor by Walker in the '40s, with the ultimate result that the two of them shared a jug.

In 1954, Tilly was the subject of a story Pittsburgh Pirates' general manager Branch Rickey, Walker's old St. Louis manager, told his troops in an effort to get them to play harder. Describing Walker as a player with all the ability of Ty Cobb, but not the desire, Rickey told the Bucs of a game where Walker hit an apparent game-winning home run in a fenceless ball park on a barnstorming tour in Texas, only to be thrown out at third for the game's last out due to lack of hustle.

"The Mahatma" compared this feat to one involving Cobb. Cobb reached base against Rickey's team via a walk, stole second, then went to third on an overthrow. The throw from the centerfielder was on the mark and in time, but Cobb kicked it out of the third baseman's glove and scored. The centerfielder who had Cobb dead to rights? Tilly Walker.

Tilly served on the Highway Patrol until 1957 and passed away suddenly on September 21, 1959 at his brother Winni's home. Surprisingly, the press did not give much coverage to his passing, and the obituaries were filled with inaccuracies. But he was remembered well by those who knew him. More than a dozen highway patrolmen served as pallbearers at his funeral and burial in the Urbana Cemetery. Those who knew him still smile at the mention of his name.

Last year, the ne Tennessee Chapter of the Society for American Baseball Research adopted the name "Tilly Walker Chapter" in his honor.

Unlikely home run headlines

One August 24, 1904, Wee Willie Keeler hit two home runs in a game for the only time. The solo, inside-the-park rockets came off Barney Pelty of the visiting St. Louis Browns. Pelty lost the game, 9-1, to "Curveless" Al Orth. Keeler poked only 33 home runs in sixteen full seasons. Pelty (92-117), the "Yiddish Curver" gave up only 22 longballs in 1,918 innings over ten years (seven in this season), a pretty good ratio even for the deadball era. These were the only roundtrippers Keeler hit in 1904. Ex-Boston outfielder Patsy Dougherty, who hit 17 career homers in ten seasons, was the only other batter to thump Barney twice (both hit as a Highlander—one in the same contest as Keeler's duo). Willie, who got the first American League New York franchise hit and run scored in 1903, also hit Kid Carsey, Doc Parker, and Win Mercer for two homers each over the years. Of Pelty's 22 gopher balls, seven were were to Highlanders/Yankees and five (of his last eight) to Boston swatters.

—Dixie Tourangeau (homer information supplied by David Vincent and the SABR Home Run Log)

Red Barber said Hoyt could tell baseball stories better than any man who ever lived.

Waite Hoyt, Conveyor of Baseball Memories

Rob Langenderfer

In late 1941, when Burger Beer hired Waite Hoyt, a noted former pitcher for the New York Yankees, as the principal radio broadcaster for the games of the Cincinnati Reds, few ex-players had announced baseball games for major league clubs. Although Hoyt had voiced his desire to do so many times, he had been denied a chance to audition for an announcing job by three teams, including the Yankees. Ellen Frell, his niece, wrote an article about her uncle entitled "Waite Hoyt: The Broadcast Years in Cincinnati" for the summer, 1988 issue of *Queen City Heritage*. In the profile she revealed, "In the 1930s, a sports broadcast booth was not an acceptable arena for an ex-player...[The upper management of baseball teams and radio stations believed that former players] lacked the verbal ability to announce." Hoyt, however, was talented, articulate, and ultimately successful. He was the Reds' primary radio broadcaster from the 1942 through the 1965 seasons.

When Hoyt began his radio career as a play-by-play man in 1942, baseball broadcasting was still developing. Not every major league team had a radio announcer, and those that had one did not air every game. Some owners were fearful that people would stay home and listen in on the radio instead of coming out to the ball park. The only former players who had succeeded as announcers before Hoyt were Harry Heilmann and Dizzy Dean. The success of Dean and

Hoyt, especially, helped set the trend for other former players to take their places behind the microphone.

In the 1940s and the 1950s, radio broadcasts brought baseball regularly into the households of fans unable to attend games and strengthened the bonds they felt with their teams. Hoyt, with his famous rain-delay stories and unique personality, connected with his audience on a personal level. He conveyed the game at its most dramatic and its most humorous, helping to preserve the history of the game in the nation's collective memory.

Waite Hoyt was born in Brooklyn, New York, on September 9, 1899. His father, Addison Hoyt, was a vaudevillian. His mother, Louise, was a freelance writer. Both parents were very well educated and they passed an appreciation of culture down to their son. This, along with the familiarity with the entertainment industry he gained from observing his father's career, helped Hoyt make an easy transition to radio. Hoyt's father may have affected him in a more subtle fashion, however.

He remembered his father as a dreamer who was light-hearted, never truly grew up and always thought that he would make it big tomorrow. In looking back on his own career, Hoyt reflected that while he sacrificed his youth in pursuit of baseball, he, like his father, never truly grew up because he enjoyed the game so much.

Passionate about baseball and a superstar pitcher at Erasmus High School, Hoyt broke into the major leagues in 1918, but attained his greatest success for the great Yankee teams of the 1920s. He won 237 games in his career and was inducted into the Baseball

Rob Langenderfer *is a longtime fan of the Cincinnati Reds. He wrote a longer version of this article in 1998 in achieving his M.A. from the University of Cincinnati. His ideal dream would be to make a living doing baseball research and collaborating on or writing baseball books. He lives in Florence, Kentucky*

Hall of Fame in 1969.

After the Dodgers released Hoyt in 1938 to end his career, he wanted to go into radio. "Radio had long seemed the logical choice," he explained years later. "I would still be in the entertainment business and still be able to make it in the circles I had grown used to. And if I could work my way to the top, I would have an income comparable to what baseball had brought me."

He got his start in radio hosting a general three-hour radio program on WMCA in New York called "Grandstand and Bandstand" that introduced many celebrities from opera and theater coming from as far away as Europe. The tobacco company he worked for chose him for the job because it knew that he was a popular figure in New York. The broadcast provided him some valuable experience in radio.

Hoyt went on to host a fill-in show on WOR following the Red Barber-Al Helfer play-by-play of the Brooklyn Dodger games in 1940. The program's length was based on the needs of the station and the sponsor at any particular moment, so it varied from day to day. Hoyt was forced to perfect his ability to tell baseball stories in a casual, extemporaneous style, and to call them up from memory to fill the time available.

In 1941, Hoyt signed with the William Morris Agency, and it soon found him a potential baseball broadcasting job in far-off Cincinnati. In his audition before executives of the Burger Brewing Company, Hoyt told a compelling story about a little boy rather than calling an imaginary ballgame. He was chosen for the job, and he accepted tit at once. During his first season, two other stations were also broadcasting the Reds games. Burger soon acquired exclusive rights, and Hoyt became the voice of the Reds.

Hoyt's peers placed him among the best broadcasters baseball had to offer. Russ Hodges, the legendary radio announcer for the New York Giants, said this of Hoyt in the mid-1950s:

"Waite Hoyt is authoritative. When he gives a statement there is no doubt as to its accuracy. He gives a clean-cut description of the game, drawing a clear, positive picture for his listeners. His voice is really very fine. During the occasional lulls he dips into a vast

Waite Hoyt during the 1923 World Series

Transcendental Graphics

store of baseball knowledge. His stories of associations with such immortals as Babe Ruth, Lou Gehrig, John McGraw and countless others are a delight for Waite's fans. One thing I'm positive about is the fact that he is just as fine an announcer as he was as a player."

Ritter Collett, retired sports editor for the Dayton *Daily News*, noted that the secret to Hoyt's success was his ability to make the listeners feel as if he were broadcasting the game to each of them as individuals, simply telling his friends what was happening in the game. It was important to Hoyt that all these friends get accurate information, and he didn't hesitate to correct a colleague if an error was made on the air. In his unpublished autobiography, Hoyt tells a story about the time that his partner, Dick Nesbitt, noted on the air that Stan Musial was in a slump after going 0 for 3 in a game. Hoyt then commented quietly that Musial had been 14 for 15 prior to that day's game. Nesbitt simply said, "Oh."

In very limited circumstances, however, Hoyt would occasionally engage in some "cleverness" of his own. Until 1956, he did not travel with the Reds on their road trips. Instead he was fed information about the game via Western Union Morse code and teletype, and he called the game in the radio studio. Once when Cincinnati was playing in St. Louis, over the wire came the news that Cincinnati's Lonnie Frey had walked. The bases were loaded and a run would have tied the game. Hoyt reported it that way. But the ticker continued that that Frey had walked…out of the batter's box! Hoyt quickly ad-libbed that the umpire had said that the call of the pitch was strike 2 instead of ball 4. Hoyt also had to concoct a call of time by the umpires to get the runner back to third. He even had the Reds' manager, Bill McKechnie, go out to the field and argue the call. As it turned out, Frey eventually reached base and the run did score.

Hoyt revealed in his autobiography that big league officials condoned a slightly different type of chicanery in baseball broadcasts. He said that announcers were ordered to make three deliberate mistakes during a game so that pirate broadcasts could be identified.

Hoyt's long career as a major leaguer gave him the

background to include gritty, realistic details in his recreations from the 38th floor of the Carew Tower. A Western Union teletype machine, operated by Al Hunefield, delivered thin strips of paper that contained symbols like S1C (strike one called) and S2S (strike two swinging). Hoyt used his knowledge of pitching to make an educated guess about what kind of pitch had been thrown, and he tossed in other likely "action" as well.

While Hoyt tried to adhere to a distinctly positive tone in his broadcasts, he neither ignored bad news nor put on false airs of happiness when there was nothing to cheer about. Hoyt recalled in Curt Smith's book, *Voices of the Game*, that Reds president, Warren Giles, asked him in 1946 why he was not as enthusiastic as Cubs broadcaster Bert Wilson. Hoyt's response? "Why the shit *shouldn't* Bert Wilson cheer? They won the pennant last year, didn't they? They've got a great park to play in and they've got some stars, they win some games. But us…your top hitter's a lousy .267 or whatever the hell it is. Your top pitcher's won eight games. What is there to *cheer* about? Christ, if I cheered like Bert Wilson with the bums we've got, people would think I was blind or the village idiot…or maybe both."

But even when the team was losing, Hoyt focused on memorable players, such as Ewell Blackwell, Ted Kluszewski, Frank Robinson, and Vada Pinson. Hoyt commented to Smith, "I would have been a jerk to talk about our team; we were almost always hopelessly out of it. So I spun some stories and built up the stars worth talking about."

Hoyt was known for his fairness to the other team. In a 1976 interview for the Cincinnati *Enquirer*, Hoyt addressed the topic of how an announcer should call a game. "You have to be the local man; you're paid a handsome salary to be the booster of your team. But you also have to be a fair person. When you say the other team was terrible, yet your team won, what you're saying is that your team didn't have enough talent to win except against inferior players."

In contrast to Dean, the other former player who was a great success in the 1940s and early '50s, and who would launch into any story that came into his head at any time, Hoyt believed that a broadcaster should call a game as if he were describing it to a blind man. He never allowed a digression to interfere with his reporting of the action on the field. He would never interrupt the game with a story when a pitch was thrown. He used proper English, rather than Dean's more colorful language. Hoyt was famous for broadcasting in the past tense, something no other broadcaster has done. He explained that he did it because the action in the game had already occurred when he called it.

Cincinnati TV news anchor Nick Clooney commented that Hoyt was very sophisticated in his broadcasts and that every once in a while he would use a word that a listener would have to look up in a dictionary. Glenn Sample, Cincinnati's official scorer since 1978, commented on Hoyt's style and personality in and out of the booth: "He had a wonderful vocabulary. He was very intelligent. He was so wonderful to listen to…Waite Hoyt had a laugh that was unbelievable. He would laugh at himself." Curt Smith wrote of Hoyt, "He was the first to combine knowledge of the game (a player's strength) with literacy (a professional announcer's)."

There were far fewer books about baseball history available when Hoyt was broadcasting than today, and fans were interested in hearing anecdotes about players. In their 1988 history of Cincinnati baseball, *The Cincinnati Game*, Lonnie Wheeler and John Baskin wrote, "Hoyt's story-telling did justice to the vivid baseball life he led, and through the rain and some lean Cincinnati seasons, he became the unofficial historian of the game's pre-war years. [Red] Barber said that Hoyt could tell baseball stories better than any man who ever lived."

What made Hoyt so memorable for fans both serious and casual was his ability to tell stories about the great figures of baseball's past in a way that entertainingly conveyed the drama or the humor of the situation. His stories raised spirits, made the listener feel good about baseball and about the human race in general and gave them something to tell their sons and daughters to interest them in the game.

Hoyt's stories had a similar effect on fans who loved baseball history. His tales strengthened and solidified the place reserved for baseball stars such as Ruth and Gehrig in the hearts and minds of America. Having played alongside many of baseball's greatest figures in one of the game's most glorious periods. He served as a living promoter and transmitter of much of the game's magic.

Special thanks to Curt Smith, whose book, Voices of the Game, *proved invaluable in the writing of this article and who was always helpful with his insights and suggestions. Special thanks also to the staff of the Cincinnati Historical Society Library who aided the author in his examination of the Waite Hoyt Collection of papers and other materials. Donn Burrows, whose video,* Waite's World: The Life and Times of Waite Hoyt, *was of great assistance to the author, is also deserving of thanks for the generous amount of time he spent with the author discussing the subject. Greg Rhodes was of invaluable assistance in the completion of this piece both through his comments and through his book (co-authored with John Erardi),* Cincinnati's Crosley Field: The Illustrated History of a Classic Ballpark. Day By Day in Cincinnati Reds History, *by Lloyd Conner and John Snyder was also of assistance.*

The 1907 Pacific Coast Baseball Championship Series

Tom Larwin

When asked about the first professional baseball championship series for a San Diego team, most fans in San Diego will recite the 1984 World Series in which the National League Padres played the Detroit Tigers of the American League. Some might recall Padres Pacific Coast League series in 1937, 1964, or 1967.

But the first championship contest for San Diego was in November, 1907. Immediately following the 189-game PCL season a five-game series was organized between the 1907 champion Los Angeles Angels, or Looloos as they were also called, and the San Diego Pickwicks, champions of the Southern State League. As PCL champs, the Angels came into the series as the favorites.

Because of this series, it might be accurate to say that San Diego's first Hall of Famer was Walter Johnson. The Big Train pitched in three games for the Pickwicks.

The 1907 series was billed in San Diego as being played for the "Pacific Coast Championship." In addition to the Hall of Famer Johnson, 13 of the 25 players who took the field played for major league teams at one time or another. This was pretty high quality ball.

Language of the day—Researchers can never ignore the language used by writers of the day. Pitchers were invariably referred to as "twirlers." Home plate was referred to as the "pan." If you were designated for

pitching duty, then you were being prepared for "slab service." Fans were called "rooters." The ball was a "sphere." Pitchers with good curves were known for their "twisters" and "benders." Screwballs were "outshoots." The batters connected with "leather" and fielders got their "mitt on the horsehide," "hooked in" a pop fly, and "hauled in old gentleman Spalding." The pitcher's mound was the "box." Batters went "fishing" for tough-to-hit pitches, and hoped to "find" the opposing pitcher. Bases were "bags," or "sacks."

Nicknames included "Kitty," "Chief," "Pop," "Cap," "Dolly," Rube," "False Alarm," "Soldier," "Happy" and "Hap," and "The Big Train." And, how about helping your chances to win by putting the "kibosh on the champs!" Pop ups were characterized as being "dinky," grounders were "slow," and teams got a "trimming." Further, the "leather was propelled," the "sphere was slammed," batters having a bad day were "filled with wrath," strikeout victims would "wrench their vertebrae out of joint," inaccurate pitchers were "wild as a March hare," misplays were "rank errors," base hits were apt to be described as "pretty," and a fast fielder "scooted like a scared rabbit." When a team needed a hit, they hoped for a "bingle" and that their best hitter would be at bat "to pull off the stunt." A good umpire was a "first class handler of the indicator."

Home teams were expected to give their competitors "a hard rub." In addition to the "Looloos" and the "Pickwicks," PCL teams in 1906 and 1907 were called the "Commuters," "Beavers," "Seals," "Siwashes," and "Raisin Growers." They were often referred to as "aggregations" or, derisively, "griefers" and "bushers."

As all researchers know, this colorful language

Tom Larwin *is president of the San Diego Ted Williams SABR Chapter. He is a professional engineer and serves as general manager of the San Diego Transit Development Board.*

Cartoon by Gale from Los Angeles Times, *November 3, 1907.*

makes reading about the events great fun.

Background—On Sunday, November 3, 1907, the Los Angeles Angels completed their season as champions of the Pacific Coast League with a record of 115 wins and 74 losses—a total of 189 games played. The Angels won the four-team Pacific Coast League by 13 games over San Francisco:

	W	L	Pct.	GB
Los Angeles Angels	115	74	.608	—
San Francisco Seals	104	99	.515	13
Oakland Commuters	97	101	.489	22.5
Portland Beavers	72	114	.388	41.5

A depressed but realistic San Francisco writer for *The Sporting News*, Will J. Boradori, wrote on October 24 that Los Angeles would win the pennant. "Los Angeles will carry away the honors because the Angel City is represented by the best team...Under the capable management of Captain Frank Dillon, the Looloos have played ball every inch of the way....All credit is due Dillon, for he knows the game in all its finer points and instills a great deal of his knowledge and spirit into his players with the result that they were continually playing 'inside' base ball, oftentimes to the great discomfiture of their opponents."

Boradori went on to note that "...the Angel team is composed of a fast aggregation of ball players and I dare say would give the majority of teams in the major leagues a hard rub.

"...behind the plate, always working for success, are Bobby Eagar and 'Happy' Hogan...the club's star twirlers are 'Dolly' Gray who has won more games than any other pitcher in the league, and 'Bill' Burns, who has been drafted by Washington...Hosp, Nagle, Randolph and Bergeman have helped materially also in slab service...at first base, Dillon is in a class by himself...Bernard, at second, is of big league caliber...Bert Delmas, at short, is a San Francisco lad, who has played such wonderful ball this season that Boston bought his release...Jud Smith played third up to a month or six weeks ago when he broke his collarbone, his place being taken by 'Kitty' Brashear, one of the best in the league...the outfield is composed of Carlisle, Ellis and Cravath. The former and latter have already been sold to major league teams and both should easily make good, for they are fast fielders and great hitters."

The November 2 issue of *The Sporting Life* also had an article that complimented the leadership of player-manager Dillon, listing all of the injuries he'd had to deal with over the course of the season: a broken shoulder bone, malaria, a bum ankle and tonsillitis, two bad hands, a broken finger, sick in bed for two weeks, a sprained ankle, split hand, stomach trouble, general debility, and a bad knee.

"The team has played pitchers in the outfield, infielders in the outfield, outfielders in the infield and all sorts of lineups imaginable, on very few occasions being able to present all players in their proper positions."

Anticipation—San Diego had a population of about

17,700 in 1900. By 1910 the population had more than doubled to 39,578. The area was beginning to boom.

The Pickwick's ballpark for the series was called "Athletic Park" or "Palmer Park" (operated by Palmer Bros., lessees), which was located in a block near 26th and Main Streets, just southeast of downtown and about a mile and a half from where the new ballpark is to open in 2002. This general site was a primary venue for San Diego baseball from 1887 through the first two decades of the 1900s. In 1907, fans got to the park on the Logan Avenue streetcar line.[1, 2]

The Angels came to town by train on Wednesday, November 6. They brought most of their starting nine, with several notable exceptions: Gavvy Cravath, Bert Delmas, and Jud Smith.

In the Thursday, November 7, 1907 edition of the San Diego *Union* the series was advertised as follows:

BASE BALL
CHAMPIONSHIP SERIES
NOV. 7, 8, 9, 10—TWO GAMES SUNDAY
ADMISSION 25¢, GRANDSTAND 25¢
LOS ANGELES LEAGUE TEAM,
CHAMPIONS OF PACIFIC COAST,
VS. SAN DIEGO PICKWICKS,
CHAMPIONS SOUTHERN STATE LEAGUE
THURSDAY AND FRIDAY GAMES AT 3 P.M.
SATURDAY AND SUNDAY AFTERNOONS AT 2:30
AND SUNDAY MORNING GAME AT 10.
TAKE LOGAN AVENUE CAR TO 26TH AND
MAIN STREETS.

Reprinted by Permission.

OH, LOOK WHO'S HERE!

SAN DIEGO FAN—*"Well, old man, here's another victim. You have won one game, now you will have to go some to win the rest."*

Cartoon by S. R. Hofflund from San Diego Union, *November 8, 1907.*

Earlier in the week the Los Angeles *Daily Times* also prepared its readers for the series with a front page sports section cartoon in its Sunday, November 3, 1907 edition that was entitled BARNSTORMING! (see Figure 2). The barn in this case was San Diego. In its Thursday, November 7 edition the *Times* (by direct wire to the Times) had an article that touted the upcoming series under the headline, SAN DIEGO BASEBALL—LOS ANGELES COAST CHAMPIONS WILL PLAY TODAY IN FIRST GAME OF FIVE WITH GRIEFERS. The article noted that "Interest in the series between the Looloos and Pickwicks is very great and local sports are betting on Palmer's[3] aggregation to win the series, as the team is strong."

The *Union's* November 7 edition headlined: COAST CHAMPIONSHIP HANGS IN BALANCE. The article continued that it will "...prove a fight worth going miles to see. The possibility of getting the two teams together is something that has been discussed for weeks...the 'rooters' of this city have for some time been of the opinion that they had a team which could take the measure of the Angels." The paper added fuel to the mix by suggesting that the Pickwicks were not being taken seriously by the Angels.

The mound staffs for the two teams included two leading pitchers at the time: Dolly Gray for the Angels and Walter Johnson for the Pickwicks. Gray was a southpaw considered by many as the best pitcher in the Coast League. Johnson was already being touted as someone who could toss the "sphere over the pan with the speed of a bullet and in addition to this he has all the twisters that a first class twirler could desire."

Game 1: November 7
San Diego 1, Los Angeles 0
San Diego Leads Series 1-0

Fans in attendance for the first game of the series watched a pitching duel. Headlines told the story. *The Sporting News*, November 21:

SUPERB PITCHING.
CANTILLON'S[4] TWIRLERS MEET ON PACIFIC COAST. JOHNSON WON FROM SOUTHPAW BURNS, BUT LATTER'S DEFEAT WAS DUE TO POOR SUPPORT.

The Los Angeles *Daily Times*, November 8:

WHITEWASHED
JOHNSON FANS SIXTEEN MEN.
LOOLOOS UNABLE TO HIT YOUNG BIG LEAGUE PITCHER. HOSP'S ERRORS AT SHORT THROW AWAY THE GAME. NEITHER BERNARD, CRAVATH NOR DELMAS IN LINE-UP.

The San Diego *Union*, November 8:
PICKWICKS WIN FIRST GAME; SCORE 1 TO 0 JOHNSON FANS 16 MEN; STAR PLAYS ARE FEATURES

COAST LEAGUE CHAMPIONS ARE PUT DOWN TO DEFEAT BY SAN DIEGO TEAM— DILLON GOES INTO TRANCE OVER RESULT

The front page of the *Union's* sports page on November 8 had a cartoon that mocked Los Angeles with the banner OH, LOOK WHO'S HERE! (see Figure 3). Further, the lead article began "Poor old Los Angeles! To think of the Pacific Coast League champions, the pride of every Angel city rooter, going through an entire season making monkeys of all the nines they went against, and then, coming to San Diego to receive the trimming they have so often handed out to their adversaries. If there was ever a surprised bunch of champions it was yesterday afternoon. After the last man had gone out in the last inning it took them nearly five minutes to recover from the catastrophe. Captain Dillon was so surprised he could hardly speak, and his faithful minions did not have the heart to bring him out of his trance."

As might be expected, the *Times* took a different slant, and emphasized the fact that three Angels players were missing from action. It also noted the importance of Johnson: "The Looloos were unable today to find Johnson, the Anaheim wonder..." The writer gave credit to both teams for playing "first-class ball" and declared that the game was "worthy of a better crowd than turned out." According to the *Times*, the attendance was a mere 300.

The Sporting News on November 21, and *The Sporting Life* on November 23, also covered Game 1.[5] They noted that Johnson, a Washington rookie, went up against Burns, who had been drafted by Washington.

Johnson was certainly the star of the game. According to the *Union* "Johnson certainly had the kibosh on the champs. Every man on the team, with the exception of Captain Dillon, fanned at some time during the game. And dinky pop-ups or slow grounders were the best that the leader of the gang could do. Sixteen Angels had their wings singed by the Pickwick twirler, to the enthusiastic delight of the loyal San Diego crowd."

Dillon had apparently passed on an opportunity to sign Johnson for the Angels in 1906.[6] San Diego fans were reportedly shouting during the game, "There's the boy you turned down last season."

Only five batters reached base against Johnson: three hits, one walk, and one a base on error. Burns also had a good game. He held the Pickwicks to five hits and one walk, but was hurt by five errors, three by Franz Hosp, a pitcher filling in at short for Delmas.

The Pickwicks scored their winning run in the seventh inning. First baseman Langdon reached second on a boot and bad throw by Hosp. Hanrahan sacrificed him to third for one out. Johnson then hit a long fly to Hogan in right to score Langdon.

Meyers went 3-for-4 for the home team and was

robbed by a good play by Hosp for his only out of the day. Umentioned in the press was the fact that the umpire for the game was Pickwick player Karns. Later in the series he would become more prominent.

LA	0 0 0	0 0 0	0 0 0		0	3	5
SD	0 0 0	0 0 0	1 0 x		1	5	1

WP - Johnson LP - Burns
Time of game: 1:28

Game 2: November 8, 1907
Los Angeles 5, San Diego 2
Series Tied 1-1

The second game of the series had the Angels's star pitcher, "Dolly" Gray going up against "Soldier" Carson. The *Union* reported that Carson threw with some speed, and he was later to have a short stint in the major leagues, but at the time had little or no professional experience. The headlines again told the story from the differing perspectives of the two towns. The San Diego *Union,* November 9:

LOOLOOS WIN GAME FROM CARSON, 5 TO 2
PICKWICKS PUT UP POOR SUPPORT AND VISITORS HIT HARD

The Los Angeles *Daily Times,* November 9:

SAME OLD STORY
BUSHERS ARE EASY VICTIMS
DOLLY GRAY HAS NO TROUBLE IN WINNING GAME.
TIMELY HITTING ACCOUNTS FOR CHAMPIONS RUNS.
PITCHER KARNS FAILS AS AN UMPIRE.

San Diego had its hopes pinned to Carson, and he was not rapped hard according to the *Union.* But he was wild as a March hare. His wildness combined with five errors behind him did the Pickwicks in. The Angels had eight hits, three walks, and a hit batsman.

Gray pitched a fine game, allowing six hits. He shut down the home team for eight innings, but then he allowed "...one of those old-time rallies for which the Pickwicks are famous...." The Pickwicks lost the services of Chief Meyers when he took one of Carson's outshoots on a fingertip, forcing him to abandon his catching duties and move to first base for the remainder of the game.

The *Times* had a different slant. The Pickwicks scored their two runs "...when Gray eased up," and "the Looloos played rings around the San Diegans, who showed up in true busher form when Johnson was on the bench."

As for the umpiring, all the *Times* would say was that "Karns proved an unsatisfactory umpire."

LA	0 1 1	1 0 0	1 0 1	5	8	0
SD	0 0 0	0 0 0	0 0 2	2	6	5

WP - Gray LP - Carson
Time of game: 1:42

Game 3: November 9
Los Angeles 8, San Diego 4 (12 innings)
Los Angeles Leads Series 2-1

Most of the story line on Game 3 was about the umpiring: "after two days of agonizing decisions," wrote the *Union,* "nine out of ten which favored the Los Angeles team...Umpire Karns left the grounds...there is not the slightest doubt that Karns is one of the most unpopular umpires who ever handled an indicator on a San Diego diamond. And there is every reason why this should be so. There has been hardly a time during the present series when his decisions did not seem to favor the visitors."

In the ninth inning, Dillon stole second base and the ball rolled about ten feet away. Dillon made a motion toward third base, and Umpire Karns gave him the bag on a call of fielder's interference. This, according to the *Union,* "...aroused a strenuous protest, not only from Pickwick players, but from fans." Too much to take apparently, because Karns left the field and was replaced by one Clements. The *Union* noted that "he showed an inclination to be governed almost entirely by the wishes of the Los Angeles players and as a result, allowed the game to continue when it should have been called on account of darkness."

The Angels scored four times in the twelfth. The *Union* summed up San Diego feeling: "the Angels won the game, but it was with the aid of the umpires and the shades of evening."

LA	0 1 0	0 2 0	1 0 0	0 0 4	8	15	3
SD	0 1 0	0 0 0	2 1 0	0 0 0	4	6	10

WP - Nagle LP - Bergeman
Time of game: 2:12

Game 4: November 10
San Diego 4, Los Angeles 3
Series Tied 2-2

Game 4 was the morning half of a twin bill on the fourth and final day of the series. Karns, who had umpired the first three games, was on the mound for the Pickwicks. Franz Hosp toed the slab for the Angels.

The Pickwicks won with a four-run fifth tht included no hits. Walks, errors, and other misplays aided the home team. The fourth and decisive run scored on a steal of home while the Angels's players were arguing a call.

Karns had given up six hits and three runs for the Pickwicks with one out in the top of the sixth when he hurt his hand trying to scoop up a bouncer. Walter Johnson relieved with the bases loaded, one man out, and Rosy Carlisle up. Johnson got out of the jam when Carlisle bunted into a double play. He held the Angels scoreless for the next three innings, allowing only one hit and striking out three to pick up the save.

After three games of alleged bad umpiring, this game's new umpire, Frary, "gave eminent satisfaction to the crowd" according to the *Union*. "He clearly showed that he knew his business. His decisions are given in firm and business-like manner that stamps him first-class handler of the indicator."

Oh, and how times have changed when it comes to umpire-player relationships! Umpire Frary "...is not the kind of an umpire who will submit to the abuse of players. This was demonstrated in the morning game yesterday when Nagle called him a name. Umpire Frary responded in a manner entirely unexpected, at least by 'Judge' Nagle. Mr. Frary promptly put his good right fist to the aforesaid 'judge's' jaw, and the latter lost no time in reaching his playing position. During the balance of the game he kept as far away as possible from the umpire."

LA	0	0	0		1	0	2		0	0	0	3	7	4
SD	0	0	0		0	4	0		0	0	x	4	3	4

WP - Karns LP - Hosp Save - Johnson
Time of game: 1:52

Game 5: November 10
Los Angeles 9, San Diego 2
Los Angeles Wins Series 3-2

The largest crowd, according to the *Union,* "that has ever passed through the gates of Athletic Park" was on hand for the Sunday afternoon game. By the time of the second game's start the "crowd had spread out on either side of the field and threatened to encroach upon the playing territory."

This deciding game of the series was to be a match between the teams's two best pitchers, Dolly Gray and Walter Johnson. The *Union* noted that "with Johnson in his usual form the Pickwicks should have won the game." But Johnson pitched a sore-armed seven innings, allowing 11 hits (nine over the last four innings), and striking out five. The paper reported that his "sore arm prevented his doing any more than lobbing the ball over the pan after the third inning."

Then there was poor "False Alarm" Shaw! He not only made six errors for the Pickwicks in the series but "unfortunately it seemed as though every time the Pickwicks would get men on second and third bases it was "False Alarm" Shaw who had to come to bat." His base-running was equally dangerous. In Game 5, Shaw reached second with Hartley on third and no outs. Shaw tried to advance on a ground ball, while Hartley held at third. "This compelled Hartley to once more leave the sack and when it was all over Shaw had gained his point—Hartley was out and he was on third. This was as far as he got, however."

The game was the poorest of the five played. Los Angeles got 15 "bingles" while San Diego had ten. But it was the poor play that did the Pickwicks in according to the *Union*: "The Pickwicks put up a most listless and stupid game in the field...many of the misplays do not show in the error column. If they did, two rows of figures would probably be necessary in order to get them all in."

LA	1	0	0		2	1	0		3	1	1	9	15	2
SD	0	0	0		0	0	0		0	2	0	2	10	1

WP - Gray LP - Johnson
Time of game: 1:43

Los Angeles clinched the 1907 "championship of the Pacific Coast," though the San Diego Pickwicks, led by Walter Johnson and Chief Meyers made it close. San Diego's first crack at a professional baseball championship went down to defeat. Fans in San Diego would have to wait until 1936 before getting a team in the Pacific Coast League, and 1969 before the Padres became members of the National League.

Rosters
Los Angeles Angels

Curt Bernard, 2B. Primarily a second baseman for the Angels, he played 94 games there in 1907, and 47 in the outfield, hitting .271 from the left side in 111 games. Played for New York NL, 1900-01 hitting .238 in 43 games. Missed the first two games of the series and still ended up tied with most hits (6) and a batting average of .375.

"Kitty" Brashear, 3B. Played in 65 games at third and 95 at second. Hit .270 in 159 games. Played for St. Louis NL in 1902 hitting .276 in 110 games. Six for 22 in the series, an average of .273.

William "Sleepy Bill" Burns, P. The lefty won 23 and lost 16 in 1907. After season, drafted by Washington and eventually pitched for five major league teams, 1908-1912 (30-52). Living in Cincinnati in 1919, Burns was an agent between players and gambling interests during the Black Sox scandal, and apparently lost money.[7] Pitched in and lost one game in the series—Johnson's shutout. He gave up only five hits.

Walter 'Rosy' Carlisle, LF. Switch hitting outfielder batted .259 in 179 games in 1907. Led PCL with 14 home runs. Major league career consisted of three games for Boston AL in 1908, going 1-for-10. Went 3-for-19 in series and struck out nine times. However, his three hits were all triples.

Frank "Pop" Dillon, 1B. Manager, also known as "Cap," batted from the left side. Born at Normal, Illinois in 1873 and began his baseball career with Omaha in 1894. From there he played with Dubuque (1895), Rockford (1896), Reading (1897), Buffalo (1899), Pittsburgh NL (1899-1900), Detroit AL (1901-02), Baltimore AL (1902), Brooklyn NL (1904), and Los Angeles (1903-15). Played 181 games in 1907, batting .304, good for third place in the league. On April 25, 1901 he doubled home the winning run to cap a 10-run bottom of the ninth for a 14-13 comeback victory in Detroit's initial game at their new Bennett Park.[8] Over his major league career he batted .252 in 312 games. According to Lange, Pop was "...not only an A-1 base player in his position, but was also a great general on the baseball field. A fine hitter and fielder, having all the earmarks of a real baseball player. He was respected by the fans and players alike, a model for a young player to copy."[9] Dillon led all players in the series with four runs scored and four stolen bases.

Ted Easterly, C. Lefty hitter batted .225 in 11 games with the Angels. He played for San Diego at one time and he was taunted as "traitor" in game one, according to the *Union* and reportedly sent fans into "paroxysms of joy" when he struck out against Johnson with a runner on base. Later in that same game Easterly came to bat still "some sore" from striking out earlier. He was determined to "...slam the sphere somewhere. Three times he tore up the earth within a radius of six feet of the pan, and as often he missed the leather by from one to six inches. When he went back to the bench for the second time during the game Easterly was so filled with wrath he could have bitten a tenpenny nail in two." Easterly played in the majors for Cleveland and Chicago AL 1909-1913, hitting .300 over 704 games. He hit .286 in the series and led both teams with five runs batted in.

George William 'Rube' Ellis, CF. Batted and threw from the left side. Hit .239 in 171 in 1907. With St. Louis NL, 1909-12. Hit .260 in 555 major league games. Batted .250 in the series.

William "Dolly" Gray, P. The lefty went 32-14 in 1907, and led the league in win percentage and wins. Pitched in the majors for Washington AL, going 15-51, 1909-11, with a 3.52 ERA and 46 complete games. Nickname came from "goodbye Dolly Gray" a popular Spanish-American War ballad. Gray also was noted for losing a one-hitter when, after a two-out error, he walked seven straight batters on 3-2 counts.[10] Gray was 2-0 for the series allowing only four runs in his two games. He also hit the only home run in the series.

Wallace Lewis "Happy Hogan" Bray, C. Real name Wallace Bray, but as ballplayer known as "Hap" or "Happy" Hogan. Born in Santa Clara in 1876, he began his baseball career with Sacramento in 1902-03. After that stint he played with Tacoma (1904-05), Fresno (1906), Los Angeles (1907-08), and Vernon (1909-11). Managed Vernon until his death in 1914. A catcher and outfielder, he caught in 109 games and hit .168 for the season. Lange noted that Hogan was "...an enthusiastic and happy baseball player, giving all there was in him to make his career a success. He was well liked by the fans and players, and a general on the baseball field...always ready to pull off some play that was not expected."[11] He was 6-for-21 in the series, tying for the most hits.

Franzel 'Franz' Hosp, SS, P. Batted only .118 in 36 games for the Angels, ten of them at shortstop. However, he went 12-7 as a pitcher. Hosp at one time played for the Pickwicks. He was 5-for-19 for the series and lost Game 4.

Walter "Judge" Nagle, 2B, SS, P. Hit .249 in 69 games, 11 at shortstop, five at second base, and 11 in the outfield. Also had a 16-14 record as a pitcher. Pitched for Pittsburgh NL and Boston AL during 1913 (13 games, 5-3).Won the extra-inning Game 3, going all twelve innings and allowing six hits and four runs. In the series, he also played second base until Bernard showed up and shortstop when Hosp was on the mound.

San Diego Pickwicks

Fred Bergeman, CF, P. Pitched for the Angels during the 1907 season, going 6-5 and hitting .135. Pitched in two series games and gave up nineteen hits over fourteen innings.

Alex "Soldier" Carson, P. Appeared for the Portland PCL team in 1909 and pitched ten hitless innings in a game. Pitched for Chicago NL in 1910 going 0-0 in two games. He took the loss in series Game 2, but struck out nine.

Jack Clynes, LF. Played in the Northwest League in 1907. In a November 28, 1907 game report, he was said to have a "wing" that was the envy of his teammates. He had a good series, going 6-for-19 with three doubles.

Tom Downey, 2B. Played in majors 1909-1915 (Cincinnati, Philadelphia NL, Chicago NL, Buffalo FL) with a career batting average of .240 in 651 games. Batted .217 for the series.

Hanrahan, RF. Hanrahan made an outstanding play in game one. In its November 8 edition the *Union* described it as follows: "...Brashear poked a short fly out midway between center and right and about 40 feet back of second base. As soon as the ball was hit Hanrahan started for it. Over the ground he scooted, like a scared rabbit, but it was safe to say, that there was not a person on the grounds who thought the Pickwick right fielder would get his mitt on the horsehide. But he did. And it was only after the hardest of a run that he managed to get close enough to the ball to extend his arms to their fullest capacity and haul in old gentleman Spalding." Hanrahan went 1-for-10 in the series. No other record could be found for him.[12]

Jack Hartley, CF. A local star as early as 1896; he started out as a southpaw pitcher but became an outfielder because of his hitting ability. Batted 2-for-16 in series.

Walter "The Big Train" Johnson, P. The outstanding player of the series, even with the Game 5 loss. Original Hall of Fame inductee. Just turned twenty, he already had a year in the majors with Washington (5-9). After 1907 season he went on to win 411 more major league games through 1927. A fair hitter, with .237 lifetime average. Drove in the winning and only run in Game 1. This 1-0 victory would be common for Johnson in his career. He had 38 such wins in the majors, an all-time record.[13]

Karns, P. Another player not identified by a first name. Pitched and won Game 4. Umpired in games 1-3 with some notoriety.

Langdon, 1B, C. No first name cited in any of the coverage. For the series he had one hit in 17 at-bats.

Austin "Duke" LeBrandt, C. In 1907 he played with Omaha of the Western League. Filled in at catcher when Meyers injured finger in Game 2. The *Union* on November 9, 1907 reported that LeBrandt was "a red-hot favorite with San Diego fans and will be given a warm welcome when he appears in a Pickwick uniform." He ended the series going 2-for-12 with no RBIs.

Joseph "Cannibal Joe" McCarty, SS. Another mystery player we don't know much about, other than he lived at 1099 9th Avenue while in San Diego. McCarty went 3-for-21 in the series.

John Tortes "Chief" Meyers, C, 1B, CF. Also called 'Jack,' this college man from Dartmouth played for New York, Brooklyn, and Boston NL, 1909-1917. Appeared in 992 major league games and batted .291. Hit .290 in four World Series. Went 6-for-9 in this series. Unfortunately for the Pickwicks, he hurt his finger in Game 2 and missed most of two games.

Issac "Ike" Rockenfield, RF. The *Union* referred to Rockenfield as "Rockenfielder." Clear, though, that "Rockenfield" is correct. The *Times* on November 11, 1907 reported that Rockenfield played with St. Louis NL in 1907. According to the *Baseball Encyclopedia* he played with St. Louis AL, 1905-1906, hitting .221 over 122 games. Lived in San Diego until his death in 1927. Went 1-for-8 in the series.

"Big Leaguer" or "False Alarm" or "Hunky" Shaw, 3B. All references to Shaw use a nickname, so his first name remains uncertain. Two different Al Shaws played in the majors during this era. One was primarily a catcher and the other an outfielder, but both saw limited duty at third. Apparently not well thought of judging by the newspaper accounts of the series. In Game 4 the *Union* noted that he "made his usual fumble." For the series he made six errors, along with seven putouts and seven assists. He wasn't much better on offense, going 2-for-15.

OTHER PARTICIPANTS

The umpires included **Karns** for Games 1-3 (until the ninth, when he left the field in a huff), **Clements**, who finished Game 3, and **Ralph Frary** who took over for Games 4 and 5. Frary, who caught for Nashville, came to San Diego that weekend to play with the Ralstons club after the close of the Southern State League. He had considerable experience as an umpire in the Northwest League (*Union,* November 11, 1907). There was a Frank P. Frary who was Mayor of San Diego from 1901-05, but there is no evidence that the two Frarys were related.

William H. Palmer was manager of the Pickwicks. A councilman, 1905-09, and head of Palmer Bros. house moving company. Brother Scott Palmer was the manager of the Pickwick Theatre at 1029 4th.

Sources:

Baseball Encyclopedia, 9th Edition, Macmillan Publishing Co., 1993.

Brandes, Ray, and Bill Swank, *The Pacific Coast League Padres, Lane Field: The Early Years, 1936-1946,* Published by the San Diego Padres and the San Diego Baseball Historical Society, Vol. I, 1997.

Dodge, Richard V., *Rails of the Silver Gate,* Golden West Books, September 1960.

Lange, Fred W., *History of Baseball in California and Pacific Coast Leagues, 1847-1938,* 1938.

Los Angeles Daily Times, November 3, 7-9, 11, 1907.

San Diego Union, November-December, 1907.

Shatzkin, Mike, ed., *The Ballplayers,* William Morrow and Co., 1990.

The Sporting Life, November 2, 1907, November 16, 1907, and November 23, 1907.

The Sporting News, October 24, 1907, October 31, 1907, November 21, 1907, and December 12, 1907.

Thomas, Henry W., *Walter Johnson, Baseball's Big Train*, Farragut Publishing Co., 1995.

Vetter, Nick, ed., *Low and Inside,* special June 1993 edition.

Notes:

1. Nick Vetter, ed., *Low and Inside,* special June 1993 edition.

2. Ray Brandes and Bill Swank, *The Pacific Coast League Padres, Lane Field: The Early Years, 1936-1946,* Volume I, 1997.

3. This was a reference to Will Palmer who was team manager; also of interest, the *Union's* advertisement for the game noted "Athletic Park, Palmer Bros., Lessees."

4. This refers to Joe Cantillon who was manager of Johnson's Washington A.L. team in 1907.

5. However, *The Sporting News* article reported the game to have been played on November 13 instead of the actual date, November 7.

6. Henry W. Thomas, *Walter Johnson, Baseball's Big Train,* 1995, pp. 15, 16, 24.

7. Mike Shatzkin, ed., *The Ballplayers,* 1990.

8. Thomas, p.171.

9. Fred W. Lange, *History of Baseball in California and Pacific Coast Leagues, 1847-1938,* 1938, p.127.

10. Shatzkin.

11. Lange, p.127.

12. San Diego *Union,* March 22, 1936.

13. Shatzkin.

San Diego Pickwicks, 1907. Left to right. Walter Johnson, Karns, Chief Meyers, Jack Clynes, Alex "Soldier" Carson, Manager Will Palmer, Fred Bergeman, Jack Hartley, Langdon, "False Alarm" Shaw, Joseph "Cannibal Joe" McCarty, Tom Downey, Hanrahan. Photo by H. R. Fitch, San Diego Union, November 10, 1907. Copyright, 1907, San Diego Union, and San Diego Historical Society, Reprinted by permission.

Player Summary Statistics

Name	Pos.	AB	R	H	2B	3B	HR	RBI	Sac.	SO	W	HBP	SB	BA	SA	OBA
Los Angeles																
Nagle	2B, P,SS	17	2	3	0	0	0	1	2	4	0	0	0	0.176	0.176	0.158
Bernard	2B	16	2	6	0	1	0	1	0	1	1	0	2	0.375	0.500	0.412
Carlisle	LF	19	3	3	0	3	0	1	0	9	4	2	1	0.158	0.474	0.360
Dillon	1B	21	4	5	0	0	0	2	0	1	3	0	4	0.238	0.238	0.333
Brashear	3B	22	3	6	1	0	0	2	0	8	1	0	2	0.273	0.318	0.304
Ellis	CF	20	2	5	0	1	0	2	1	2	1	0	1	0.250	0.350	0.273
Easterly	C	21	3	6	2	0	0	5	1	3	0	0	0	0.286	0.381	0.273
Hosp	SS, P	19	2	5	0	1	0	4	0	3	1	1	2	0.263	0.368	0.333
Hogan	RF	21	0	6	0	0	0	2	0	4	0	0	1	0.286	0.286	0.286
Burns	P	3	0	0	0	0	0	0	0	3	0	0	0	0.000	0.000	0.000
Gray	P	6	4	3	1	0	1	1	1	1	1	0	0	0.500	1.167	0.500
Totals		**185**	**25**	**48**	**4**	**6**	**1**	**21**	**5**	**39**	**12**	**3**	**13**	**0.259**	**0.362**	**0.307**
Pickwicks																
Downey	2B	23	1	5	1	0	0	0	0	2	0	0	1	0.217	0.261	0.217
McCarty	SS	21	0	3	0	0	0	0	0	1	1	0	0	0.143	0.143	0.182
Clynes	LF	19	2	6	3	1	0	1	0	3	1	2	0	0.316	0.579	0.409
Meyers	C, 1B, CF	9	1	6	2	0	0	2	0	0	1	0	0	0.667	0.889	0.700
Shaw	3B	15	3	2	1	0	0	0	0	0	2	3	1	0.133	0.200	0.350
Hartley	CF	16	0	2	0	0	0	2	0	1	1	1	0	0.125	0.125	0.222
Langdon	1B, C	17	3	1	0	0	0	1	0	1	2	0	0	0.059	0.059	0.158
Hanrahan	RF, PH	10	0	1	1	0	0	2	1	2	1	1	0	0.100	0.200	0.231
Johnson	P	6	0	0	0	0	0	1	0	1	0	0	0	0.000	0.000	0.000
Carson	P	4	0	0	0	0	0	0	0	2	0	0	0	0.000	0.000	0.000
Bergeman	CF, P, PH	8	0	1	0	0	0	0	0	1	1	0	0	0.125	0.125	0.222
LeBrandt	C	12	2	2	0	0	0	0	0	0	0	0	0	0.167	0.167	0.167
Rockenfield	RF, PH	8	0	1	0	0	0	0	0	4	0	0	0	0.125	0.125	0.125
Karns	P	2	1	0	0	0	0	0	0	0	0	0	0	0.000	0.000	0.000
Totals		**170**	**13**	**30**	**8**	**1**	**0**	**9**	**1**	**18**	**10**	**7**	**2**	**0.176**	**0.235**	**0.250**

Name	W-L	G	IP	R	H	SO	W	HB	ERA	K/IP
Los Angeles										
Burns	0-1	1	8	1	5	0	1	0	1.13	0.00
Gray	2-0	2	18	4	16	10	5	4	2.00	0.56
Nagle	1-0	1	12	4	6	4	2	2	3.00	0.33
Hosp	0-1	1	8	4	3	4	2	1	4.50	0.50
Totals	**3-2**		**46**	**13**	**30**	**18**	**10**	**7**	**2.54**	**0.39**
Pickwicks										
Johnson	1-1	3	19.2	7	15	24	2	0	3.20	1.22
Carson	0-1	1	9	5	8	9	3	1	5.00	1.00
Bergeman	0-1	2	14	10	19	4	4	2	6.43	0.29
Karns	1-0	1	5.1	3	6	2	3	0	5.07	0.38
Totals	**2-3**		**48**	**25**	**48**	**39**	**12**	**3**	**4.69**	**0.81**

note: ERA includes total runs scored

Free Agency in 1923?

Steve L. Steinberg

Urban Shocker is one of baseball's forgotten stars. One of the American League's dominant pitchers in the 1920s, he won 156 games in that decade, most with the lowly St. Louis Browns, despite the fact that his last decision was in 1927. After going 37-17 for the great 1926-1927 New York Yankees, Shocker died of heart disease in 1928.

Even more forgotten is Shocker's challenge to the reserve system and his fight for free agency, a matter that became the cause célèbre of the 1923 winter baseball meetings. Ultimately, Shocker did not win his bid for freedom, but he shook the very foundation of baseball. The incident precipitated a showdown between Commissioner Landis and the owners of baseball that almost ended Landis' reign a mere three years after it began.

The triggering event was straightforward, though unusual in the days when the role of a ballplayer's was in the home. Shocker wanted to take his wife along on the final Browns road trip in September, 1923. Shocker's nephew, Roger Shockcor (the original spelling of the family name before the pitcher changed it to simplify matters for reporters), remembered that Urban's wife Irene loved to be "a part of the action." The response of the Browns was swift and clear: They had a well-established rule that wives did not go on road trips. (According to the St. Louis *Globe-Democrat* of December 31, some teams, like the Giants, Reds, and White Sox, allowed wives on trips, while others,

like the Pirates and Tigers, did not.) When Shocker did not head east with the club, he was fined $1,000 and suspended.

The Sporting News was very much on the side of management, writing on September 27 that the rule was "justified by experience, and for the general good of a team on the road." *TSN* editorial writer John Sheridan wrote that one of the great values of baseball was "no outsider can help a baseball player in this game of rugged individualism." This sort of logic was unclear to many, as the St. Louis *Post-Dispatch* wrote on September 20: "A tactical blunder appears to have been made, since the presence of a player's wife on a trip certainly should contribute to his good conduct, if he is the least inclined to waywardness."

Shocker felt his personal liberty had been infringed upon, since the team was interfering with his family affairs. On September 27, he asked to be declared a free agent, claiming the team had voided his contact by suspending him. The New York *Times* wrote on December 4, just before the winter meetings began, "Stripped of its legal verbiage, the case simmered down to the question of whether a club had the right to discipline a player as it saw fit."

Commissioner Kenesaw Mountain Landis was the wild card in this dispute once Shocker appealed to his office. Hired by the owners in 1920 after the Black Sox scandal, Landis had shown indications that he could not be counted on to rule in the owners' favor in disputes with players. The Associated Press reported on December 30 that Landis was reluctant to take a position that might cause the players to feel they were "baseball slaves," as had been asserted in the Federal

Steve L. Steinberg *is working on a biography of Urban Shocker and can be reached at ssteinberg@trinorth.com. He owns a retail apparel company and has a profound love for the history of the game of baseball. He lives in Seattle with the wife and three children.*

The inscription here says it all.

League suit against organized baseball. Years later, Leo Durocher said, "He [Landis] was always on the side of the ball player. He had no use for the owners at all." Maverick owner Bill Veeck wrote that Landis admonished players, "Don't go to those owners if you get into trouble, come to me. I'm your friend. They're no good." During the December, 1923, meetings, Landis ex-

plained his support of the underdog: "When he [the player] comes into court against a club owner, he sometimes is not adequately represented."

The Sporting News was clearly worried. "One can never tell what stand Landis will take. He is quite capable of assuming arbitrary jurisdiction in the Shocker case." Landis did just that, which *TSN* declared, would cause "the fur to fly." Shocker then strongly intimated he'd go to court if the case went against him, challenging the reserve rule, which "would open the door for a legal fight that might shake baseball to its foundation."

In the meantime, the new manager of the Browns, the great first baseman George Sisler, entertained trade offers for his unhappy star. Since 1920, Shocker had been the winningest pitcher in baseball, going 91-51 (.641) on a team that won only 53 percent of its games. So it was not surprising that many teams inquired about Shocker. The New York *World*, for example, reported that the Yankees offered future Hall of Famer Waite Hoyt. The Yankees had been trying to get Shocker back ever since they'd traded him in January, 1918. The trade, in which Shocker was a last minute throw-in, was Miller Huggins' first major action as Yankee manager and one of the few mistakes the Yankees made as they built their powerhouse.

The backdrop to the winter meetings was the ongoing battle between Landis and American League President Ban Johnson. On December 10, a St. Louis *Post Dispatch* headline shouted, AMERICAN LEAGUE REPORTEDLY READY TO WITHDRAW IF LANDIS DECIDES SHOCKER CASE AGAINST BROWNS...MAN HIGH IN THE COUNCILS OF ORGANIZED BASEBALL TELLS SPORTS EDITOR WRAY THAT OWNERS WILL REFUSE TO ACCEPT VERDICT IN FAVOR OF ST. LOUIS PITCHER. Wray wrote, "Landis is a friend at court for all ball players—and it may cost him his official hand." That very day, Landis, ever the tactician, postponed a decision until after the meetings. But he was still on the offensive. As the meetings opened on December 12, he made a preemptive move, denouncing Johnson and threatening "Any time you [the owners] assert by your votes that I am not wanted, that moment I will tear up that contract." Johnson's AL owners quickly fell into line, giving Landis a sweeping victory. It was Yankee owner Colonel Jacob Ruppert who rose in support of Landis and rallied the owners. "Ruppert's speech kept Landis in baseball," declared the headline in the *World*.

On January 18,1924, just days before the hearing, Shocker surprisingly withdrew his case. Red Sox president Bob Quinn, who had been the Browns' business manager earlier in the 1923 season, helped persuade him to accept a settlement. Credit was also given to Sisler, whose close friendship with Shocker played a role. (Before the winter meetings ended, Sisler telegraphed new Browns business manager Bill Friel that he wanted to keep Shocker, and the Browns then took Shocker off the trading block. When asked by the *Post Dispatch* on January 19 if Shocker would remain a Brown, Ball said, "That is strictly up to George Sisler...There will be absolutely no interference from the business office."

But the key figure behind the scenes was Ban Johnson. On January 23, the *Globe Democrat* reported

that Johnson, acting as duly appointed proxy by the Browns, signed Shocker to a 1924 contract. On January 31, *The Sporting News* reported that Johnson had intervened with Quinn to avert a situation that might have forced the league to walk away from Landis and operate independently. Attorneys for both Shocker and the Browns said that reports of the settlement were news to them. Even owner Phil Ball, a close friend and ardent supporter of the league president, said he knew nothing, but that he had received a wire from Johnson that the case had been settled. Ball's support for Johnson was boundless. He would tell the *World* in February, 1926, "I am with Ban Johnson, first, last, and always."

The *Post-Dispatch* reported that Johnson protected Ball's feelings by letting the fine stand, and protected Shocker by substantially raising his salary to reimburse him for the $1,000 fine. Exactly what financial incentives were given to Shocker to settle can only be speculated upon. But he said he was completely satisfied and treated better than he anticipated. "If everyone had friends like him [Bob Quinn], there wouldn't be any enemies in this world...Manager Sisler can count on me to pitch my head off once the season starts."

Baseball owners breathed a collective sigh of relief. Back on December 4, Irving Vaughn of the Chicago *Daily Tribune*, had seen the explosiveness of this case: "...more than a mere dispute between player and club. It involves points that threaten the whole structure of organized baseball, and Landis realizes this." George Daley, sports editor of the *World*, wrote that Landis was saved "from making a decision on a most delicate question." *The Sporting News* summarized the closure this way:

> The temperamental and probably ill-advised player had refused to admit the errors of his ways, to take his punishment...Shocker escaped the full consequences of his rank insubordination, but better that than the possible—nay probable—consequences of a decision by Commissioner Landis subversive of club rights and league sovereignty.

Just how Landis would have ruled in this fundamental case can only be surmised, but what the *Post-Dispatch* on December 14 called his "tendency to give the players a chance" almost precipitated fireworks that the paper on December 26 said "would make the Last Days of Pompeii look like a wet match." But it is not surprising that during these winter meetings, all sixteen baseball owners secretly agreed, according to the *Post-Dispatch* on December 13, to incorporate into standard player contracts a clause that required the player to abide by all present and future team rules, for the purpose of discipline.

Saint Matty and the Prince of Darkness

Martin D. Kohout

It would be hard, on the face of it, to find two major league contemporaries more different than Christy Mathewson and Hal Chase. Mathewson, arguably the greatest pitcher in National League history, dead of tuberculosis at the age of forty-five, a member of the first class of inductees of the National Baseball Hall of Fame at Cooperstown, is remembered as one of baseball's shining heroes, a sort of Galahad in baggy flannel and spikes.

By any measure, Matty was one of the all-time greats. Granted that his major league career (1900-1916) occurred during the so-called Dead Ball Era, when pitchers routinely compiled statistical records that are amazing to modern fans, and granted that he benefited from playing in New York, even then the nation's media center, and for a team that won five NL pennants during his tenure, no matter how you slice it, Mathewson was a true superstar. The most recent edition of *Total Baseball* rates him the best pitcher in the NL seven times and the best in the majors four times.

Moreover, he was immensely popular with fans and fellow ballplayers. His catcher, Chief Meyers, recalled, "How we loved to play for him! We'd break our necks for that guy…. He had the sweetest, most gentle nature. Gentle in every way." Another teammate, Fred Snodgrass, concurred. "Matty was the greatest pitcher who ever lived, in my opinion. He was a wonderful, wonderful man, too, a reserved sort of fellow, a little

hard to get close to. But once you got to know him, he was a truly good friend."[1]

Chase, on the other hand, has gone down as baseball's Judas goat. He was perhaps the game's greatest villain, a shadowy figure repeatedly accused of throwing games, offering bribes, and betting against his own team, indicted in the infamous Black Sox fix. Said one contemporary, Bill Wambsganss, "He was a cheater right from the beginning and everybody knew it."[2]

For all of this, though, at a point early in their major league careers, Mathewson and Chase seem to have been friendly. As a result, the subsequent course of events which drew them back together years later with disastrous consequences has the awful inevitability of myth. Indeed, Eric Rolfe Greenberg used Mathewson and Chase as paired symbols of good and evil in his novel *The Celebrant* (1983), and the story of their relationship, beginning in friendship and mutual admiration but ending in accusations and mutual loathing, reveals much about the ambiguous nature of moral and ethical standards which governed pre-lapsarian (i.e., pre-Black Sox) baseball.

Fine but flawed—During his major league career (1905-1919), which also fell entirely within the Dead Ball Era, Chase was regarded as a competent, even dangerous, hitter and baserunner, but it was his defense that made him a star. No less a personage than Babe Ruth claimed that "For my dough, Hal Chase was the greatest first baseman who ever lived." George Kelly, Chase's successor as the Giants' first baseman, and a member of the Hall of Fame, said, "Oh, Gehrig

Martin D. Kohout *lives in Austin, Texas. Like Hal Chase, he is a native of the Bay Area who bats right and throws left. Unlike Hal Chase, he has never had the opportunity to influence the outcome of a major league game. He is writing a biography of Chase.*

and Terry were good. But Chase could do everything they could—and better."[3]

Despite such praise, Chase will never join Mathewson in the Hall, because Prince Hal was apparently a confirmed cheater—a gambler who repeatedly threw games, who bet against his own team and then tried to ensure that it lost. So gifted an athlete was he, in fact, that he could dazzle fans, sportswriters, and even fellow ballplayers with his ability, his grace, and his coordination—while playing to lose. Perhaps he would hesitate before starting after a ground ball, waiting just long enough for it to elude his reach by the barest of margins. Perhaps he would break a split second late to cover the bag, his teammate's throw just eluding his desperate stab. "I remember a few times I threw a ball over to first base and it went by to the stands and a couple of runs scored," recalled shortstop Roger Peckinpaugh, who joined the Yankees in 1913, Chase's last season with the club. "It surprised me. I'd stand there looking, sighting the flight of the ball in my mind, and I'd think, 'Jeez, that throw wasn't that bad.' Then I'd tell myself that [Chase] was the greatest there was, so maybe the throw was bad. What he was doing, you see, was tangling up his feet and then making a fancy dive after the ball, making it look like it was a wild throw."[4]

Chase was accused in 1908, 1910, and 1913 of "laying down" on his team, but managed to beat the rap each time. After finally wearing out his welcome in the major leagues after the 1919 season, he was indicted as a go-between in the Black Sox scandal, but was never convicted of any crime. He was banned from Pacific Coast League ballparks in the wake of another bribery scandal in 1921, and the rest of his life was a slow but steady decline into alcoholism, poor health, loneliness, and poverty.

Common ground—As young stars of seemingly limitless promise in New York, however, Matty and Prince Hal had much in common. Mathewson, born in Factoryville, Pennsylvania, on August 12, 1880, began his major league career with the New York Giants of the National League in 1900. Chase, born in Los Gatos, California, on February 13, 1883, began his major league career with the New York Highlanders (later renamed the Yankees) of the American League in 1905. Both men struggled in their first major league seasons: Mathewson posted an undistinguished 0-3 record and 5.08 earned run average in six games during that 1900 season, while Chase batted only .249 as a rookie five years later. Despite their less-than-overwhelming first seasons, however, both men had obvious potential and were quickly recognized as stars in the making.

Moreover, both became famous (or, in Chase's case, infamous) for more than their considerable athletic ability. Matty was handsome, intelligent, articulate, and

modest, perhaps the first professional athlete widely looked upon as a role model even by parents and teachers. The fawning press made much of his being a "college boy," with all the wholesomeness associated with higher education in those days, and he stood in stark contrast to the crude, unsophisticated, harddrinking louts who seemed to predominate in major league baseball. The combination of Matty's character and his good fortune in playing in New York, where a number of newspapers were covering and celebrating sports with unprecedented enthusiasm, ensured that "No player before his time—or after—(that includes Babe Ruth, Ty Cobb, Ted Williams, Mickey Mantle, Willie Mays, and Stan Musial) ever captured the public fancy the way Matty did."[5]

Chase was almost immediately hailed as the potential savior of the AL franchise in New York, which was desperately seeking a box-office attraction to compete with the older, better-established, and more successful Giants. Chase was initially seen as the American League Highlanders' answer to Mathewson—that is, a handsome, articulate college boy, a hero worthy of emulation not just for his athletic accomplishments but for his character and even his appearance. Chase was described in terms similar to those applied to Mathewson, as "a tall, handsome-looking chap, with light hair and complexion" who "has the appearance of an athlete. He bears himself confidently and like the well-bred college boy he is."[6] Indeed, Chase was even said to resemble Matty physically.[7]

In actuality, Chase had considerably less right to be called a college boy than did Mathewson. While Matty left Bucknell after his junior year to pursue a professional baseball career, his academic record was strong—his biographer Ray Robinson noted that Mathewson's lowest grade as a freshman was a 90 in analytic geometry—and he was president of the freshman class, a member of several literary societies, played the bass horn in the college band, sang in the glee club, and was a member of the Phi Gamma Delta fraternity and the Theta Delta Tau honorary leadership society.[8]

Chase, on the other hand, spent two years at Santa Clara College, but apparently was recruited solely as an athlete. In fact, the Santa Clara archives contain no evidence that he ever attended a class.[9] Indeed, there is some doubt that he even graduated from high school.

Matty and Prince Hal were both inordinately fond of games of chance, as were many ballplayers (and others) in those days. Chase soon earned a reputation as a card sharp. Gabby Street, a teammate of Prince Hal's in 1912, later recalled watching him produce a pair of kings apparently out of thin air to win a huge pot in a poker game. "Funny thing, I never really thought of it as cheating," reflected Street. "More like beating the system. For some reason, Hal was showing off for me. He wanted to show he could palm a pair out of his sleeve in that tough company and not get caught. But it's like he wanted somebody to know it."[10] In 1921, during a second divorce trial, his landlord testified that "Chase was what was known as a crooked gambler," and said that once, when Prince Hal was discovered to have won $1,500 shooting craps with loaded dice, he escaped only by jumping through a window and running away.[11]

Mathewson excelled at chess and checkers and was so accomplished a card player that Giants manager John McGraw, no stranger to games of chance himself, once felt it necessary to fine his star pitcher $500 for playing poker with some of the other Giants. The manager justified the fine on the grounds that Matty should have realized the potentially disastrous effects of playing for sizeable sums of money with teammates he was assured of beating. "I'd fine anyone else twenty-five or fifty dollars," said McGraw, "but Matty should know better, so the fine is five hundred."[12]

Diverging careers—The pugnacious McGraw was another thing the two stars had in common. Despite the apparent differences in their personalities, and despite the unusually stiff fine, McGraw was deeply and sincerely fond of Mathewson. So close were they that in the spring of 1903, Matty and his new bride, Jane, moved into a new seven-room apartment at 85th Street and Columbus Avenue with John and Blanche McGraw.[13]

Three years later, with the Mathewsons expecting a baby and looking for a place of their own, the McGraws moved to the Washington Inn, a residential hotel at 155th Street and Amsterdam Avenue. Among their new neighbors was "a well-mannered, pleasant twenty-two-year-old Californian" named Hal Chase.[14] We do not know with certainty when Chase and Mathewson first met, but meet they did, most likely through McGraw, and they seem initially to have been on friendly terms.

Hal Chase

In fact, Matty gave Chase a signed presentation copy of his ghostwritten book, *Won in the Ninth,* a thinly veiled roman á clef for juvenile readers about an earnest young first baseman named "Harold Case," in 1910.[15]

Despite their apparent similarities, however, Matty and Prince Hal's careers followed strikingly different trajectories. Matty won 373 games in his seventeen major-league seasons, tying him with Pete Alexander for the all-time NL record. Against those 373 wins, he lost only 188 games, for a .665 winning percentage that ranks eighth all-time. His 79 career shutouts rank third in major league history, and his career earned run average of 2.13 ranks fifth. He led the NL in wins and shutouts four times, in ERA and strikeouts five times.

By contrast, Chase played fifteen years in the major

leagues, compiling a lifetime batting average of .291 with 57 home runs, 941 runs batted in, and 363 stolen bases, but does not rank among the all-time leaders in any statistical category. He led the National League in batting once and the Federal League in home runs once. His career did not quite live up to expectations, though it is possible that his career numbers might look better had he always been playing to win. On the other hand, even when he may not have been on the take, Chase seems to have taken his baseball career rather casually. His son insisted, with some plausibility, that "money never meant anything to him," except perhaps as a means of keeping score. Certainly he could be lavishly generous, especially when he wanted to seem like a big shot.

Trouble—Matty and Prince Hal's paths crossed again in late July, 1916, when McGraw traded his protégé to the Cincinnati Reds so Mathewson, his days as a dominant major league pitcher behind him, could assume the managerial reigns. Many assumed that the Giants were hoping to give Matty some managerial experience before summoning him back to New York as McGraw's successor with the Giants, and indeed when the deal was struck the Giants tried to retain the right to recall Matty after two years. The Reds, understandably, objected. Acquiring Matty, even if his pitching days were over,[16] was a major box-office coup for a team that was on its way to finishing either seventh or eighth for the fourth year in a row.

With the Reds Matty was reunited with Chase, who had joined the team that spring after the Federal League, for which he had abandoned the White Sox in midseason 1914, folded. For a time, it had seemed that Chase's major-league career might be over. He was persona non grata in the American League, and had come close to signing with the San Francisco Seals of the Pacific Coast League before joining the Reds in early April. Now, as if to thumb his nose at his many detractors, Chase was on his way to perhaps his best season. He would finish 1916 with the best batting average in the NL at .339 while also ranking first in hits, second in runs batted in and slugging percentage, and third in total bases.

The Reds, however, finished tied for seventh place with a 60-93 record, and their winning percentage after Mathewson took over was actually lower than it had been under his predecessor, Buck Herzog. But Matty, having apprenticed under McGraw, was expected to teach the Reds how to win, and most observers were willing to withhold judgment on his managerial abilities until he had a full season under his belt. Sure enough, in 1917 the Reds improved to fourth place and posted their first winning record since 1909. Chase's batting average fell to .277, but he again finished second in the league in runs batted in.

The Reds' improvement continued in 1918, as they rose to third in the NL. They finished the season, however, without their star first baseman. On August 7, the day after Chase had raised his batting average to .301, Mathewson suspended Prince Hal for "indifferent playing." At first the press attributed the suspension to nothing more sinister than Prince Hal's notorious lack of punctuality, as Matty implied publicly that Chase would soon be back in the lineup—"I think a layoff will do him good," he explained[17]—but soon hinted at more serious crimes. "Hal Chase will never play another game for the Reds so long as Mathewson is manager or at any other time," wrote Jack Ryder in the Cincinnati *Enquirer.* "After Matty has a conference with President Herrmann [Garry Herrmann, president of the Reds], it is probable that Chase's baseball career will be ended. It's a tough finish for a player of pleasing personality and great natural brilliance, but it is inevitable."[18]

In fact, according to Ray Robinson, Mathewson had long been suspicious of his old friend's inexplicable errors or misplays, and his suspicions had been confirmed on July 25, when pitcher Pete Schneider asked Matty to start another pitcher in that afternoon's game against the Boston Braves. Schneider made his unusual request, he told his manager, because he had heard that Chase and second baseman Lee Magee had bet on the Reds to lose the game. In fact, Magee tried desperately to throw the game. He committed an egregious error in the bottom of the ninth inning, allowing Boston to tie the score, and then, having reached base on a bad-hop single in the top of the thirteenth, dragged himself around the bases so reluctantly on Edd Roush's drive into the leftcenter-field gap that Roush almost passed him on the bases. Roush, yelling "Run, you son of a bitch!" at his teammate, barely beat the throw home for an inside-the-park home run.

Ironically, Magee's run proved to be the game-winner, as the Reds held on to win, 4-2. The scheme did not become public knowledge until 1920, when a Boston gambler named James Costello testified that Chase and Magee had indeed bet $500 apiece that the Braves would win the game. When the unfortunate Magee had subsequently stopped payment on his check to Costello, the gambler threatened to expose the scheme, whereupon Prince Hal promised to make good on Magee's debt. Costello recalled, however, that he did not collect the full amount until he brought suit against Magee in Boston Municipal Court in June, 1919.[19]

Years later, however, sportswriter Tom Swope offered another explanation for Matty's action against Chase. Swope covered the Reds for the Cincinnati *Post* for forty-one years beginning in 1915. In a 1960 letter to Lee Allen, Swope claimed that "practically all the Reds knew Chase bet regularly on the club's games, sometimes that the Reds would win, more often, likely, that they would lose." This, however, was not the reason for the suspension. The issue that finally brought Matty's wrath down on Prince Hal, according to Swope, was a card game.

Swope recalled that Mathewson and Ryder of the *Enquirer,* both of whom were "stingy and grasping in financial matters," were avid bridge players. Early in the season they recruited Chase and pitcher Mike Regan to make up a foursome, and proceeded to beat them regularly. "After a few sessions," wrote Swope, "Chase, always a crook, told Regan that they were up against a bad situation in bridge and should do something to even the competition because they knew so little of the game." Chase devised a system of signals involving "the way he handled his ever-present cigar." When Regan was drafted into the military in August, however, the thought that he might die with his involvement in this dishonest scheme still on his conscience drove him to confess the plot to Matty. Only then, according to Swope, did Mathewson do "what other Reds had been asking him for weeks to do [i.e., suspend Chase]."[20]

Regardless of what the truth was behind the suspension, Herrmann announced his support of his manager: "Matty is sure that he has the goods on Chase and we will go to the limit to find out the exact truth with regard to his action in certain games. It is a shame that a player of such great ability and brilliant qualifications should fail to give his best efforts on all occasions. He will never play another game of ball for us, and I rather think that his baseball career is completely over. There can be no halfway measures in a case of this kind."[21]

In response, Chase went on the offensive. He threatened to sue the Reds for salary lost during his suspension, and unabashedly confirmed the charges against him. "Let's not dodge around the bush," he told *The Sporting News.* "I'm accused of betting on ball games and trying to get a pitcher to throw a game for money. I'm accused of frequenting pool rooms and making baseball bets. I've gone into pool rooms and made bets on horses, but I say right here have made no baseball bets and have never thrown the team. As a result, rumors have it that I was wagering $100 at a crack. Who would either take or offer a baseball bet running up into the hundreds? As a sample of the wild talk, I was accused in New York not of betting against the Reds, but of offering a certain Giant pitcher $800 to let us beat him."[22]

The pitcher in question was Pol Perritt, whom Chase had probably met in the spring of 1916, which both players spent with the San Francisco Seals. Chase had approached Perritt before an August 6 game at the Polo Grounds and engaged him in a conversation, the exact details of which remained unclear. Perritt, however, reportedly assumed that Chase was trying to

bribe him, and reacted angrily. Another Giant player, outfielder Ross Youngs, also reportedly had had "serious talks with Chase," but refused to go on the record.[23] McGraw, to whom Perritt reported his encounter with Chase, told *The Sporting News* that "Perritt refused to go into details, except to say that he should have punched Chase in the eye for what he said. Perritt added that Chase should be put out of baseball." McGraw, however, seemed disinclined to take the matter seriously. "It is hard to believe the charges against Chase. He may have been kidding Perritt. He is a practical joker and says many things he doesn't mean."[24] The same issue of *The Sporting News* reported, however, that several of Chase's teammates, including Sherry Magee (no relation to Lee), Heinie Groh, and Greasy Neale, had also accused him of offering bribes, and that during the Reds' last Eastern trip opposing players had taken to yelling at Chase, "Well, Hal, what are the odds today?"[25]

Close call—Chase now admitted having placed bets on Reds games, but only on his own team to win. At least one Cincinnati reporter believed him, confidently dismissing as "a skyrocket flight of romance" the story that Chase had offered Perritt $800 to throw a game.[26] A few days later Chase hired Cincinnati attorney Robert S. Alcorn, filed suit against the Reds for $1,670 in back salary lost during the suspension, and decamped to New York.[27] Matty, meanwhile, no doubt disgusted by the whole Chase contretemps, applied for a captain's commission in the Chemical Warfare Service and left for France in late August.[28]

There, during a botched drill that autumn, Matty accidentally inhaled mustard gas. One of Mathewson's fellow officers in the CWS was the Detroit Tigers' great Ty Cobb. Years later, Cobb described the incident and its aftermath in his memoirs: "I can recall Mathewson saying, 'Ty, when we were in there, I got a good dose of that stuff. I feel terrible.' He was wheezing and blowing out congested matter."[29] Matty was still hospitalized when the armistice was signed on November 11, and the Reds were unsure if he would return for the 1919 season. Herrmann sent a number of messages and cables to France, but received no reply. Finally, feeling he could not afford further delay, he hired Pat Moran as manager.[30] Moran had just signed a contract to coach McGraw's pitchers, and when the Giant manager selflessly gave him permission to negotiate with Herrmann, cynics wondered whether McGraw would extract some payment in return.[31] When Matty finally returned stateside, he was out of a job.

The long, drawn-out battle of charges and countercharges concerning Chase culminated in a closed hearing before National League President John Heydler on January 30, 1919. By then, public sentiment seemed to have shifted in Chase's favor. Several reporters dismissed the evidence against him as circumstantial and flimsy, and criticized the National League's handling of the affair.[32] Also, McGraw was reportedly interested in signing Prince Hal if he were cleared of the charges. Such a move would seem to be a slap in the face to McGraw's former protégé Mathewson, but Herrmann dismissed the rumor: "One of the men who filed an affidavit against Chase is John J. McGraw, so I do not take much stock in the story that the New York Club is trying to clear Chase so as to sign him to play first base for the Giants."[33] Matty was in France and unavailable to testify, though he sent an affidavit. Perritt sent word from his Louisiana farm that he would also be unable to attend. The Reds did not trouble to send an official representative to the hearing, though three Cincinnati players—Regan, pitcher Jimmy Ring, and outfielder Greasy Neale—testified, as did McGraw. Chase arrived for the hearing with three attorneys, including his brother-in-law Rudolph M. Cherurg, and a stenographer.

The hearing lasted some five hours, with Chase on the stand for most of the time. Heydler's decision, announced on February 5, did not surprise those who had followed the case closely. "It is nowhere established that the accused was interested in any pool or wager that caused any game to result otherwise than on its merits," declared the National League president. "The testimony showed that Chase acted in a foolish and careless manner both on the field and among the players, and that the club was justified in bringing the charges in view of the many rumors which arose from the loose talk of its first baseman. Chase did not take his work seriously, and was entirely to blame for the position in which he found himself. There was, however, no proof that he intentionally violated or attempted to violate the rules in relation to tampering with players, or in any way endeavored to secure desired results in the outcome of games."

Final chance—Two weeks later, McGraw traded Bill Rariden and Walter Holke to Cincinnati for Chase. The Reds clearly wanted nothing more to do with Prince Hal, having already acquired Jake Daubert from the Brooklyn Dodgers to play first base. On March 4, Chase announced that he had settled his suit with the Reds and signed a contract with the Giants. Three days later Matty signed on as the team's pitching coach.

McGraw smugly predicted that his firm management would forestall any trouble between the two. "I do not anticipate a bit of trouble in that direction," he said. "Chase has told me within the past few days that his relations with Matty prior to the episode were always most cordial and that he does not feel the slightest resentment toward him now. Matty, too, is quite willing to let the dead past bury its dead. And even if they were still at swords' points I would not hesitate to have them both on the club, for while I remain as manager there can be no conflict between them."[34]

A frightening incident during spring training in Gainesville, Florida, seemed to belie McGraw's optimism. During batting practice on March 22, Mathewson was inadvertently struck in the stomach when Larry Doyle lost his grip on his bat. Matty was not seriously injured, but while Doyle and the other Giants rushed to his side, Chase, who had been awaiting his turn at the plate, did not move.

"At least," said one witness, "he had the grace not to laugh out loud. But from now on Larry can get anything he wants from him."[35]

Despite the frosty relations between two of McGraw's favorites—"During the season Matty and Chase never exchanged a word," according to Ray Robinson—the Giants got off to a good start. But the Reds stayed right on their heels, and moved into first place in early July.

The two teams met for a crucial series in Cincinnati during the first week of August. The Giants won only the last of the three games, after which "a horde of rabid fans" followed the New York players and issued "threats of bodily harm." An incensed McGraw responded by rashly yelling, "We beat you today and we'll be glad to get out of the home of the Huns." Such a remark, coming so soon after the end of World War I and in a city with a substantial German-American population, could not fail to provoke a hostile response. A park policeman swung wildly at McGraw and hit Chase instead, whereupon Prince Hal knocked the policeman's hat off. A riot was barely averted by a mounted policeman who drove off the enraged Cincinnati fans.[36]

A little over a week later the two teams faced each other again in New York. This time the Reds won four of the six games, and effectively ended the Giants' pennant hopes. Fred Lieb of the New York *Sun* wrote afterward that "Chase has been playing through the entire series as though in a trance."[37] Prince Hal sat out eight of the next nine games, supposedly because of a sprained wrist, and played infrequently thereafter. And then, on September 11, McGraw announced that he had suspended third baseman Heinie Zimmerman without pay for the remainder of the season. Rumors quickly arose that Zimmerman had offered bribes to three teammates: pitchers Fred Toney and Rube Benton and outfielder Benny Kauff. And Zimmerman's main accomplice was said to have been none other than Hal Chase.[38]

McGraw took no public action against Prince Hal, who remained with the team as a pinch-hitter and base coach until the night before the final day of the season. Even then, McGraw did not implicate Chase. "He's sick," said McGraw. "He hasn't been feeling well for a long time."[39]

McGraw later claimed that he had suspended Chase as soon as he learned that Prince Hal's former teammate in Cincinnati, Lee Magee, had admitted that he and Chase conspired to throw games during the 1918 season.[40] But since John Heydler himself swore that Magee had not confessed until February, 1920,[41] how could that information have influenced McGraw in September 1919? Perhaps McGraw took no action against Chase because he wanted to let his old friend bow out of the big leagues gracefully. No such solicitude governed McGraw's treatment of Zimmerman, with whom he had clashed repeatedly. Or perhaps McGraw did not want to admit publicly that he had been so disastrously mistaken in his assessment of Chase's character.

The big scandal—The upcoming World Series between the Reds and the White Sox soon overshadowed the Zimmerman–Chase situation. Most fans considered the White Sox heavy favorites, but a few observers noticed some peculiarities in the betting line before the series, and rumors that the series had been fixed began to circulate. Hugh Fullerton of the Chicago *Herald-American,* a long-time baseball reporter, was among those who wondered whether the rumors were true, and arranged to sit beside Matty, who was covering the series for the New York *Evening World,* in the press box. Fullerton asked Matty to note any plays that appeared suspicious to him. In the words of Ray Robinson, "At the end of the Series, won by the Reds, five games to three, …Matty's scorecard was cluttered with red circles."[42]

Matty had apparently intended to coach again in 1920, but his health precluded his return to the Giants. He was diagnosed with tuberculosis, and in July his doctors ordered him to Saranac Lake, New York, a well-known center for recovering TB patients. In September, 1921, McGraw's pennant-winning Giants played an exhibition game against an old-timers' team made up of Matty's former teammates, raising almost $50,000 for the beloved former star. In January, 1923, he felt strong enough to accept Judge Emil Fuchs's offer to become president of the Boston Braves, but in the spring of 1925 his health worsened and in July he gave up his duties with the Braves. He died on the night of October 11, 1925.[43]

The red circles that Matty drew on his scorecard in 1919 had helped Fullerton begin the chain of questions that resulted in the September, 1920, exposure of the so-called Black Sox scandal, which ended with the permanent expulsion of eight White Sox players alleged to have accepted bribes from gamblers to throw the Series to the Reds.[44] The full story of the fix will probably never be known, but Rube Benton, his former teammate on the Giants, testified that Prince Hal had won $40,000 betting on the Series. Chase, back in California after being cut loose by the Giants, was indicted as a middleman in the scheme, but avoided extradition to Illinois and thus never came to trial.[45]

Final days—Unwelcome in organized baseball, Chase spent most of the 1920s playing semipro ball for various towns in Arizona. At the time of Matty's death, Prince Hal was in Douglas, Arizona, having convinced Buck Weaver, Lefty Williams, and Chick Gandil, three of the expelled Black Sox, to join him on the Douglas Blues. In December, 1933, several New York sportswriters rediscovered him in Tucson as they accompanied the Columbia University football team to the West Coast for the Rose Bowl game.[46] By that time age and alcohol had begun to take their toll on the once-dazzling Prince Hal, and the ensuing years were hard ones. He bounced from Arizona to California and back, was hospitalized in 1940-1941 and again in 1944[47], and by the time of his death, he was living on the charity of his sister Jessie and her husband, who owned an orange ranch in Williams, California. His brother-in-law, Frank Topham, despised Chase and refused to let him in the house, so he built a tiny cabin for the old ballplayer.[48] Chase died on May 18, 1947,[49] and is buried with his parents in San Jose.

Ultimately, it is a work of fiction that seems to have best captured the contradictions of the real Hal Chase. In *The Celebrant,* Jack Kapp, an idealistic young jewelry designer, idolizes the saintly, almost godlike Mathewson. Jack's profligate brother Eli befriends the sinister Chase, with disastrous results. During the final week of the 1911 season Jack takes his young son Matthias (known as Matty) to his first baseball game at the Polo Grounds: "Matthias was delighted to find his Uncle Eli in the box; I was something less enchanted to discover his guest, Hal Chase. Matthias, though, immediately took to the Yankee, whose huge hands held him gently."

The action of the game holds little interest for Matthias. "Finally he fell asleep in Chase's arms, which charmed the player. I offered to take him, but Chase insisted he was no trouble…. Matthias stirred, and he soothed the child by stroking his hair. 'Good-looking kid. I probably have a few of my own out west.'"[50]

The fictional Chase's genuine and tender affection for young Matthias, combined with his offhand reference to illegitimate children (Chase was in fact a notorious philanderer),[51] captures something of the maddeningly contradictory nature of the factual Prince Hal, his undeniable personal charm and his equally incorrigible amorality. Chase was a grinning, back-slapping, cigar-chewing extrovert, and no doubt much better company than the quiet Mathewson, who seems downright priggish by comparison. The differences between them make their similarities, and their curiously entwined fates, all the more intriguing. Indeed, Mathewson and Chase stand in much the same relationship as do God and Satan in John Milton's *Paradise Lost*. We know we should admire the first of each pair, who stands for rectitude and good, but we can't help finding the second vastly more fascinating.

Notes:

1. Lawrence Ritter, *The Glory of Their Times* (1966; New York: Collier, 1971), 88 (2nd quotation), 168 (1st quotation).

2. Paul Green, *Forgotten Fields* (Waupaca, Wisc.: Parker, 1984), 44.

3. Richard Scheinin, "Hal Chase's Son, Grandson Say He's Being Treated Unfairly," Knight-Ridder Newspapers, March, 1993 (1st quotation); unidentified clipping in possession of Hal Chase Jr. (2nd quotation). Among the other notables on record as considering Chase the greatest first baseman ever are Nick Altrock, Jimmy Austin, Ed Barrow, Ty Cobb, George Davis, Billy Evans, Kid Gleason, Clark Griffith, Hughie Jennings, Willie Keeler, Connie Mack, Clyde Milan, and Edd Roush.

4. Quoted in Lawrence Ritter and Donald Honig, *The 100 Greatest Baseball Players of All Time* (New York: Crown, 1981), 129-131.

5. Ray Robinson, *Matty: An American Hero* (New York: Oxford University Press, 1993), 7.

6. *Sporting Life,* July 28, 1906.

7. Ibid., Apr. 8, 1905.

8. Robinson, *Matty,* 20, 25.

9. An informational biographical form on Chase compiled by the Santa Clara athletic department after his death includes the following notation: "While Hal Chase is listed in the 'Registry of Students' printed in the College catalog, I do not find him listed in the Registrar's Book or in the 'Librum Voti' (grade book) for the year." Hal Chase clipping file, Santa Clara University Archives.

10. Gib Bodet, "The Life and Times of Prince Hal Chase" (unpublished ms., n.d.), 19-20, 21 (quotation).

11. Cincinnati *Commercial Tribune,* Jan. 27, 1921.

12. Robinson, *Matty,* 44.

13. Ibid., 42; Charles C. Alexander, *John McGraw* (1988; New York: Penguin, 1989), 102.

14. Alexander, *John McGraw,* 119.

15. I am grateful to musician and composer Dave Frishberg for bringing this literary connection to my attention. Frishberg, who once tried to write a musical about Mathewson, found this signed copy in a second-hand book store in Soquel, California. Dave Frishberg to Martin Kohout, July 29, 1990.

16. Matty pitched in only one game for the Reds, a rematch with his old rival Mordecai Brown in the second game of a Labor Day doubleheader in Chicago. Both pitchers were hit hard as the Reds won, 10-8. After the game Mathewson promised his team, "If I ever go into the box again I will buy every one of you a suit of clothes." Cincinnati *Enquirer,* Sept. 5, 1916. He never had to make good on that promise.

17. *The Sporting News,* Aug. 15, 1918; Cincinnati *Enquirer,* Aug. 8, 1918 (quotation).

18. Cincinnati *Enquirer,* Aug. 10, 1918.

19. Robinson, *Matty,* 187; Cincinnati *Enquirer,* July 26, 1918, June 8, 1920; Alexander, *John McGraw,* 207 (quotation); Harold Seymour, *Baseball: The Golden Age* (1971; New York: Oxford University Press, 1989), 291-292. Schneider, who Chase and Magee had said was in on the fix, was waived out of the NL without explanation at the end of the 1918 season. Seymour, *Baseball: The Golden Age,* 291.

20. Tom Swope to Lee Allen, June 23, 1960, in Hal Chase file, National Baseball Library, Cooperstown, N.Y.

21. Cincinnati *Enquirer,* Aug. 11, 1918.

22. *The Sporting News,* Aug. 22, 1918.

23. Cincinnati *Enquirer,* Aug. 19, 1918; Alexander, *John McGraw,* 207. Youngs, one of McGraw's favorite players, was also mentioned in connection with the Jimmy O'Connell-Cozy Dolan bribery scandal in 1924, but was exonerated by Commissioner Kenesaw Mountain Landis. See Alexander, *John McGraw,* 256-257.

24. *The Sporting News,* Aug. 22, 1918.

25. Ibid.

26. Ibid.

27. Cincinnati *Enquirer,* Aug. 27, 1918.

28. Robinson, *Matty,* 188.

29. Ty Cobb with Al Stump, *My Life in Baseball: The True Record* (1961; Lincoln: University of Nebraska Press, 1993), 190.

30. Alexander, *John McGraw,* 212.

31. Cincinnati *Enquirer,* Dec. 12, 13, 1918, Jan. 26, 1919.

32. See, for example, *The Sporting News,* Feb. 6, 1919; New York *Globe,* Jan. 22, 27, 31, 1919. In a cartoon entitled "Keeping It Dark," Robert Ripley, the cartoonist who later gained fame as the originator of "Ripley's Believe It or Not," depicted an anxious-looking baseball player, labelled "National League," sneaking down the "Back Stairs" of National League headquarters at night. Over his shoulder he carried a bag, labelled "Chase," from which emanated the yowls of an angry cat. The worried player was saying, "Wonder where the nearest river is?" New York *Globe,* Jan. 31, 1919.

33. Cincinnati *Enquirer,* Jan. 27, 1919.

34. New York *Globe,* Mar. 8, 1919.

35. Frank Graham, *The New York Giants: An Informal History* (New York: G. P. Putnam's Sons, 1952), 110.

36. Alexander, *John McGraw,* 214; Cincinnati *Enquirer,* Aug. 4, 1919.

37. New York *Sun,* Aug. 16, 1919.

38. Ibid., Sept. 12, 1919; New York *Times,* Sept. 24, 30, 1920.

39. Graham, *The New York Giants,* 115.

40. Chicago *Tribune,* Sept. 29, 1920.

41. Cincinnati *Enquirer,* June 9, 1920.

42. Robinson, *Matty,* 199, 200.

43. Ibid., 203-204, 208-215.

44. Seymour, *Baseball: The Golden Age,* 294-310, 324-330.

45. Ibid., 300, 325.

46. See, for example, *The Sporting News,* Jan. 4, 1934; New York *Evening Post,* Dec. 26, 1933; New York *Herald Tribune,* Dec. 27, 1933; New York *Sun,* Dec. 29, 1933.

47. *The Sporting News,* Sept. 18, 1941; Sacramento *Union,* Apr. 22, 1944.

48. Frank Cloak Jr. to Martin Kohout, Feb. 6, 1991 (interview). Cloak, Chase's grand-nephew, helped care for the old man. He recalled playing catch with him—using oranges instead of baseballs—and being astonished by his still-remarkable reflexes.

49. New York *Times,* May 20, 1947; *The Sporting News,* May 28, 1947.

50. Eric Rolfe Greenberg, *The Celebrant* (1983; New York: Penguin, 1986), 170-171.

51. In 1966 Lee Allen, author of *The National League Story: The Official History* (New York: Hill and Wang, 1961), which contains a discussion of Chase, received a letter from a J. L. May of Metairie, Louisiana, who claimed to be Chase's (illegitimate) son. No record of Allen's response remains. J. L. May to Lee Allen, May 6, 1966, in Hal Chase file, National Baseball Library, Cooperstown, N.Y.

The Dreaded Stickball Game

Ev Parker

In those late 1930's and early '40s
The Great Depression still clung to all of us.
You could feel it all around you,
You could smell it and taste it.

Few families could afford a telephone,
The corner candy store our communications link.
Fewer still owned autos,
No parking problems on our streets.

It was on those streets where stickball games
Were played, with laughter and some shouting.
A sewer cover was home plate,
Another sewer cover, second base.

First base and third base
Were chalked onto what we called the gutter.
A rare auto would chance to park upon a base.
"Move it mister, will ya?"

Neighbors, elbows on pillow
Watching from second and third floor open windows
Spectators enjoying a game, free
From upper tier boxseats.

A kid who could hit a ball
Three sewers
Was the local DiMaggio or Ott,
A big man on the block—a "Three Sewer Man."

But occasionally a problem arose.
An old lady tired of the noise
An affluent enough to own a phone, used it,
Called the police.

The crank call, the "dreaded stick ball game run,."
Dislike by every cop in NYPD.
Yet, the sector car would have to respond—slowly.
"Break it up boys, the game's over."

Years later, a copy myself,
The police radio directing us
To another stickball game, played by other kids.
How cops hated that call.

I've always wondered
How many kids over all the years,
Were banished from those dreaded stickball games
And introduced into something far worse.

Ev Parker, *a retired New York City policeman, now writes and spends
time with his grandson in Napa, California.*